CAN YOU
LEARN TO BE
Lucky?

CAN YOU LEARN TO BE

Lucky?

Why Some People
Seem to Win More Often
Than Others

KARLA STARR

PORTFOLIO / PENGUIN

Portfolio/Penguin
An imprint of Penguin Random House LLC
375 Hudson Street
New York, New York 10014

Most Portfolio books are available at a discount when purchased in quantity for sales
promotions or corporate use. Special editions, which include personalized covers, excerpts,
and corporate imprints, can be created when purchased in large quantities. For more
information, please call (212) 572-2232 or e-mail specialmarkets@penguinrandomhouse.com.
Your local bookstore can also assist with discounted bulk purchases using the Penguin
Random House corporate Business-to-Business program. For assistance in locating a
participating retailer, email B2B@penguinrandomhouse.com.

ISBN: 9781591846864 (hardcover)
ISBN: 9780698139817 (ebook)

Printed in the United States of America
10 9 8 7 6 5 4 3 2 1

Book design by Ellen Cipriano

While the author has made every effort to provide accurate telephone numbers, internet
addresses, and other contact information at the time of publication, neither the publisher nor
the author assumes any responsibility for errors, or for changes that occur after publication.
Further, the publisher does not have any control over and does not assume any responsibility
for author or third-party websites or their content.

To my mother, Sandy,
whose endless encouragement has
given me everything

P.S. I'm sorry but you can't take it back.

CONTENTS

CAN YOU
LEARN TO BE
Lucky?

INTRODUCTION

What We Talk about When We Talk about Luck

n January 2003, my friend Jordan and I were two of the thirty-five hundred people in Homer, Alaska. When we moved there, we wanted to be surrounded by snow and nothingness and beauty and dreamed of watching the northern lights on a nightly basis. But after several months of peeing our pants with excitement whenever the temperature hit the double digits, we would have slaughtered the mailman for the chance to leave for a bit. Jordan was lucky; all he had to do was call his rich mother to get some money to travel.

While Jordan was away, I agreed to leave the big farmhouse where I lived with four others and take care of his cabin, truck, and new puppy for two weeks. *Lucky.*

After driving four hours from Homer to the Anchorage airport, Jordan hopped out at the unloading zone. Leaving the engine running, he grabbed his black duffel bag and camera equipment from the bed of the pickup and gestured for me to slide over to the driver's seat.

He leaned in. "There's cheese in the fridge, that big brick of cheddar. It's still good. And there's plenty of dog food for the puppy. And lettuce, I think. And beer."

"You said you were going to leave me food for the two weeks. And pay for gas for the truck. It's on empty." I unearthed my wallet to show him the $5 bill and lack of a credit card.

"Yeah, about that," he said, his eyes shifting toward the terminal. "Listen, my plane is about to leave." He gave me a pair of twenties for gas. My nostrils flared. *Unlucky.*

I stopped for the traditional Alaskan refill of gas and Taco Bell, then left and took to the road. Within minutes, signs of sprawl and chain stores gave way to snowcapped mountains and earnest moose-crossing signs. The sky was cornflower blue, crisp, and cloudless; the road was clear. I thought about spending the next two weeks in Jordan's cabin taking care of his puppy and editing the novel I'd finished writing the week before. *Lucky.*

And then life happened.

I veered around a wide bend and down a hill onto a section of the road that some damn omnipresent trees were protecting from the sun. The entire stretch of asphalt before me morphed into ice.

Despite the plentiful experience driving on ice that accompanied learning how to drive in my hometown of Buffalo, I could tell that this time was different. I couldn't do anything. Something was wrong.

Time stood still; the truck did not.

The rear end fishtailed until the truck was perpendicular to the road and started flipping. The world and horizon spun around me. The highway appeared to my left, where the window should have been. Random dents in the door and windshield arrived, uninvited. Shattered glass joined me, spinning around in the cabin. I stuck out my hand to protect my head, and the bones in my wrist popped out of the skin.

The truck rolled over five times before coming to a rest on the side of the road heading in the opposite direction. I spent half an hour staring at my own bones and blood before an ambulance arrived. A helicopter returned me to Anchorage, where an orthopedic surgeon quickly went to work on my wrist and later liberally used the word "shattered," estimating that I'd broken it in over thirteen places before fusing it with a plate and six screws.

"It's your left hand, at least!" people exclaimed, trying to console me. *Lucky.*

"I'm left-handed," I replied. *Unlucky.*

The internal bleeding from my fractured skull collected into a subdural hematoma, a coagulated blood clot placing substantial pressure on the inside of my skull that surgeons removed days later.

I spent the next few months watching Conan O'Brien on Vicodin on my mother's couch in California. Without health insurance—I was stupid, young, and on a budget and didn't even know how that would have worked—I quickly accumulated over $200,000 in medical bills. I was always tired and in a daze. Everything was bright and loud.

My friend Jordan kept calling and asking me to pay the deductible for his car insurance.

I declared bankruptcy the following year to get rid of my medical debt.

Why did this happen to me? I constantly wondered.

My inquiry was not put to bed by the good folks at State Farm, who concluded (in what was surely a rigorous theological inquiry) that my accident was an act of God. Yes, God could have just sent me a letter saying, "Cherish each day!" but then I would have needed to find another story to begin this book, and as anyone who knows me can verify, when given the opportunity to do anything in the world, I will always opt for a burger and a nap.

In legalese, an act of God—or *damnum fatale*—refers to damage caused by an unavoidable, nonhuman entity that can otherwise be referred to as fate. When insurers can't go after someone else's policy, they say it's God. From this, we can draw two conclusions: First, insurance companies have been using the Bible to get out of paying claims for centuries. Second, in attributing my accident to an act of God, State Farm *really* meant that my carnival ride from hell was neither my nor someone else's fault, but something inevitable caused by an "extra- or superhuman element." It just happened.[1]

It just happened.

This fact, as you can imagine, was of no comfort whatsoever.

This book is about navigating life's hidden patterns. While there's no way to account for *every* variable influencing a situation, this doesn't make the world entirely unpredictable. Enough regularities exist to give us a rough guide to their causes and the best ways to deal with the unforeseeable. Randomness is a poor teacher. Organisms need to accomplish tasks while adhering to biological laws of energy usage—succeeding as lazily as possible—which evolution has accounted for by shaping the brain into an efficient, action-oriented predictor.[2] It behooves living beings to see the world as understandable and manageable; meaning, continuity, and a sense of control keep us sane.[3] Making accurate predictions allows us to anticipate the environment and plan our actions, which is why feeling unsure about our ability to handle the future makes us anxious.[4]

No species deals with uncontrollable events very well. In a famous experiment, the University of Pennsylvania's Richard Solomon began studying fear's influence on learning by restraining dogs in hammocks and playing a tone before their back paws were shocked. Later, those dogs and a newer group were transferred to another condition; after hearing that ominous tone, they could jump over a barrier within ten seconds to avoid being shocked entirely. Researchers predicted that the previously shocked-and-restrained dogs would learn how to escape faster than the others.

That did not happen. "After a few trials, they passively 'accept' shock and fail to make escape movements," wrote the surprised researchers.[5] Dogs from those initial trials in the hammock transferred the idea that *escape was impossible* onto their new condition, never learning that the underlying rules had changed. Researchers define the feeling of futility accompanying prolonged, uncontrollable shitty situations as learned helplessness.

After my accident, I couldn't help but wonder how I could have avoided spending time in a snow-covered ditch with a fractured skull. What if I'd never traveled to Seward's Folly? Had always given snow the cold shoulder? Steered clear of it? Run away from any location offering the possibility of both precipitation and freezing temperatures? Should driving never have been a *thing* in my life? But *it just happened,* and nothing could ever erase that; they're called freak accidents for a reason. Something even worse could happen any second that I'd be completely powerless to prevent, unable to control.

Cultures set the stage for our beliefs about how much we can control life. Since humans and chimpanzees split from a common ancestor over six million years ago, evolution has gently tweaked *Homo sapiens'* genetic material roughly fifteen to twenty million times.[6] Our ancestors only triumphed over their physical superiors by hunting together, which shaped our species' brain to master the art of shared intentionality, or goal-oriented collaboration. This shared sense of reality known as culture establishes our expectations of how the world works by defining the social norms that dictate both behavior and beliefs, enabling groups to run smoothly.[7]

An unwavering belief in its ability to sway the unseen forces that influence what we can't directly control, coupled with the belief that divine intervention can fill in all the gaps, would create a culture unbelievably optimistic in its own agency and perception of how much it can control. It's the culture I was raised in, a family belief that goes way back.[8]

In 1620, my brazen and litigious great-great-great-great-great-great-great-great-great-great-grandfather Edward Doty stepped off the *Mayflower* with over a hundred of his fellow passengers and crew members, creating the second-oldest colony of English settlers in North America. Along with other Puritan settlers, Doty helped establish the cultural norms of the United States on the premise of the self-made man, hoping to create a Christian utopia, a "redemptive community of God's chosen people," free from the corruption of the modern world and with a very specific freedom of religion: freedom to not have a government interfere with their particular reading of the Bible and their adherence to its values of thrift, hard work, and temperance.[9]

"Underpinning this formula for success was . . . the belief that a benevolent God operating in a universe of reason and law would reward virtue with worldly success."[10] Rejecting Europe's class-heavy consciousness, they believed in equal opportunities, that God would help those who helped themselves.

The Protestant work ethic was made into law in Massachusetts in 1648, a law that stated that no person shall "spend his time idlely or unprofitably under pain of such punishment as the Court of Assistants or County Court shall think meet to inflict."[11] These upwardly mobile behavioral norms were a huge boon to this country's economic success.[12] This "we make our own luck" belief—that our actions and beliefs influence *everything*—developed unimpeded, separated from other explanations by oceans for centuries.[13] Emphasis on "character ethic had rested on the belief that in an open society anyone who was morally deserving might rise to social and economic prominence."[14] Idealizing self-reliance and the importance of character is easy when we're surrounded by proof that hard work and honesty lead to success, which was the case when small groups of farmers and artisans embedded in their churches, families, and communities formed the core of the nation's economy.[15]

Over time, railroads, industrialization, urbanization, and mass immigration pushed American life to cities and centralized the economy. Benjamin Franklin's model of success through constant self-improvement morphed into a view of success as a competitive game of social Darwinism, where a winner-take-all society played by a different set of rules.[16] "The virtues of patience, hard work, and prudence were being undermined by the spectacle of men who seemed to blossom into millionaires overnight."[17] Sudden wealth and visible inequality eroded the collective belief that success stemmed from merit, frugality, and faith alone.[18] Elements of chance seeped into American life.[19] Hard work, a good character, and faith in a benevolent God were no longer enough in America: you needed luck.[20]

In 2001, Argentina's economy collapsed, and its currency was devalued after the country defaulted on billions of dollars in loans. Overnight, the city that was once more expensive than Paris became an economic war zone with sky-high unemployment and a cash shortage. Because the depression made it relatively cheap for foreigners like me to make dollars and spend pesos, several years after my accident I moved to Buenos Aires to experience life abroad. Life could end at any time, and I wanted to make the most of mine.

At the end of 2007, I watched the economy of the United States collapse while living in South America. A restaurant TV relayed the telltale images: bankers vacating buildings and unemployment lines snaking around the block. My waiter just sighed. *Mala suerte,* he said. *Bad luck.* People who view causes entirely beyond their influence have an *external* locus of control, the opposite end of the can-we-do-anything-about-this spectrum as Pilgrims. My arguments with Argentines (as well as the existence of my Argentine ex-husband) attest to culture's sticky sway in shaping our view of how the world works, including the presence of luck and the controllability of life.[21] Despite the repeated, unwelcome appearance of randomness in my life, I had come to believe that doing *something* was better than shaking your head and saying, "That's life."

Humans work together by sharing beliefs about what shapes the world and what, if anything, we can do to guide the future. When the connection between our actions and the outcomes seems tenuous, cultures may reason that a greater, unseen power is at work, easing our anxiety by offering a larger sense of meaning and narrative to the unfolding events. How and how much we can influence that divine power controlling these events depends on the beliefs of a culture's religion or an individual's spirituality.

After a few years in Buenos Aires, I returned to the United States at the height of the Great Recession. Up close, I couldn't explain the floundering and flourishing; it seemed as if the entire country had gotten into a car accident, but only some people had fractured their skulls. Life was characterized by visible, drastic inequality decided by factors beyond pure merit, eroding my optimistic belief that success was entirely self-made. In addition to hard work, a good character, and confidence in your future, you needed something beyond your control: You needed luck.

. . . .

After my accident, I dealt with randomness by watching TV on Vicodin. Sadly, the glorious nothingness of bitching about the world in sweatpants yielded little but an expanding waistline. Post-Argentina, however, I soothed myself by falling down a rabbit hole and researching everything I could about luck: I wanted a sense of certainty about uncertainty.

I didn't realize it at the time, but taking action was the first, right step. Any successful outcome that I wanted but couldn't completely control— getting a job, a book deal, a new apartment, an expanded social circle, money, or a sense of purpose or getting off my mother's couch—required action on my part. Doing nothing resembles learned helplessness. Doing something, even when it looks like a meaningless superstition and isn't always as fun as self-righteous apathy, leads to better outcomes than bemoaning the state of the world in sweatpants.

I discovered not only that many "random" outcomes *do* have predictable causes, but that we can prepare for these and nudge the system toward our favor. I learned that getting the luck of an unplannable collision depended on how willing I was to put myself in a place where those encounters were more likely to happen. Once I started connecting to people, I quickly realized how small the world really is. I opened up to friends about living back at home and was offered a gig house-sitting at a vineyard in Oregon. I met someone looking for fellow writers and joined a writing group. The scientist James Austin called this the Kettering Principle, named after that prolific inventor: "Keep on going and the chances are you will stumble on something, perhaps when you are least expecting it. I have never heard of anyone stumbling on something sitting down."[22]

Sometimes life fractures our skulls. Sometimes it takes our money. Sometimes it shocks our paws. Sometimes it passes over our superior résumés because we didn't list the right hobby. Sometimes it grades someone else's performance on a curve. Sometimes it sends us more horrible first dates than we know what to do with. Things happen. While it's realistic to accept that uncontrollable events or external luck exist, it's *maladaptive* to believe that we're completely powerless to influence the outcomes. Understanding what is and isn't out of our hands can increase our chances of finding success by allowing us to focus on what we can change.

Decades of studies conducted since the original dogs were shocked have led to a major revision in the model: passively accepting the status quo is the *default* response to ongoing shitty situations. The lazy path of inaction known as learned helplessness is normal when bad things persist; it's easier to ignore or rationalize whatever circumstances you're in—both the fact that you're hurting and *why* you're hurting—than to try to change them. Thankfully, life is not a psychology lab, and the rules governing situations constantly change. The escape doors might open at any time, and the positive, adaptive approach to life must be learned.

This book will show you how.

1

Best in Show

Why Lucky Timing Is out of Our Hands

t's the third day of the nineteenth annual Motor City Tattoo Expo in the GM Renaissance Center in downtown Detroit, and I'm on my seventy-second straight hour of immersion in tattoo subculture. I've learned about the latest advancements in ink color, needles, and removal procedures. I've learned to not ask about the significance of names, because those conversations tend to turn to children, the deceased, or deceased children. I've also learned to not ask how many tattoos people have, because when you start doodling and wind up with a page full of interconnected scribbles, the correct answer to the question "How many drawings are on the page?" is both "a million" and "one." I've lost count of how many times I've been approached by artists making suggestions about how they'd cover the rare, blank canvases that are my arms and neck.

Like portly men descending upon a European beach, the tattooed are quick to expose skin upon entering a nonjudgmental environment. There are flames, there are fairies, there are flags. So. Many. Skulls.

Not only have I never seen so much living body art in my life, but it's multiplying. Most of the booths have been rented by tattoo artists; the air squawks, buzzes, and hums with the sounds of needles leaving permanent marks. Blank butts and upper arms enter, emerging colored and transformed. The freshly inked walk around, some with their body parts wrapped in Saran wrap to stop the bleeding, but most holding up paper towels or cloths, as though having recently returned from the front line.

But I am not here for the tattoos; I'm here for the competition. It's the third day, so the biggest contest most worthy of analysis has finally arrived: Best in Show.

There are three judges, two men and a woman, Sheri, who smiles when asked her age. "Twenty-two," she purrs in her Sweetwater, Texas, drawl. "And I've been tattooing for thirty years." She has long strawberry blond hair and in an alternate universe would make a great school librarian but in this universe has a sleeveless pink button-down shirt revealing full sleeves on each arm. All the judges have a few decades' worth of expertise, allowing them to excel at recognizing patterns and detecting details invisible to others. Knowing *how* the sausage is made allows them to spot cured meats made with an objectively trickier technique, whereas others would merely smile and say, "Tasty!"[1]

I've talked my way onstage to see the judging in action, and seeing the tattoos from here is to appreciate the detailing, the shading, the colors, and the placement on a new level. I'm so close to countless bloodstained Wet-Naps used to blot new tattoos that I have to actively suppress the idea of running out for a hepatitis shot. After the last contestant leaves, the judges confer with one another before calling back three final contenders: a middle-aged man named Jay with a thigh tattoo of a blue and green face that merited pointing and *ooh*ing and *aah*ing, a cute boy with an even cuter blue jay on his forearm (my gaze follows, confirming my undying love for brunettes with nice arms), and a friendly faced girl named Tanya with a brightly colored gecko on her left forearm. The judges peer at the inked flesh yet again, their mouths agape. The finalists leave.

Those onstage huddle to pick a winner. The judging for Best in Show starts with a strongly worded campaign against the face led by Mike Siderio: *"I don't know about those colors."* They agree that the texture was amazing—those details, those lines!—but they also agree that the colors were flat. Perhaps both the artist and the owner of the thigh *wanted* it that way, but the judges are the experts and the experts are pronouncing it flat. The face is out. Jay will be devastated. Alas, the only tissues around the stage are covered in blood.

The blue jay: "The branch and feathers were amazing. But the detailing of the stomach was a little soft and underdone." Of the three, the blue jay was my favorite. It's possible that the guy who served as its canvas—who is currently somewhere out there breaking hearts—swayed my opinion of the tattoo.

The last: "Those gecko hands were super-detailed," Sheri says, nodding.

"It gets at least a half a point higher. It had more impact," says the gray-ponytailed Brian Everett. (Note: Everett had no scorecard and was not an actual judge, but *just some dude sitting onstage.*)

"I'm a skull guy, so if I liked the frog, then that really means something," says Jason "Swany" Swanson, a barrel-shaped man who has flown in from Spokane, Washington, for the extravaganza. The frog/gecko seems to be gaining momentum. Sure, it was a great tattoo, but was it *really* the best that had been inked during the entire convention? The judges lean in and whisper. The MC, Carl—head shaved, goatee fiery red, voice thick from a lifetime of Marlboros—has had enough cans of Red Bull to dissolve his adrenal glands and seems to want to call it a day. But if they wanted to award the absolute best, wouldn't they chug some more Red Bull and look at every tattoo? Someone hands Carl a sheet of paper.

"And the winner," announces Carl, "is . . . oh boy, this isn't surprising. The gecko!" Tanya jumps in the air and smiles. Trophies are collected onstage. Photos are taken. Life is good.

A few hours beforehand, I'd spoken to the head judge, Mike Siderio, an industry legend and native of Wildwood, New Jersey, bearing a faint resemblance to the love child of Richard Petty and Tom Cruise, who discusses tattooing with the vigor of a Siberian husky approaching newly fallen snow.

I asked him about his scoring strategy.

"You've got to leave a little room at the top," he said, crossing his arms across his chest. "You can't just give a ten to the first thing you see."

Perhaps no type of competition on earth selected its victors more elegantly than gladiator fights in ancient Rome, but today's tournaments require more nuanced measurements than "Who is still alive?" Sporting activities with objective winners use values like speed, distance, and weight—hence, the Olympic motto *Citius, Altius, Fortius,* which is Latin for "Faster, Higher, Stronger." (Being all three of these in ancient Rome conferred a fourth distinction: "Aliver.")

Today, to see the margin of a sprinter's victories, we can use a device like a laser at the finish line that speaks only the universal language of math and is therefore our friend. But as the components influencing victor selection move from robotic calculation to subjectivity—from "who was fastest" to "was that traveling" to "which evening gown was fiercest"—the number of opinion-based judgments outside the contestants' control increases, transforming the winner from *indisputable best* to *judges' favorite.*

Waiting until each contender has been seen to render a verdict—like the judges evaluating those tattoos—is called "end of sequence" judging, which typically favors the final entries. When we look at a sequence of items, our attention snaps to whatever is interesting and shiny about each new thing; even if that feature isn't terribly noteworthy, it's what we notice and appreciate in the moment. As a result, the first things get the short end of the stick.[2] When viewing entries for Best in Show, Mike Siderio couldn't have looked at that first tattoo and said, "We'll never see another tattoo in the next twenty minutes with such accurate, detailed lines!" When someone in middle school asks you out, there's no way to gauge that date against all future nights ending in vague suggestions for future plans. Newbie house hunters can never exclaim, "This will be the only house we'll ever see in our price range with a decent yard!" It's the *last* contestants, tattoos, and songs that make us shriek with pleasure. "*Those gecko hands!*" indeed.

If we don't wait until the end, we engage in step-by-step judging, rendering verdicts piecemeal and rating each item as it comes up. (My mother has invented a third alternative—judging everything before having seen anything—which appears to be largely lacking in diagnostic validity.) Artistic sports with subjectively scored elements like diving, synchronized swimming, and gymnastics use this method, evaluating each performance after it ends. Lots of life's little auditions also do this, sizing up your first-date cardigan, Rutgers application, or slapdash entry to the science fair right then and there.

Because appearing toward the end increases your chances—making others judge your term paper, job interview, or first-date skills more favorably—victory can depend on where you fall in that person's schedule, something outside of your control and subject to luck.

One analysis of the 1994–2004 European figure-skating championships found that the final performers had a 14 percent chance of winning, whereas the odds of the first skater emerging victorious was a mere *3 percent*.[3] At the 1998 Winter Olympics in Nagano, Japan, Michelle Kwan was considered the top contender on the U.S. figure-skating team. Her closest rival, Tara Lipinski, was her junior by two years. While Kwan looked the part, the *New York Times* said that Lipinski's outfit for the long skate that year conveyed a very specific image: "I'm going to my first Communion and I intend to yodel."[4]

Kwan's flawless performance in the long program in Nagano failed to get gold-medal-worthy scores because perfection, when appearing too early in the night, does not get perfect marks. Lipinski skated later. Just two years after finishing fifth in the junior world championships, Lipinski became the youngest woman to walk away with the gold medal, pulling off the biggest upset in figure-skating history.

A month beforehand, Kwan had been given a stream of perfect 6.0s at the national championships. For the same performance later at the Olympics, judges gave her a 5.9 for presentation. Just imagine being a judge in Nagano, Japan. How could you see *one* figure-skating performance and declare it the absolute best? You'd behave like the tattoo judge Mike Siderio, giving it a high score and leaving some room at the top, just in case you were truly floored later.[5] And then, when you saw those later performances and tattoos, you'd be unduly impressed by whatever they bring to the table that nothing else has.

The benefits of performing later have consistently been found in competitions using step-by-step judging as diverse as a Nebraska state high school gymnastics meet, the Eurovision Song Contest, the World Championship in Synchronized Swimming, and the Queen Elizabeth competition for classical violin and piano.[6]

Scorecards are predictable because order influences the *context* of judgments. Our lazy brains make use of whatever information, ideas, processing power, and emotions are most accessible at that moment.[7] We judge early entries against what's most available to our brains at the time: our *perfect ideals,* crafted by a lifetime of wishing and learning, because we have no idea what awaits us in the actual pool of applicants. Over time, the context changes as we get an idea of what's actually out there. We may spend our twenties searching for a triathlete/CEO/philanthropist/underwear model to settle down with, but by our late thirties we may be willing to settle for someone who isn't legally obligated to inform his neighbors whenever he moves. We dream of hiring the COO of Snapchat while writing a job ad, but soon become smitten by each literate letter from an applicant who isn't trying to sell SEO optimization. Scoring talent competitions and tattoo contests mimics the rest of life: Eventually, we lower our expectations—without even realizing that we're doing it—if we'd like to leave without crying.[8]

The Bigger Takeaway: Our Brains Are Lazy

Sometimes, the last competitors don't get lucky. In 2010, three researchers from Columbia University in New York and Ben-Gurion University in Beersheba, Israel, examined an Israeli parole board's rulings over the course of ten months.

To avoid any conflicts of interest, the judge, the social worker, and the criminologist on the board weren't aware of which cases they were going to see before that day, so they had to take in the entirety of each case at once. Evaluating between fourteen and thirty-five cases per day only gave them an average of six minutes per case. Food divided their day into three discrete parts, with breaks for a late morning snack around 10:00 a.m. and a lunch around 1:00 p.m.[9]

After crunching the data on 1,112 rulings, researchers didn't have to look far to find visible patterns.

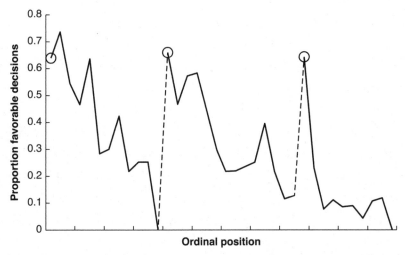

Shai Danziger, Jonathan Levav, Liora Avnaim-Pesso, "Extraneous Factors in Judicial Decisions," *Proceedings of the National Academy of Sciences* 108, no. 17 (2011): 6,889-92, doi: 10.1073 /pnas.1018033108

The board was most likely to grant parole at the beginning of the day and immediately after the two breaks. When freshly seated in court, judges ruled in favor of the prisoners in 65 percent of the cases, and over the next few hours the likelihood of their granting parole fell to nearly *0 percent*. Researchers accounted for potentially complicating factors and found that the chances of getting parole had nothing to do with a prisoner's gender or ethnicity or the severity of the crime. They also ruled out personal biases, because these numbers were crunched from two parole boards without quotas to meet that had seen the prisoners at random. The biggest factor determining a prisoner's fate was simply how much time had passed since the judges' last break.

In the Olympics and the nineteenth annual Motor City Tattoo Expo, the last contestants got lucky, but at the Israeli parole board, the last ones got screwed. Knowing *why* this happens is one of the most important things we can learn about our luck.

We probably don't want to know how much our lives have been influenced by the state of other people's brains when we pop up in their schedules. In one famous study, psychologists played with fire by toying with hungry college students, telling subjects to not eat for at least three hours before an experiment that they were told was about taste perception. Two bowls were placed in the lab (which, the researchers note, was filled with "the delicious aroma of fresh chocolate and baking"). One bowl was piled with freshly baked chocolate chip cookies and chocolates; the other one held red and white radishes.

After placing students onto either Team Radish or Team Chocolate, the experimenter left the hungry undergrads alone for five minutes to eat two or three of the food items from their assigned bowls.[10] Subjects completed questionnaires testing their mood, waited for fifteen minutes, and were then asked to complete an allegedly unrelated puzzle to analyze their problem-solving savvy. They were given ample pencils and pieces of paper for multiple attempts and access to a bell they could ring if they gave up before actually finishing. There was just one caveat: The puzzle—which required students to trace a geometric shape in one stroke, with no pencil lifting or line retracing allowed—was impossible to solve. While members of Team Chocolate worked for nearly twenty minutes, the students on Team Radish only tolerated eight minutes of this madness before ringing the bell.[11]

The behaviorist Clark Hull started work in 1929 at Yale's Institute of Human Relations, and after developing "a bad case of physics-envy from reading Newton's *Principia Mathematica*" with its ability to explain phenomena with objective mathematical certainty, he began a quest to develop a unified theory of behavior that would allow him to formulate quantitative models to explain and predict rats' actions.[12]

In a classic example of If You Work in a Really Young Discipline,

Developing Painfully Obvious Concepts Can Get You Tenure at Yale, in 1943 Clark Hull outlined the "law of less work" in his book *Principles of Behavior*.[13] "If two or more behavioral sequences, each involving a different amount of energy consumption or work have been equally well reinforced an equal number of times," he wrote, "the organism will gradually learn to choose the less laborious behavior sequence leading to the attainment of the reinforcing state of affairs."[14] The law of less work, dubbed "the law of least effort" by the Nobel Prize–winning psychologist Daniel Kahneman, applies to mental tasks as well as physical ones: When two paths lead toward the same goal (whether a piece of cheese, credit for an undergraduate psych class, or choosing a decent tattoo), our default is the shorter, easier route. Unless we're motivated to make more of an effort (that chocolate! a nap!) or given a form of error correction, our brain opts for the elegance of laziness.[15]

Like tax season or being weighed by an accurate scale, errors are inherently threatening. They imply that we've wasted energy by doing something wrong and that we have to adjust our mental model of how the world works, which requires even *more* energy.[16] One key component of our brain's error-detection unit—a way of signaling That Did Not Pan Out—is the anterior cingulate cortex. ACC activity is a sign that we have to exert *more* mental control by trying a little harder, learning something new, or changing our thinking. When we get feedback that we've made a mistake or our expectations aren't met, we experience a negative-reward prediction error, a sudden drop in dopamine levels that recruit the ACC, which we automatically experience as aversive. Being wrong simply sucks on a biological level, but it's how we learn.[17]

Becoming more proficient at a task allows our brain to downshift from the metabolically taxing prefrontal cortex to the basal ganglia, an older, more efficient area that's responsible for motor control. Experts can deliberate for longer than novices before wanting to call it a day because their superior pattern recognition skills use less processing power.[18] But even experts get tired, and whenever we start feeling that our time would be better spent elsewhere, we unknowingly choose what is easiest and save energy (without realizing it) by thinking less. Eventually, everything that is not edible or pillow shaped becomes unimportant. Our brain is constantly lazy, but only in situations when we can hold one variable constant can we see its effects so clearly.[19]

But do judges ever find out that they've made an error by going with the default choice, bestowing luck upon the last singer or the first prisoner? Are they told about their biased judgments? Nope. When it comes to comparing one Olympic-level feat with another, *the judges never receive objective feedback on their ratings*. There's no way for them to see all of the routines again in a different order, learn how the sequence altered their scores, and use that information to minimize any bias caused by the order of the ratings.

Receiving corrective feedback is just as important as being rewarded: It's how we learn. Because group living is so important for humans, simply discovering that we disagree with others whose opinions matter to us also recruits the anterior cingulate cortex, our brain's That Did Not Pan Out signal. Judges assess their own ratings by conferring with peers on the parole board, at the ice-skating rink, or at Detroit's Renaissance Center, all of which are run by fatigue-prone brains that eventually make the easiest call and arbitrarily bestow luck upon some of the participants.[20] As the philosopher Bertrand Russell once remarked, "Even when the experts all agree, they may well be mistaken."[21]

Can You Plan to Compete Last?

The comedian Kurt Braunohler and his girlfriend met as teenagers at Johns Hopkins University in Baltimore, moved to Brooklyn after graduation, and spent the next thirteen years together.[22] One October day when they were both thirty, Kurt wanted to know something quite simple, given the length of their relationship.

"Why do you think we haven't gotten married yet, or even talked about it?"

His girlfriend replied, "Well, I think that before we get married, we should probably sleep with other people."

Braunohler—who was then in a thirteen-year relationship with the second woman he'd ever slept with—gave the matter some thought.

"I was like, 'Okay, if that's what you think.'" The pair decided, as couples tend to do, to borrow an idea from the Amish. *Rumspringa*—which translates to "running around"—is the period after the Amish turn sixteen and can participate in activities that violate any of that community's sundry moral, religious, and ethical codes. Braunohler and his girlfriend agreed on a thirty-day relationship *Rumspringa,* when they could do whatever and make up for whatever activities they felt that they were denied in their twenties. Braunohler decided to spend this time collecting as much data as possible.

"I was in a race. I was in a thirty-day race to sleep with as many people as I possibly could. Because after thirty days, I was going to go back and then get married." On January 3, he moved in with a friend for the month and went on a date the next day.

"There was no number I was shooting for; I just thought of it like a limited-time engagement. If there was a day that went by when I wasn't trying to sleep with a random stranger, then I was failing. It was my job."

Braunohler's moment of insight occurred at Crash Mansion, a hip bar on the Bowery on New York's Lower East Side. A female bartender kept placing free drink tokens on the bar in front of him. She asked if he wanted to smoke a cigarette; they went to the back room and started making out. "Then I was like, 'Oh, we're going to have sex.' So I just kept drinking until she got off." Her shift ended at 4:00 a.m., closing time in New York.

"It is fascinating to see—if you stay at the bar until four in the morning—all of a sudden . . . all these people are pairing off." Braunohler's Golden Rule of Getting Laid has two parts. "Anyone in New York City, I feel, can have sex any night of the week if they just follow two rules: Stay at the bar until four in the morning and dramatically lower your standards."

Closing time is history's greatest matchmaker. James Pennebaker studied this notion at three bars in the 1970s.[23]

"They were around the University of Virginia in Charlottesville," says

Pennebaker. "So they were all college bars."[24] On a Thursday night, six research assistants strolled into bars that closed at 12:30 a.m. They asked patrons two questions: "How would you rate the others here tonight?" and "If you were a member of the opposite sex, how would you rate your own sex here tonight?"—on a scale of 1 (not attractive) to 10 (extremely good-looking) at nine, ten thirty, and midnight. While people reported being surrounded by stunningly average individuals at 9:00 p.m., they found themselves in a roomful of hotties just half an hour before closing time.

American Idol voters, Olympic judges, tattoo experts, house hunters, and bar hoppers begin by comparing what's in front of them with their ideal standards. Reality sets in. Standards unknowingly soften. We discover that someone we fancied at 10:00 p.m. has since vacated the premises. Mild panic becomes a possibility. Another contender gives us the cold shoulder. We become enamored with the unique qualities of whoever is in front of us as the night goes on, continuously calibrating our barometer of the options.[25]

I asked Braunohler if this closing time experience informed his subsequent hookup strategy. "I would just do that every night. I would be at a bar until it closed every night for that month." Economists have another term explaining the appearance of acceptable smooching partners at 4:00 a.m.: scarcity. As judgment and decision-making researchers write in what is destined to become a classic Valentine's Day card inscription, "It is better—in terms of long-term reproductive output—to mate with the last person on the island (by finding him or her 'attractive enough') than not to mate at all."[26]

"You see it a lot," says Braunohler. "When people hit a certain age, they all of a sudden end up marrying somebody. You're like, 'That person, really? You used to date people much better than that.' But late in the game, you're just like, 'I gotta do this.'"[27]

It's easy to see how people choose whatever is good and available and in front of them when they get tired and have to make up their minds in settings like the Olympics or *American Idol,* where we know precisely how many options we have. When you're being judged based on subjective criteria, you want to make your case as close to the end as possible and high-light your unique attributes. It's not simply that we find people *more* attractive at closing time, a tattoo more artful at the end of a long convention, or a figure skater more skilled in the closing performance of a competition.

If being with anyone is better than being alone, or choosing trumps not making a choice, then the available options stick out because they help you accomplish what you fundamentally want to do. We don't see tattoos, per-formances, and women getting prettier at closing time. We simply see that the answer to our question has conveniently appeared in front of us—right at the moment we have to decide.

Notes for Those Who Want to Use the Fine Art of Timing to Get Lucky

- When there is a fixed number of entries, go last. In one analysis of 165 episodes of *American Idol* and seven other international versions of that show, researchers found that "with the exception of the first position, moving one position closer to the end of the show provides an additional 5 percentage points chance of being safe for a contestant."[28] Contestants at the beginning get the short end of the stick when the phone lines open because we simply don't *remember* them as well.

- Be memorable. Who gets lucky? Whoever comes to mind when it's time to choose. If you're seen early in the morning for an in-terview, send a reminder email later that day. If you're trying to win over the protagonist in a romantic comedy, wear a yellow bow tie. Flaunt that connection to a foreign dignitary.

- Emphasize your added value. Point out what you uniquely bring to the table.

- Frame a loss as a learning experience.[29] Losses are only fatal blows if you're laser focused on the outcome. Being able to look into the camera and say that you're "*just here to learn as much as possible!*" translates to more adaptive coping strategies. Saying that you "desperately need to prove to my family that I'm not a disappointment!" will make recovery more difficult.

- Don't take it personally. Many of the aforementioned contests have a fixed number of entrants, but hiring managers, casting directors, and singletons can stop their search once they've found a decent candidate. As we get tired, we go with the default choice (our boss's nephew) because mental effort counts as a cost. We probably don't want to know how much our lives have been influenced by how tired other people are when we pop up in their schedules; fortunately, we don't.

- Stay until closing time. Lower your standards. Sixty percent of the time it works.

2

The Charlie Brewer Principle

How That Warm, Fuzzy Feeling Leads to Luck

could hardly sleep at all last night," says Coach Hank Carter, smiling, sitting behind his desk and twisting his wedding ring. The first practice is in a few hours. Carter is a father of two, on the brink of turning thirty-nine, and a touch under six feet tall. His face is wide, roughly 50 percent of it grin. He wears his dark brown hair closely cropped, a few specks of salt poking through. Like most of his staff of sixteen, he's fully decked out in Under Armour gear. He's a largehearted man with contagious enthusiasm who also manages to be unfailingly gentle, respectful, and spiritual. He is, in other words, Texan. He's also the director of athletics at Lake Travis High, and the athletics program of any high school in Texas and the vitality of its community orbit around the one sport where Carter is undisputed king: In 2011, the Lake Travis Cavaliers became the first team in Texas history to win five straight state championships in a row.

The Lake Travis Cavaliers picked up their first state championship in 2007. The next year the Cavs got a new pair of coaches: Morris (head coach; specialty: offense) and Carter, who had by then moved up the ranks to become a defensive coordinator.

"The first two years here we won the state championship. Coach Morris went on to coach college as an assistant, and I took over as head coach. We won two more state championships. It's been quite a run," he says. He's helped turn the team into a legitimate Texas football dynasty, but it's been a few years since they've won a trophy. The year before, a series of bizarre weather mishaps spoiled their last game, which seems to have added more urgency to this season.

I want to know how Hank Carter plans on picking the starting lineup. He claims the right answers are obvious. "We're the bus drivers. We're just trying not to screw it up," he says. Like Michelangelo summoning David from the marble, perhaps Carter already sees a viable team within this uniform-clad mob of hormones before us. "We have a lot of kids we're excited about, but spring ball is going to give us the chance to fill in the gaps and see who's ready to take the next step." If you're a linebacker, you're in luck: Most of last year's defensive starting line is graduating, leaving lots of room for newcomers.

What about the other positions? Offense always produces the breakout stars of any team, none quite like the default team captain, the starting quarterback. Does he have an idea?

Here's where Coach Carter's eyes get wide and he bounces up in his seat. A reaction so strong even *my* heart starts racing. He leans forward.

"His grandfather was a quarterback for the University of Texas. His father was a quarterback for the University of Texas. His uncle was a quarterback for the University of Texas. His brother had been a quarterback at Texas Tech University but transferred and is now the starting quarterback at Virginia Tech. His older brother, Michael, right there," he says, gesturing to one of the many triumphant photos on his wall, "won two state championships as a starting quarterback for us."

This is gold so good it can't possibly be true. But it is.

"Charlie is the next one in line."

And there you have it: the simple, tiny secret of how a junior in high school can get lucky enough to earn the distinction of being selected as the starting varsity quarterback of the first team in history to be Texas state champs for five consecutive years. All you have to do is be bona fide Texas quarterback royalty, descended from multiple generations of starting quarterbacks from the University of Texas. You have to share 50 percent of your DNA with the former starting quarterback of that very team, the one who helped kick off the spree of state championships. You have to be a gifted athlete whose mother used to host the weekly team dinners during the regular season when your older brother played. You have to already be embedded into the tapestry of the town and team, beginning the season from a position of legacy and an air of inevitability.

You have to be Charlie Brewer.

Why is it so hard for some people to break into a new scene while the Charlie Brewers of the world have their dreams hand-delivered to them? In this chapter, we'll learn what got Hank Carter's heart racing and how we can use this information to maximize our own luck.

Those Marbles! That Scale! And How They Influence Your Luck

Amitai Shenhav of Brown University researches factors influencing decision making. In one of his studies, he analyzed which regions of the brain were most active after asking subjects to choose between two items. Having observed his subjects undergo the process of gathering information, considering its options, and finally choosing, he came to view the orbitofrontal cortex, or OFC, as a key region.[1]

"You're collecting evidence for one option or another and considering positive attributes of each one," says Shenhav. He likens our brain's OFC response to options as a process of gathering marbles. Each new piece of information that we gather about an item is akin to your brain collecting a marble that corresponds to that item's value. After you viewed a high-value item like a free phone, your brain would show a larger OFC response (games! a camera!) than after you viewed a lower-value item like a piece of gum (five seconds of flavor!).[2]

"Marbles are collecting, more marbles are collecting, and the size of those marbles scales with the value of those attributes," he says. When we're deciding between two things, we're comparing the overall weight of the "phone" marbles versus the "gum" marbles. In the case of this decision— phone or gum—we'd place the hefty "free phone" marbles on one side and the pebble-sized "free gum" marbles on the other side. Deciding wouldn't take long, because the positive qualities of one clearly outweigh those of the other, making the scale's tilt immediately clear.

When the difference between values isn't as clear—two colors of the same phone; getting a raise or extra vacation time—the decision becomes trickier. Comparing equal or less-quantifiable values is like collecting a bunch of marbles that are roughly the same size, making the scale wobble evenly back and forth. You imagine life with a little more money and add a marble to one side; you imagine life with a little more free time and add a marble to the other side. This we can do forever.

"In the case of having to choose between two high-value items, you have additional evidence collecting. It's reflecting the overall value of those different things you're considering," explains Shenhav. We deploy our attention to make sense of the world.[3] Spending additional time looking at something gives us more of an opportunity to learn new, positive traits about an item, accumulating more evidence and marbles until the scale clearly tips over. (In fact, when the options are relatively simple—like two kinds of snacks—researchers can often manipulate preferences simply by presenting one of them more.)[4]

While we contemplate our options—but before we even know what we're going to end up choosing—eventually the scale starts tilting in one direction. After it passes a certain threshold, a funny thing starts to happen: We start getting picky about which marbles we collect, favoring the ones we can put on the side that's tipping.[5] Our gut is drawn to information that's easier for us to process, or thoughts that are easier for us to have. This economy of effort promotes predictability and consistency and allows for more energy-efficient categorization of new information. In addition to being faster to handle, *fluent* information triggers a positive emotional response. It just *feels* right. Down to the neuron, the brain is lazy.[6]

Our hunches steer our attention and how we interpret that information, both of which give us more ammunition to present those hunches as fact. One real-world study examining the attitudes of Italians on the expansion of a U.S. military base found that people's gut responses influenced what news they read over the following weeks.[7]

"They systematically expose themselves to information that is consistent with their implicit evaluations. They then use this information to make up their mind about this topic, and then they come to a conclusion later," says the study's author Bertram Gawronski, a professor of social psychology at the University of Texas at Austin.[8] From picking tattoos to quarterbacks, we use our feelings to decide—but we're often not even aware of where those good feelings are actually coming from. All things being equal, we prefer information that fits into our brain's preexisting filing system; things that are easier to process just feel right, making it easy to add marbles to that side of the scale.[9]

Before we ever start picking up marbles, consider this: Everything you know and love in the world was at one point unknown; other people are no different. Learning about people is just another form of learning, a process of developing an association between someone and his or her value. To get lucky, other people need to add a bunch of big, positive marbles to our side of the scale—the same way that Coach Carter did when he chose Charlie Brewer to be the quarterback. The first Charlie Brewer principle is easy: *Just be there.*

The Greatest Networking News for Introverts in History

In 1945, MIT built two housing projects to handle the influx of students studying under the GI bill after returning home from World War II. Finished in early 1946, Westgate and Westgate West were isolated from the rest of campus housing, surrounded by fields, highways, factories, and the Charles River, creating a perfect setup to examine the formation of actual friendships and relationships.

In his seminal analysis, the social psychology pioneer Leon Festinger discovered one key variable influencing how likely two people were to become friends: proximity, the social equivalent of good product placement. When asked to name their closest friend at the complex, two-thirds of the residents picked someone in the same building; two-thirds of *those* named someone living on the same floor, most frequently naming their next-door neighbor. More important than physical distance was "functional distance"; meters matter most by leading to opportunities for actual interaction. Simple stairwell placement could make the difference between lifelong friends and two dudes who sort of recognize each other at a bowling alley five years later.[10]

Proximity can lead to luck because of the mere exposure effect. In his original study, Robert Zajonc, one of the leading social psychologists of the twentieth century, exposed subjects to foreign characters or Chinese ideograms—figures and characters that meant nothing to the English speakers—and later asked how much they liked them. Seeing a symbol more frequently led them to report liking it more later; "merely" being exposed to something makes us like it more, hence the term "mere exposure effect." One of Zajonc's graduate students, Richard Moreland, tested this theory in action with four "average"-looking women.[11]

Moreland asked the women to enter the large lecture hall where he taught Intro to Psychology, which sloped down toward the front like a movie theater. The women entered after class had already started, slowly descended the stairs so that everybody could see them, and sat in one of the front two rows. After spending the entire time pretending to take notes in silence—perfectly impersonating my college career—they left without saying a word. One woman performed the "Karla at NYU" routine at fifteen lectures, another ten, and another five times. One didn't show up at all. At the end of the semester, everyone in Moreland's class was given a questionnaire with four photos of the women and a few questions: Do you like this one? Do you think you're similar to this other one? How attractive do you think she is?

And did the students really know what this was all about?

"They had no idea what was going on," says Moreland, explaining the thought process of both the study's participants and anyone who has ever been in a relationship with me. "Most of them weren't even aware that these women had been coming to class."[12] Even though they hadn't spoken to anyone, the pencil-wielding goons in Moreland's class rated the women who attended more lectures as more likable, attractive, and similar to themselves, even though the vast majority of students reported never having seen them before in their lives. This study easily represents the greatest networking news for introverts in history. You can get ahead in the business world without actually talking; just showing up at office parties and briefly lingering near the snack table will put you miles ahead of lazier introverts. Woody Allen was right: 80 percent of success is just showing up.[13]

People are unlike anything else on earth, capable of introducing great pleasure and pain into our lives because they come with the potential for reciprocity. Whatever we can do to others—threaten, ignore, love, cover in Silly String, impeach, mock, stuff into a locker at the YMCA, cut off in traffic, or post poorly lit photos on Facebook suggesting a disappointing number of chins—they can do right back. We can't see their motivations or intentions, so we end up making inferences about what they're likely to do in the future by observing them over time.[14]

The mere exposure effect is the head-slappingly obvious process where we come to associate a person with something vital to survival: *the absence of bad things.*[15] In the words of Robert Zajonc, our brain likes the known (even things we don't recall having seen before) because "if it's familiar, it hasn't eaten you yet." Increased familiarity decreases activity in a part of the brain called the amygdala, which rapidly orients us toward things in the environment worth knowing about.[16] From a survival standpoint, it makes sense that the unknown grabs our attention—it's potentially dangerous—which is why every benign interaction with someone adds a marble to the "safe" side of the scale. Simply meeting people who remind us of others we've already judged to be safe automatically adds a few "this person is safe!" marbles to the scale.[17]

From picking quarterbacks to rating women in lecture halls to awarding tattoos, our feelings cast the final votes, even if they have the same vague, unknowable origin story as gas station hot dogs or the tooth fairy. Even when we're not aware that something has been innocuously looming on our periphery, the sense that someone is safer makes that person more likely to get lucky.[18]

Getting to Know You

One shortcut to the luck-enhancing Charlie Brewer principle is to be close. The *woonerf* is a style of extra-wide, curbless street that originated in Amsterdam in the 1970s, exemplifying the urban planning moment known as New Urbanism. It maximizes space by throwing slow-moving cars and pedestrians together. Americans are initially untethered by the idea of multiuse streets; we're apt to stay in our cars and stick to our overflowing schedules. Wandering, we argue, is for Europeans and the elderly. But get us out of our cars, strip away the traffic lights, and the curious, social, people-watching animal in us all emerges. When Microsoft's Paul Allen wanted to build up Terry Avenue North in Seattle for his massive investment firm, Vulcan, he wanted a community.

What urban planners designed seems like entropy, with cars, pedestrians, and bicyclists all duking it out. But as the nearby bustling, multiuse Pike Place Market demonstrates, controlled chaos works. Drivers are forced to connect and communicate with the pedestrians. Neighbors and co-workers might bump into each other. Gossip and news get passed on. None of it's planned, yet all of it is. The "structured accidentalness" of New Urbanism is designed with these kinds of community-fortifying, life-enhancing encounters in mind. Unexpectedly seeing a friend can alter the course of your day ("Want to get lunch?"), your week ("Tennis on Thursday?"), or your life ("I'll introduce you to my coach"). When we take the time to slow down and get to know the things around us, we give ourselves the opportunity to learn about them and like them more. When we slow down and let other people get to know us, *they* get the chance to like *us* more.[19]

A researcher developed the "interaction time-cost" theory in 1935, when examining the effect of physical proximity—propinquity—on marriage. "The amount of potential interaction is inversely related to a time-cost function; the greater the cost, the less the potential interaction. The time-cost function is directly related to distance," he wrote. Translation: Being close gives everyone the chance to get to know one another. Each interaction adds a marble to the scale, but it's easiest to collect marbles from those nearby; the search for a quarterback, study buddy, collaborator, or spouse starts wherever we are. (If you live outside a major city and are trying to date urbanites, remember: From your perspective, they're all the same distance away; from their perspective, you may not be hot enough to make the trek to New Jersey.)[20]

Friendships are more likely to form between college students living on the same floors in dormitories. And students living closer to the ground floor wind up with more friends than those living on higher floors. People on the twenty-sixth floor can stop by the twelfth or fifth floor while coming or going, and the twelfth-floor crew has lots of opportunities to visit that fifth-floor dorm room. Inhabitants of the fifth floor—a lower floor near an elevator is even better—are like people living on parade routes or families with inground pools: Isn't it an odd coincidence how many friends they end up having? Aren't they *lucky*?[21]

In one classic study, how close two police recruits usually were to each other—determined by the alphabetical order of their surnames—was a key predictor in their becoming pals. "The closer two Maryland State Police trainees are in the physical structure of the group, the more likely they are to choose each other as friends."[22] Another study examining the social dynamics among elementary and middle school teachers over the course of a year and a half found that friendships were most likely to emerge from those who taught on the same floor and took breaks at the same time.[23] Children who sit in the middle of the classroom are more likely to be considered popular—not because they're cooler, of course, but because it's easier for everyone in class to get to know them.[24] Seating arrangements, assigned randomly on the first day of class, can determine friendships over the course of a semester.[25] Physical proximity even influences how likely researchers are to collaborate.[26] We're willing to pay more for centrality, too; one longitudinal study in Denmark found that while married couples were more likely to move from the city to the country, singles appear to tolerate the higher cost of city living because it gives them access to more potential mates.[27]

Alas, these ongoing interactions that come from being close to others won't *automatically* make them like you, because we repeat experiences if they're positive. There are only so many hours in the day, so in order to maximize life's rewards, we tend to steer clear of others after the scale has tipped to the "that person is a jerk" side. Negative early impressions are hard to reverse. Not only do we opt out of future interactions with others once we've gathered enough "jerk" marbles (and in the beginning, it only takes one), but when we do cross paths, it also becomes easier for us to pick up negative "that person is a jerk" marbles. We're generally motivated to have pleasant encounters with others, which is why most of our interactions are nice. Proximity tends to lead to increased liking and luck because, in part, the process of compiling marbles is both ongoing and two-sided: *Both parties benefit from having a good reputation.*[28]

"The unknown is innately both threatening and promising," states the psychologist Colin DeYoung. "The balance between those two responses, as they play out in competition with each other, explains a lot about human behavior and about individual differences."[29] How long it takes someone else's scale to tip and declare that you'd make a fine friend or quarterback varies greatly, depending on the situation and how risk averse someone is. Luck grows over time when you show up, avoid giving other people negative marbles (sarcastic, tardy, offensive) to add in the beginning, and check yourself, which gives others additional opportunities to learn about you and pair "you" with your positive traits. Coach Carter observed Charlie longer than the other athletes, giving him more opportunities to confirm that Charlie had the qualities he deemed important in the athlete-coach relationship. We may start the process of learning about the world as a random walk of information sampling, but eventually we're drawn to the kind of information that's easier for us to process.[30]

Sometimes, It's out of Your Hands

Charlie had control over a few components of his luck: He showed up, so he seemed less risky. He knew Coach Carter and was an outstanding student athlete, thereby emphasizing his personal value to the coach. The final aspect of the Charlie Brewer principle is out of our hands. Our prediction-loving brain is so smitten with cues that the mere act of connecting dots in the universe makes us happy, meaning that how quickly others collect those "you are right for the job" marbles depends on your resemblance to others who have succeeded in the past. The scale tips faster for some people.[31]

"A lot of times, you don't even stop to think about it very explicitly if somebody matches well with the idea of your expectations about what somebody should be like," says the researcher Mark Leary. "Only when you get mismatches do people give it much thought; otherwise, it feels good."[32] How closely someone aligns with our mental image of what that person should look like also affects our evaluations of his or her performance.

Researcher Noola K. Griffiths recorded female violinists to examine if their clothing influenced ratings of "proficiency, musicality, appropriateness of dress and attractiveness."[33] Women in a "nightclubbing dress" that included a "tightly fitted top and short skirt" were rated less technically and musically proficient than those wearing formal concert attire or jeans, even though the same master track was dubbed over each video. Repeat: Identical performances received lower scores when the women weren't wearing the expected attire. We give higher scores to people who dress the part. For example, patients rate doctors' trustworthiness, empathy, and competence highest when they wear a traditional white coat compared with sartorial alternatives like casual attire or a business suit.[34]

"It's more likely that mere exposure effect has to do with a feeling of *familiarity* or fluency. Things are familiar to you, and because it's familiar, this feeling of familiarity leads to a feeling of liking," states the learning researcher Jan De Houwer. Thinking of Brewer as the quarterback was a fluent thought for Coach Carter, just as it was easy to imagine a Bush as president or that handsome brunette as our future life partner.[35]

We Do What Feels Right
(Not What *Is* Right)

Swiping a debit or credit card at a point-of-sale machine to make a payment is the first step in a long and complex process that ends, as most things in life do, by taking your money. My little credit union in Oregon doesn't own all of the infrastructure required to let me buy noodles in Singapore with my debit card, so it has to outsource some of the steps for this twenty-first-century game of telephone: reading a magnetic strip, communicating about funds, paying noodle vendors—all of which require speed, encryption, compliance, and perfection. One company that helps facilitate your cash-free morning latte is Opus Systems.

The director of hiring and sourcing Farokh Daruwala has invited me to oversee his process. The Opus Systems office is on the second floor of an upscale business park office in Princeton, New Jersey, across from a Westin and a Jim's Steakout; the building does not lack for law offices or nubby blue industrial carpeting. Aside from the putting green, the only nonessential decoration I can find is an infographic depicting the differences between the habits of Winners and Losers. (According to a pair of androgynous figures, losers make excuses and winners make plans.)

Daruwala himself is wearing a yellow button-down shirt and khakis and speaks with a clipped Indian accent formed in his childhood in the outskirts of Mumbai. He opens up his LinkedIn account, which Opus uses for the bulk of its hiring. Farokh has heard of other companies using Facebook but prefers to use Facebook for personal use and LinkedIn for work.

"We are hiring for two very senior positions right now," he says, showing me a stack of résumés.

I sort through the pile with the job description of global alliances manager in mind.

One jumps out, a candidate who has been doing the exact same job in a high-volume environment for over ten years. He's developed and maintained an impressive international set of connections. On the next page, my eyes are drawn to a pleasant surprise: He's a former marine!

It's easy for me to imagine a marine in this position because it's easy for me to imagine a member of the armed services doing *any* job. I've garnered a positive impression of their discipline and work ethic from personal experiences and already added lots of marbles to that side of the scale. Cultural references we've all been exposed to make it easy for everyone to make associations about specific groups of people. One of those is the simple connection between "men" and "work."

In one study by Michael Norton at Harvard Business School, subjects ranked applicants for a job at a construction company and were asked to emphasize industry experience and an engineering education. The two best candidates had engineering degrees; one had five years of experience, plus extra certification from the American Concrete Masonry Association. The other had nine years in the field but lacked additional education.[36] When anonymous, gender-free résumés were judged, the applicant with extra education was chosen 76 percent of the time. When names were added (alternating, so sometimes the candidate with more education and less experience was male, and sometimes female) and the résumé with those credentials belonged to a woman and was pitted against a male candidate, only 43 percent favored her. Hardly any subjects cited gender as a factor.

One large-scale meta-analysis examining over twenty-two thousand hiring decisions found that men were typically preferred over women for traditionally male-dominated jobs—manager for a construction company being the ace in the hole here. No such preference for women was found for jobs in fields dominated by women.[37]

"Insight into the mechanism does not protect you against the effects. You make a stereotypical decision and then your next secretary is once again a woman, and all of women are secretaries," says the researcher Norbert Schwarz.[38] Schwarz's work has explored the surprisingly hazy line between thinking and feeling, demonstrating that emotion and cognition influence each other. "It's a self-reinforcing process. You do things because they feel right. It feels right because it is fluent and familiar and that's just how it wants to be."

Markets allow cultures to organize large-scale behavior and exchanges. In today's job market, we submit résumés and interview candidates because that's simply how we're used to picking new employees. But just as a judge of a tattoo competition only needs to select one that fits the bill (not the best), a culture only needs to come to a decent solution for organizing its members' lives before it catches on and emerges as a social norm. The *best* method of doing something doesn't always emerge, just whatever is efficient enough to get the job done. Cultural norms are so slow to change because constant exposure to an idea is what makes it seem normal; predictability and a sense of control are what keep us sane.[39]

Women are secretaries because the mechanization of the Industrial Revolution eventually spread to the office. The Remington typewriter was introduced in 1874—necessary, but demeaning work on a menial piece of equipment.[40] Managers wouldn't have to learn how to operate them or even train their office workers if they hired young women, which they could do at a fraction of the cost of hiring a man. In the 1880s, typewriters were advertised by pretty young things dubbed "Remington girls," making them more marketable to office managers. Secretarial work offered better working conditions, hours, and more prestige than work as a salesgirl, the other white-collar position available to women.

Like nurses, these women became commonly associated with a support role that never threatened the jobs they assisted, so employment manuals soon touted them as having natural expertise. In a 1925 treatise on office management, William H. Leffingwell wrote, "A woman is to be preferred to the secretarial position, for she is not averse to doing minor tasks, work involving the handling of petty details, which would irk and irritate ambitious young men, who usually feel that the work they are doing is of no importance if it can be performed by some person with a lower salary."[41] By 1930, 95.6 percent of the office workers employed in the United States as stenographers and typists were women.

Hiring managers see résumés and add "safe" marbles to the scale, seeing it as a good process of selecting candidates. But is it? By definition, evaluating candidates from résumés without prioritizing criteria beforehand means sizing them up on a holistic basis, just like Daruwala as he picked up each résumé. As stated in *Judging Merit*, this kind of decision makes it less likely that someone will be able to "articulate the criteria leading to his judgment and thus reduces the possibility of challenging, justifying, and improving these criteria." Using *all* of the information on a résumé or application implicitly indicates that you haven't systematically decided which traits are *most* important in a candidate.[42] When the hiring standards are flexible, people simply go with their gut, unknowingly confusing "this information is easy to process" with "this must be right."[43] For example, gender bias is typically eliminated only when hiring managers firmly commit to a set of criteria *before* looking at the résumés.[44] Otherwise, the only source of error correction that usually comes into play is when things go south and we place the blame on the most salient or noticeable difference.

"With recruiters, the only signal they get back is when they make a catastrophically bad hire," says Vivienne Ming, a theoretical neuroscientist turned start-up founder, whose work on maximizing human potential has helped uncover which traits actually help predict employee performance. "The only training they get is 'Don't take a risk.'"[45]

I pass along the résumé, which Daruwala peruses. He is impressed with this man's work history, the years of consistency and regularity, climbing the ladder in the exact position Opus needs to fill. But he quickly puts his résumé back in the pile.

"He does not have the relevant experience," he replies. This man's experience was in the *pharmaceutical* industry, but he wants another kind of applicant: someone who can hit the ground running in financial services.

"If we are working with a Fortune 500 company, they probably want someone who is working at a similar-size company with similar issues in a similar industry," says Eric Fine, a recruiter at Michael Page. "The best-case scenario is to find the person doing that job at a competitor. Ideally, you'd find someone doing the exact same job at a rival company." Getting lucky is easiest for those who already fit the bill.[46]

· · · · · · · · ·

Charlie Brewer? Of *course* he should be the quarterback. Can't you just feel the excitement? Doesn't it just seem right?

It's impossible to start evaluating Charlie Brewer without this string of associations immediately coming to mind: *His grandfather was a quarterback for the University of Texas. His father was a quarterback for the University of Texas. His uncle was a quarterback for the University of Texas. His brother won two state championships as a starting quarterback for the team.* They're all positive images and things that help us predict. It's information that we know is good in the world. We pay attention to the things that help us achieve our goals in life; it's just more efficient that way, even though it turns us all into experts at ignoring information that feels wrong to process, even though this is precisely the kind of information needed to update our mental model of how the world works and improve.

It's spring ball at Lake Travis, and scouts from Oregon State University, Stanford, and the U.S. Air Force watch from the sidelines. Division I coaches aren't allowed to talk directly to the athletes until they're seniors, but they can talk to their coaches beforehand.

"Coach Carter was telling me about all of the juniors who already have offers. Ivies," I say to the stern, black-polo-clad OSU scout as he sizes up the boys. It's in the mid-eighties, barely breezy, and cloudless, and these boys are running countless plays with all of their pads, uniforms, and helmets. This is the good weather, I'm told.

The scout crosses his arms and keeps his eyes on the field. "Well, yeah. That's when you gotta get 'em."

You've got to get them early, but not just when they're juniors: Becoming a quarterback in Texas is something that starts in middle school. "It's like a language," says Carter. "Say we speak ten thousand words here on varsity. [In middle school] they're learning, maybe, five hundred."

And there are no cuts in the Lake Travis football program, so anyone who signs up for football doesn't take standard physical education class. They learn football year-round. So technically, the University Interscholastic League "limits practice and rehearsal for each extracurricular activity to a maximum of eight hours outside of the school day per week. . . . [T]he athletic period does not count against that eight hours."[47] But it's thanks in part to this classic Texas loophole that the first day of spring ball practice at Lake Travis looks suspiciously professional. By this point in the process, there are few surprises.

As Carter told me a few months ago, "We start evaluating these kids the *first* time we see them." But before Carter and the other coaches ever saw those kids, they started building a mental catalog of successful quarterbacks from the past and developing associations about who might work in the future.

Back outside Austin, I loiter near the middle of one of Lake Travis's practice fields, a few feet behind a cluster of players led by the varsity offensive coordinator Michael Wall, a tall, lean, ruddy-cheeked blond running drills with a small group of would-be quarterbacks. It's Charlie Brewer and the others, an array of leggy boys vying for the remaining spots as Brewer's backup or on JV. They form an informal, near-circular line.

Wall is busy yelling strings of words in their language: *Fresno, California! Phoenix, Arizona! One ball, guys, set up strong and drive it! Come on!*

One at a time, the player in front hunches over and waits for Wall to bark his command before shuffling backward, following his marching orders. The two main targets are nets. The one to their left resembles a comically oversized basketball net. To the right is a net the size of a narrow bay window, vertical and rectangular, with three tiny pockets forming a diagonal line down its front, each one scarcely larger than a football.

Balls are thrown into the ground or the big net; a few are launched toward the daunting, pocketed net.

There are middle school coaches present today, including Jerrod Ackley, a coach from Hudson Bend Middle School, one of Lake Travis High's two feeder middle schools. He's new to the district, only about a year in, and is observing spring ball as a part of his professional development. The middle school and high school coaches trade notes about who's playing well ("vertical alignment," explains Carter), because the star athletes begin to emerge around seventh grade. I ask Ackley how he picks quarterbacks.

"Strength. Leadership. The way they carry themselves. If he has confidence, then the team notices that. You can usually tell at a pretty young age who's the more elite among the group." The other boys naturally fall in line behind the quarterback. It's hard to imagine a teenager as comfortable on the field as Brewer, who grew up around Texas football royalty.

We use our feelings as a source of information when making decisions without ever knowing where those feelings come from. Unless some method of error correction comes into play, there's nothing stopping us. Is there a way for Carter to find out if another athlete would have made a better quarterback? The other coaches would have chosen Charlie. There's no alternate universe in which we could turn back time and see how life would have turned out with that different choice.

"Sometimes, you're better off making a decision and sticking to it, even if it really wasn't the best decision. If you just keep . . . changing your mind, you're not really going to accomplish anything," says the researcher Cindy Harmon-Jones. "You really need to stop regretting and experiencing dissonance about maybe making the wrong choice and start derogating that other college that you could have gone to. [You need to say] 'I've really made the right decision,' and just go ahead and act on that decision in the best way possible."[48]

One, two, three, convoy! Going convoy! Ackley and I look up. Brewer moves back a few steps and looks right before throwing a perfect spiral landing squarely in that minuscule middle pocket.

Maybe someone else would have made a better quarterback than Brewer. But does it matter? The kid has a hell of an arm.

Notes for Those Who Want to Be Like Charlie

- Flaunt your similarities to those people you want to be compared with.

- Go to the party or the lecture hall. Move to that neighborhood. Length of acquaintanceship is a proxy for trust. Eighty percent of success is just showing up.

- Because we typically opt out of interactions that we suspect will be unpleasant, first impressions can be *impossible* to overturn if they're negative.

- "For young people who are lucky enough to have wealthy parents or good looks, the schoolyard is an easy place to get by. Not only do peers want to befriend them and ascribe them significant social power, but they also are willing to overlook and even reward their sometimes nasty behavior. For children who do not have such luck, the road is much more difficult."[49] In other words, you can only get away with what's known as "being a dick" if you're shielded by money or good looks, but as we'll see later on, it's not a winning strategy.

- Sit in the middle. Be nice.

- People stay in environments where they feel comfortable. If you show up someplace and feel like a stranger, push yourself and stay.

- Being considered safe or being similar to something awesome are shortcuts to establishing a good reputation—and *that's* what makes someone seem trustworthy. Consider other methods of building a good reputation: a social connection or an association with a prestigious organization.

- Showcase both your warmth *and* competence by bringing everyone delicious, homemade brownies. If they turn down your offer, run; luck cannot exist wherever brownies are declined.

3

Bitches in Glasses

The Occasionally Unlucky Side of Intuition

Today, Kristen Paladino, a casting director from New Jersey, is decked out in flip-flops, candy-pink toenails, three bracelets on her right wrist, and a long black jersey-knit dress. Her trusty assistant Steve Stancato sits beside her, clicking away on his MacBook as she tells me about one of her favorite games as a child.

"Match. I was really good at that," she says with a smile. Match, if you'll recall, is a game that begins with a grid of cards lying facedown; each player flips over any two cards at a time to reveal the cartoon faces on the other side. If the cards don't match, you flip them back over; when you manage to pick up two with identical faces, you keep both. She's always been good with faces.

Paladino somehow still looks upbeat, despite already having dealt with people in the entertainment industry for hours. We're at Silvercup Studios in New York, where projects like *Do the Right Thing* and *The Devil Wears Prada* were filmed; an episode of *Girls* is filming right now. As we speak, Paladino is casting for *Taxi Brooklyn,* a new TV series based on a 1998 film.

Her assistant Stancato scans a list of faces on the Breakdown Services website, where casting offices post descriptions of the kinds of performers they're looking to hire; agents pay a hefty fee for access to these legitimate listings, scouring them to see if any of their clients would be a good fit.[1] Stancato and Paladino have put out calls for the actors they need: a female knockout in her late twenties or early thirties who can speak fluent French. A tall Caucasian man. A teenager so scrawny as to invite accusations of a drug problem. I'm confident that I could find people like this in five minutes—we're a few subway stops away from midtown Manhattan, after all—but rules are rules, and Paladino needs to find members of the Screen Actors Guild matching these descriptions.

She leans into the monitor, scrolling through the grid of faces. For a few, she'll get a hunch that they'd be right and call them in for an audition, meaning that the screening process begins *before* actors get the opportunity to showcase their talents. Just as another athlete (given the same level of attention and training) might have been a better quarterback than Charlie Brewer, another actor might have brought a part to life even more than those who landed auditions.

I lean into Kristen Paladino's grid of faces on the MacBook and find myself getting a feeling about some of them. We use our feelings to decide, favoring information that's familiar and easy to process, and then rationalize our choices after the fact; the circuitries governing our emotions, moods, thoughts, and actions run at different speeds, influencing one another. We claim to have sound reasons for picking one head shot, online dating profile, or résumé over another, but because of the countless influences that might tip the scales at any time, the ultimate reason is simple: It's luck.

Your Face: Secret Weapon or Achilles' Heel? (Neither, It's Not up to You)

If you were a monkey in a lab who learned that a prized squirt of juice always came after a flash of light, eventually your dopamine neurons would begin firing at the earliest sign of reward: the light.[2] It's our brain's job as an action-oriented predictive processor to make sense of the world as soon as possible so we can plan efficiently without getting caught off guard; we don't just predict; we look for and lean into the predictive cue.[3] Cues help us make sense of what we encounter in the future, and for the most part, they work. In nature, similarity is a pretty good basis for figuring out what things are and what we should do with them; generalizing is efficient and, to some extent, necessary.[4] If one had to learn what "tall things with branches and leaves" were upon encountering each vaguely treelike object, Lewis and Clark would have died far before reaching the Pacific Northwest. "The dubiousness of this notion is itself a remarkable fact. For surely there is nothing more basic to thought and language than our sense of similarity; our sorting of things into kinds," noted the philosopher W. V. Quine.[5]

We learn about people this way, too. When subjects play an economic game called the Trust Game with others that can result in mutual trust (and splitting a bigger pie) or selfish deflection, eventually they get an idea of what the other person is likely to do and whether that's going to result in a reward. Over time, activity in the subjects' ventral striatum—a key motivational or reward center of the brain—shifts from the moment of cash getting and onto the instant of identity revealing, just as our dopamine neurons begin firing at the juice-predicting light.[6] We use whatever information we have about someone to predict his actions. When others unexpectedly share or act selfishly, the subjects' neural response reflects the WTF Just Happened error signal that catches us off guard and makes us rethink life itself.[7]

Because survival requires us to accurately predict whether we're seen as someone's dinner or dinner guest, humans are quick to try to predict what kinds of rules are guiding other people's actions. Our automatic response to faces starts at birth, when newborns move their eyes longer to keep looking at faces and patterns with a higher density of information in the top half, "three blobs" bearing some semblance to eyes and a mouth.[8] Every face we've ever seen, whether in person or on a screen, has shaped our brain.[9]

We all prefer potential friends and teammates. By three months old, we look longer at people resembling our caregivers—if it's familiar, it hasn't eaten you yet—and by nine months prefer toys that appear to be helpful.

Forming judgments about people is a process of collecting marbles: We see a cue suggesting that someone will play nice and plunk a huge marble on the "safe" side of the scale. These start with simple visual signs (age, gender) and become more complex over time (accent, religious preferences). Categorizing others and favoring our in-group is inevitable—hatred is not—but because we learn from what we see and hear in addition to our own experiences, by the age of six, kids with biased parents are biased themselves.[10] Eventually, our brains and real-world experiences allow for the kinds of nuanced predictions that allow us to see a name like "Brewer" and add a marble to the "great quarterback" side of the scale.

The Things You Learn from a Face

Because the brain works via prediction and laziness—and survives by being severely risk averse—we wind up making decisions about people by overgeneralizing from visible features and their non-visible traits.[11] Without realizing it, we assume that new people we encounter will share qualities with those they resemble or remind us of, meaning that we often make assumptions about people that we can't possibly know and act on them as though they were gospel. You may remember Bertram Gawronski, an expert on implicit cognition, from last chapter's study examining the relationship between gut reactions and ultimate preferences; he's also conducted many studies on the facial similarity effect.

"We automatically evaluate unknown people," agrees Gawronski. Whether or not we do it *well* is another story. We assume that visible information alludes to underlying traits based on similar people we've seen before—even people we've never met.[12] Seeing someone with even a passing resemblance to a figure we've encountered before can activate related memories without our even realizing it. We use whatever information is available when we decide, and sometimes what's most accessible is the emotional baggage that mere visual cues dredge up; it's marbles, marbles, all the way down. In the dating world, you may recognize this phenomenon as "having a type."

"People have hang-ups," says the matchmaker Lisa Clampitt. "One guy is from a dark-haired, Italian family and only wants to date blondes. You can't set him up with an Italian."[13] When someone with a strong association between "dark-haired women" and "pasta-fueled family drama" sees a brunette, the emotions and memories he associates with brunettes come to the forefront (pushy mother! hysterical sister!), *regardless of what the new person is actually like.* Ergo, people end up with decades' worth of relationship baggage and an increasingly specific "type," making blind assumptions about new people without getting to know everyone in the world who shares those traits. In neuroscience labs and on Tinder, we trade speed for accuracy, filtering and judging people based on information that doesn't matter.[14]

Certain faces benefit from their similarity to others when there are billions of dollars on the line, and we don't even know it's happening. In 2013, the famed venture capitalist Paul Graham told the *New York Times,* "I can be tricked by anyone who looks like Mark Zuckerberg. There was a guy once who we funded who was terrible. I said: 'How could he be bad? He looks like Zuckerberg!'"[15] Graham later said repeatedly that he was joking and that anyone repeating this line has an agenda to promote—I mean for Pete's sake, how could anyone use such a meaningless metric or even *believe* that— but loads of studies reveal that we do this all the time without realizing it.[16]

In a now-famous test on implicit social cognition, Pawel Lewicki gathered eighty subjects, forty men and forty women, from the University of Warsaw. Two research assistants—one with long hair and another with short hair and glasses—were instructed to ask the subjects a few questions: what their name was, what room they had been recruited from for the study, and a third, "What is your birth order?" After that third, uncommon query, each subject asked for clarification to make sure he or she understood the term correctly.

The assistant with long hair clarified the meaning of "birth order" in a friendly tone. But the second one with short hair and glasses was instructed to answer in a "slightly irritated way": *"Don't you really know the meaning of birth order?!"* Then the subjects completed some busywork that they were made to believe was the real study. But the juicy data collection began afterward, when each of them was given a sheet of paper and told to deliver it to someone in another room.

They arrived to find two women sitting down, each at her own table roughly the same distance from the door, writing but not looking up. Their traits subtly mirrored the traits of the assistants in the other room: One of them had long hair; the other, short hair and glasses. Students whose question about the term "birth order" was handled professionally gave their sheet of paper to the women at random, each lady receiving the paper about 50 percent of the time. But 80 percent of the students whose innocent question was met with a sharp, annoyed *"Don't you really know the meaning of birth order?!"* avoided handing their paper to the woman with short hair and glasses. When asked how they selected whom to give the paper to, no one mentioned her appearance or similarity to the previous bestower of mild social trauma. This lends credence to an unsavory finding made by Lewicki: "One unfriendly gesture on the part of the first experimenter was capable of producing a tendency to avoid people even roughly similar to her physically."[17]

Armed with this knowledge, I went to Los Angeles to interview more casting agents about the luck required to get roles, including Bonnie Gillespie, author of *Self-Management for Actors*. Gillespie admitted to having seen casting decisions made on the basis of arbitrary hunches.

"Those exceptions usually come from 'reminds me of my ex' or 'reminds me of the person who stole my ex.' That's the one person that disagrees with everybody else in the room, with a good reason," she says. These, of course, are the moments when a casting director or producer could *recognize* the source of that gut reaction; usually things just feel a bit off when we see someone we don't like. One study on the relationship between our choices and facial preferences photographed thirty mixed-sex couples and then used image-editing software to blend those photos with pictures of other random faces. The subjects returned a few weeks later to rate a series of images. Surprise, surprise: Subjects liked the photos that had been tweaked to share some traits with their significant others, without ever realizing why. Just like the students in Moreland's study, they never even saw it.[18]

As the model turned sociologist Ashley Mears expertly depicted in *Pricing Beauty: The Making of a Fashion Model,* booking agents in charge of selecting models for fashion shows and campaigns rely on a similar feeling when viewing faces on a wall plastered with Polaroids. Summarizing the career trajectory of professional pretty faces and bodies, she wrote, "The model . . . rides the tides of luck." Mears asked an editor in charge of hiring models to explain her process. "Though we talked for almost an hour, she could never quite find the words to explain it," she writes.[19]

The appeal of being able to predict someone's internal world from their face dates back to the first time someone's mother caught them rolling their eyes. Aristotle was the first to rigorously jot down his thoughts on the matter; over the years, this practice became known as *physiognomy.* "If the heart is habitually exercised by malice, then a malicious expression becomes habitually stamped upon the face. . . . Thus the habits of the soul become written on the countenance," wrote a success manual author in the nineteenth century.[20] Our first impressions do not emerge from divinely inspired blank slates or uncanny intuition. Can you really tell how nice, smart, or creative someone is by looking at her face? No, you cannot. But unless you're given some form of error correction, your assumptions and associations can become stronger and less accurate over time.[21]

How to Nail the First Impression (or Blow It. Honestly, There Are No Rules)

The way that others evaluate you—your photo, résumé, application, tattoo, or first-date cardigan—follows the same process of placing marbles on a scale as soon as they get any information. We form impressions of people the same way we form an impression of anything: As soon as our scale of marbles starts tipping one way, we begin to form a hunch and then start gathering evidence to back up that hunch by selectively picking up the marbles that are easiest to pick up, favoring the information that's easiest for us to process. Sometimes, that's a preexisting attitude formed when we learned to pair the seemingly benign (the font someone used on a résumé) with something of known value (Bob used that font on his résumé and *he was the worst*).[22] Because of our survival-based need to evaluate others quickly, this can even mean picking up marbles from irrelevant sources and mistakenly attributing them to a person.

In a classic study, men were more likely to call a female researcher if they met her while walking across a shaky bridge than a sturdy bridge. When you're feeling *all* the feelings when you meet a girl, it makes sense to assume that she's the cause of some of them. If people are holding a warm beverage while evaluating someone else, they pick up that "warm, fuzzy feeling" marble and conclude that the other person is extra friendly or warm. If you read dating profiles while seated at a wobbly table, your scale starts hunting for marbles to counter that, leading to a preference for people whose profiles suggest signs of stability; a firm seating arrangement could make you feel sturdy enough to favor adventurous profiles.[23]

If you want to get lucky, make other people read about your stability ("cumulative decades spent on earth, all living as a human being") while walking across a tightrope and holding a hot beverage. To soothe your soul, keep in mind that you may be spending your millionth night in with Mr. Whiskers through no fault of your own, but the fact that others were reading about you while holding a can of soda and swaying on a hammock at the precise moment that they stumbled upon your Machu Picchu photos.

Our brains are lazy and our time limited, so as we get more options, we become more superficial—about everything.[24] "Basically, we get around choice overload by ignoring most of the options that have been made available to us," says the decision-making researcher Peter Todd.[25] One analysis of eighty-four speed-dating studies found that people's criteria for potential mates depended on the size of the event; confronting multitudes makes us unknowingly switch tactics and focus on qualities that are quickly and easily assessed. When we live in a tiny town in Alaska, we'll give the whole "dating Steve" thing some real time before we gather enough marbles to say no;

on a dating app in a metropolis, we give him nothing whatsoever unless he's undeniably hot.

On the dating website OkCupid, this first information is a photo, creating a huge disparity between how many messages the most attractive people get and their counterparts with slightly less symmetrical faces. When OkCupid redesigned the website and enlarged the profile photos, the hotties got even more messages. If salaries and match percentages were prominently displayed, it'd be hunting season for late-career professionals.[26]

On January 15, 2013, OkCupid declared Love Is Blind Day and removed everyone's profile photos for a few hours. Some ballsy singletons arranged dates during this glitch in the matrix, filtering and selecting based on the information still available. People ended up enjoying themselves on these dates, even if their attractiveness rating was an 8 and their date's was a 5. "In short," wrote the co-founder Christian Rudder in his book *Dataclysm*, "people appear to be heavily preselecting online for something that, once they sit down in person, doesn't seem important to them."[27]

Consider what this switch in decision-making strategies looks like in other areas of life. Blindly submitting a grad school application, message to some sweetheart on Jdate, or a CV to 7-Eleven along with all of the other suckers leaves us open to being on the receiving end of this kind of snap, or one-step, judgment—going straight from application or photo to an assessment based on minimal information. Without realizing how stiff the competition really is, we might mistakenly assume that producers, managers, promoters, or agents will make it to the end of our reel, portfolio, demo tape, or short story. But if our website is crappy, our head shot suggests the presence of multiple chins, or the first scene builds too slowly, our dreams can easily get tossed aside. Like tattoos and Olympians, when the "best" is subjective, mere order changes who emerges victorious. As long as the gatekeepers eventually find a worthwhile partner, employee, start-up, actor, artist, or writer, it doesn't matter. Life is not a pure and virtuous luck-free meritocracy because not all merit gets a fair chance.

"A friend of mine worked reading the slush pile at a publishing company," says the cultural sociologist Katherine Giuffre. "Every day she would go into this room, and every day hundreds of manuscripts arrived in these manila envelopes, many more than she could read in one day. They were coming in faster than she was ever able to read them. So she would play these little games where she would say, 'Okay, today I'm only going to read things that come in red envelopes.'"[28] This little game can continue ad infinitum because of what the *Black Swan* author Nassim Nicholas Taleb calls the cemetery of letters: Every great masterpiece was once an unpublished pile of papers sitting on a desk, and some would-be literary masterpieces never make it past that stage. Drawing conclusions from the winners about what's *required* to find success ignores the legion of never-rans that had the misfortune of arriving at every publisher's door in the wrong-color envelopes. Some actors may never get a big break because of casting directors' hunches when they saw their faces.[29]

Think about a hiring manager evaluating a stack of résumés, one of which advertises a candidate's fluency in French. Does it matter, even if the position is for a web designer? It just might.

"Suppose the judge has a long-dormant interest in learning French to talk to her elderly aunt in Montreal. No doubt the other applicant would feel a warm glow for being offered the job," writes Warren Thorngate in *Judging Merit.* "But how would you feel about such a one-step judgment, especially if you spent 3 days preparing your résumé for the job opening but did not bother to note in your résumé that you, too, speak French[?]"[30]

I called Thorngate to ask how such haphazard processes manage to continue. "They may have overlooked some very good candidates, but they don't care," the judgment and decision-making researcher replied. "It's not a punishing error for the person who does it."[31]

The RecruitMilitary annual job fair takes place in the New Yorker hotel on Eighth Avenue a few blocks from the Empire State Building, past the lobby with throngs of tourists hunched over their rolling bags, maxed-out credit cards, and NYC guide books in indecipherable languages, past the short man in an ill-fitting suit brandishing an oversized walkie-talkie, up the elevators with art-nouveau-style detailing straight out of *Metropolis,* and over the gold and red carpeting that must have looked great in the 1930s.[32]

Most of the 508 attendees are clean-shaven men with buzz cuts and new binders, replete with promise and perfect posture, many of whom have been unemployed for months or have recently returned from tours of duty but are getting housing allowances from the GI bill or relying on the support of parents and spouses until figuring out their place in the civilian world.

A mob stands in front of the table of an employer that bridges the gap between the technical aspects of military life and a softer, horizontally structured company, one envied and known for an employee-centered culture, like Zappos or Google.

JetBlue now has fifteen thousand employees, triple its size when the manager of talent acquisition Jonathan Toppin, or JT, started working there more than a decade ago. With the exception of brown wing tips, Toppin is wearing all blue and purple, from his purple pin-striped shirt to his tie.

"My advice is to apply right now and work here while you get your AP," he says, advising someone to get his pilot license certification. "That way, by the time you get your license, we'll already know your work ethic, how you fit in. We'll be able to transition you. If you wait until you get your license to apply, you'll be an unknown."

The first, Courtney, is wearing an argyle cardigan and the characteristic slouch of a young man feeling the weight of being forced to make too many life decisions in a short period of time. His eyes are glazed over. The second young man, Garcia, has a buzz cut and is slouching at five feet nine inches. His crisply white button-down shirt is covered in perfectly symmetrical creases only seen on clothing that has been removed from packaging within the last hour. Later, when I ask him for his email address, he gives me an email address with a user name more befitting a video game forum than the job market.

"I'll make you an offer," says JT. "You email me, or you put your information into the website and mark where we met, and I will guarantee you an interview. Guaranteed."

"All right." Garcia shrugs, as though a friend had just asked to take him shopping. He doesn't seem to think that an interview is a big deal, but of the 125,000 applications that JetBlue receives a year, only 7,000 or so are brought in for in-person evaluations, making JetBlue's gates nearly as hard to open as Harvard's.

"To tell you the truth, out of all the people I speak to like that directly, fifty percent of them will actually take me up on my word," says Toppin. "The first guy that I spoke to, Courtney, I believe he'll end up doing that. The young man who just left, I think he's more of a . . . just . . ." He pauses and strains to find the right word. Something about the exchange seems to have struck a chord. "You know, he's looking around. I can only give them the offer. The rest is up to them to take advantage of it."

It's impossible to gauge someone's industriousness, intelligence, or loyalty from two minutes at a job fair; for these, you'd have to observe behavior over time in a variety of situations or ask several different types of people they've interacted with over the years, all while looking for signs of long-term changes. But today's hiring manager has to whittle down his choices and make potentially life-altering decisions based on a few seconds of interaction.

I look at JT's tie, the crown jewel in an already impressive outfit, a dark lavender number impeccably arranged in a triple knot.

"Details?" I ask.

"Details," he says, adjusting his tie with a smile.

"And how do you know if you're right?" I ask.

"That's the thing, you don't know until about six months after."

It's not a punishing error for the person who does it. "Even when the experts all agree, they may well be mistaken."[33] As long as a company eventually finds someone decent to replace Bob, Nancy in HR can disregard all of those French-free résumés with reckless abandon, bestowing luck upon the few who decided to interpret their halfway-decent pronunciation of *bonjour* as legitimate fluency in the language. Aside from getting rid of spelling errors and following industry conventions, advice on crafting the perfect résumé will always be incomplete because there's no way to know if Nancy in HR would find "Adventure Racing" or "Swarthmore" akin to plunking a big marble onto the "safe" or "would be good at this job" side of the scale.[34]

And then, the interview. But as Toppin just stated, interviews aren't foolproof. When our scale starts leaning to one side, it becomes easier to pick up marbles belonging to that side; getting a hunch about someone makes it easier to notice relevant information about them. Once we start feeling like someone might not be a good "fit," we act uneasy, which makes that person feel and act uneasy. When we like someone, our friendliness allows that person to open up with confidence. People are more confident about their judgments when they have more information about someone before the interview, but that's because they spend more time picking up one type of marble. Unstructured interviews, the most common form of hiring, are ripe with self-fulfilling prophecies.[35]

"It's one of those problems where everybody thinks that they're a good interviewer and they're a good judge of character," says the researcher Kristine Kuhn. "But obviously people just are not nearly as good as they think they are. Even [if] they met someone and judged them as a great employee and hired them, and then they turned out to be bad, that doesn't shake people's confidence. They can always explain away that it really didn't have anything to do with them not being a good judge of character."[36]

Think about that: Most of the hiring, dating, and luck-granting selection processes in use never offer corrective feedback. It would be nice if Nancy recognized that she penalizes and rewards unknown people because of their arbitrary associations to things she's seen in the past, but her job depends on being confident about her choices. When was the last time *you* got a bad feeling about someone and then genuinely tried to prove your hunch wrong? Improving your decisions requires corrective feedback—conceding that you could be completely, utterly wrong; hiring or dating someone despite getting a weird feeling about the person or not feeling a "click"; discovering the source of the aforementioned weird feeling; resolving those past issues and/or eliminating those biased sources of information; becoming less judgmental about people moving forward.

It's easier to discard the application, ignore the message, toss the unpublished novel, cross the street, and move on with our lives, ever so satisfied with ourselves for making yet another sound judgment of character—especially when the brain interprets mistakes as punishments and feeling right just feels so damn good. We never even think about proving our intuition wrong.[37] We often say that we're waiting for something to jump out at us, but *we're* the ones jumping and reacting to certain signs; the one-step process says more about the history and quirky preferences of the judge than about the person being evaluated.

Some Faces Mean Business

Our faces tell stories to others. Half of this is the setting, those relatively fixed aspects of our identity like our age, ethnicity, gender, and level of hotness that lay the groundwork for the other half, the action: What's our expression? What has our attention? What do we seem to think of it? Just as frequently linked settings and actions are easier to process (it's easier to identify someone skiing on a mountain than someone doing their taxes on a mountain), we're faster at linking up certain identities and actions. The average female face shares features with emotional expressions that evoke affiliation, like happiness. Likewise, there's quite an overlap between male facial features (square jaw) and facial expressions meant to demonstrate dominance (clenched jaw). Everyone warms up to a smiler—a sign that someone sees you as a teammate rather than lunch—but it's irksome to see dominant displays coming from beta players in the animal world, who should be cooperative and kind. Because we expect women to be more social and agreeable, non-smiling female faces are judged more harshly and severely than non-smiling male faces. Women are told to smile; men are left alone to attend to their affairs. On a guy, it's neutrality; on a lady, it's Resting Bitch Face.[38]

Other faces give you the impression that people mean business. More than two decades ago, the researchers Ulrich Mueller and Allan Mazur asked a group of students to rate the portraits of West Point's class of 1950 on one particular metric: dominance. Photos rated a 7 out of 7 were straight out of central casting, with strong jaws, high cheekbones, and rigid brow lines. Scores rated least dominant—1 out of 7—were reserved for men who looked baby-faced, with chubby cheeks, larger eyes, shorter noses, and smaller chins. Without the students knowing anything about these cadets except for how dominant their faces looked, their ultimate rating strongly correlated with their ultimate military rank at the most elite military school in the country. By their senior year, men of the West Point class of 1950 whose faces were rated "most dominant"—a face like the personification of GI Joe—were promoted *five times more* than their most chubby-cheeked classmates. That success followed them beyond West Point. Decades later, the guys who just looked like generals ended up *being* actual generals.[39]

"Facial dominance influenced career attainment, not vice versa," wrote the researchers.[40] Military career trajectories can be predicted on how square someone's jawline is; the genetic luck of having a strong browridge can serve as a lifelong cumulative advantage over other cadets at West Point. Features associated with dominance, like facial width, are associated with high levels of baseline testosterone; even though our hormonal levels can quickly rise and fall over the course of our lifetimes and days, our facial structure doesn't.

When we see a wider face, we stand up a little straighter and take that person's words more seriously; those are the faces we want on our side when the forecast calls for war. Bold, brash actions are interpreted differently when coming from people we associate with leadership roles. Aggression coming from someone who looks like he has more testosterone? It's a fluent thought that makes sense, so we like it.

Even though someone's baseline level of testosterone can't predict something as complex as his leadership ability, it predicts how we interpret his actions.[41]

Faces predict how we interpret people's actions.[42]

As we'll see in the next chapter, it's easy to be lucky when everyone has the same positive hunch about your most prominent trait.

I tell the casting agent Bonnie Gillespie about the research on faces:

Even though we may not realize it, we're searching for a prototype based on an image we already have in mind and overgeneralize facial features based on others we've known, which leads to habits that are hard to break. We pick someone who just looks right, which in turn stamps in the feeling of *rightness* for that thing.

"Oh, I can see that," she says, nodding. "You just get a feeling when you see certain faces."

Notes for Those of Us Who Have a Face

- If you aren't going to stop using your hunches anytime soon (that is, baggage based on past experiences), realize what it implies: Other people are also doing this to you, which can mean getting unfairly passed over for reasons that have nothing to do with your merit. Our failures are half chance. Knowing that you might be the victim of the Bitches in Glasses effect, you take things less personally and throw your hat into the ring every chance you get.

- Our primary motivation is survival, so flaunt cues that you're trustworthy, reputable, and safe: Smile in your head shot. Remove those jokes about serial killers and one-night stands in your on-line dating profile.

- Information that's easy to understand feels safer. Get a head shot that's mostly plain colors. Use an easy-to-pronounce version of your name.

- People start filtering out others as soon as we get *any* information—any marble that belongs on the "no thanks" side of the scale—and become more superficial as the options pile up. We might unknowingly be eliminating ourselves with shoddy envelopes, weird online IDs, unprofessional-looking websites, or goofy profile photos. Don't assume that other people will give you the benefit of the doubt; pay attention to details, spelling, and packaging.

- Our failures are half chance (that is, based on other people's unique evaluations). But *consistent* negative feedback shouldn't be ignored, especially from people with diverse backgrounds and experiences. Improving quality never hurts.

- A *lack* of feedback from gatekeepers may signal that it's time to improve what we're putting out into the ether first. Connections can only help.

- People with round, baby-like facial features are perceived as more likable and less competent, so they have to do twice as much work to be taken as seriously as people with dominant faces. It's harder for those with dominant faces to come across as safe or nurturing.[43]

- To make better decisions, figure out what criteria are important ahead of time and how to best measure that. Stick to the script.

- Ask yourself: Are you responding to the information in front of you, or to the assumptions you're making from that information? Luck is what catches us off guard, and that can only happen when you give other people a chance to surprise you.

4

How Sarah Palin Happened

The Infinite Luck of Being Beautiful

n her day, she was a looker and sometimes that's all you need.

Sarah Heath moved to Alaska with her family as a three-month-old infant in 1964. Like the vast majority of Alaskans, Heath became an active outdoors enthusiast. Her father was a science teacher and coach who passed down his love of athleticism to his daughter, whose aggressive playing style as the point guard on the state championship basketball team earned her the nickname Sarah Barracuda.

In 1984, two years after graduating from Wasilla High, Heath posed onstage and played the flute for the talent portion of the Miss Alaska beauty pageant, where the twenty-year-old won second runner-up in the contest and was named Miss Congeniality. (The winner, Maryline Blackburn, went on to earn two Grammy nominations.)[1] Heath graduated with a degree in journalism from the University of Idaho before returning to Alaska, where she worked as an on-air sports anchor for KTUU-TV in Anchorage.[2] A decade later, in 1996, Heath—who had, in the interim, married her high school sweetheart Todd Palin and earned a seat on the city council—ran for mayor of her hometown of Wasilla, defeating the incumbent by little more than two hundred votes in that town of roughly fifty-five hundred.

In an interview, one of Palin's friends recounted, "Once, while Sarah was preparing for a city council meeting, she said, 'I'm gonna put on one of my push-up bras so I can get what I want tonight.' That's how she rolls. . . . She has a horrible temper, but she has gotten away with it because she is a pretty woman."[3] Over the next decade, she was reelected mayor of Wasilla while working her way up the ladder of Alaska government.

In 2006, when she was elected governor of Alaska, she became the state's first female governor. In 2008, she received a life-changing phone call from John McCain, who asked her to join the Republican ticket as the presumptive nominee for vice president of the United States. The media and everyone's random family members on Facebook all pointed out that Palin's youthful, photogenic appearance served as the perfect contrast to McCain, himself straight out of central casting as the senior statesman with the noble wartime record. Whereas McCain looked like a president, Palin looked like the very thing that the lagging Republican nominee needed: a beautiful, brash celebrity, officially making Sarah Palin a political phenomenon.

While thin, Palin's résumé *did* exist. As the governor of Alaska, she was the only candidate on either ticket with experience in the executive branch of government. The brevity of her government-related résumé was seen as a boon to everyone tired of the Washington machine, the old boys' network, and politics as usual.

As a heterosexual female, it would take a minimal number of mojitos to get me to make out with a 1960s-era John McCain but none whatsoever to admit that Palin personifies the archetype of a sexy librarian. The very fact that Rush Limbaugh called Palin a "babe" means that her appearance has, most formidably, done the impossible: It has created a universe in which *Rush Limbaugh and I agree on something.*

The best-looking woman in American politics had the fastest, most meteoric rise in American politics. Let's be honest: Ugly women do not get jobs as on-air sports anchors or receive phone calls inviting them to run as the first female vice presidential candidate of the United States on the

Republican ticket. As Todd Purdum wrote in *Vanity Fair,* "Another aspect of the Palin phenomenon bears examination, even if the mere act of raising it invites intimations of sexism: she is by far the best-looking woman ever to rise to such heights in national politics, the first indisputably fertile female to dare to dance with the big dogs.[4]

"This pheromonal reality has been a blessing and a curse," Purdum noted. "It has captivated people who would never have given someone with Palin's record a second glance if Palin had looked like Susan Boyle. And it has made others reluctant to give her a second chance because she looks like a beauty queen." Research shows that attractiveness amplifies gender stereotypes; because of the disconnect between "feminine" and "manager," attractive women face more obstacles ascending to leadership positions than attractive men, and once in managerial positions they're judged harshly when they're attractive. But the benefits of beauty, as we'll see, far outweigh any costs.[5]

Since abruptly resigning as governor of her beloved home state, Palin has earned an estimated $13 million, including an annual $1 million contract with Fox News and $2 million for her adroitly named TLC show, *Sarah Palin's Alaska.* But Palin will forever remain the president of the Beauty Bubble, an ever-upward trajectory that can culminate in an offer for a job mere heartbeats away from the most powerful position in the free world despite having one of the thinnest résumés of the available, viable candidates and a tendency to stick her foot into her mouth whenever opening it in the absence of a teleprompter.

Is Sarah Palin a lucky woman? You betcha.

Hot or Not?

In the last chapter, we learned how our luck can depend on random assumptions that people make about us: If Nancy in HR is tacitly reminded of a grade school bully when seeing your photo on LinkedIn, your application could get tossed aside, crushing both your soul and your chances of replacing Bob in accounting. In this chapter, we'll see what happens when *everyone* gets the same hunch about a beautiful person's most prominent feature and what that ultimately does to her luck.[6]

Imagining life in Palin's Beauty Bubble first requires us to venture back to 1908, when a man walking around the British Isles noticed—as men are prone to do—women on the street, each of whom he classified into an "attractive, indifferent, or repellant category."[7] This wouldn't be news were he any other man in history, but this man was Francis Galton, polymath, cousin of Charles Darwin, and obsessive measurement taker of the human species.

Galton's method of classifying beauty remains the basis for how researchers measure attractiveness today. Imagine looking at a series of photos of faces, all photographed in exactly the same way, and rating each on a scale of 1 to 7. Get a group of people to do that for each photo, and average everyone's rating for each photo.[8] Having several people judge the faces eliminates the arbitrary "she's ugly because she looks like Megan" biases covered in the last chapter; having them rate the faces individually eliminates arbitrary consensus effects.

One of Galton's later obsessions was laying several photographs atop each other and assembling portraits from the composite images. Doing this, he discovered that the fusion of faces appeared to be quite datable. "The first set of portraits are those of criminals convicted of murder . . . the features of the composites are much better looking than those of the components. The special villainous irregularities in the latter have disappeared, and the common humanity that underlies them has prevailed."[9]

Attractive faces generally have symmetrical, average features—no single attribute sticks out; everything just goes together. Think about it: People get cosmetic surgery to *remove* their perceived villainous irregularities. All of which leads researchers to conclude that "beauty lies in the processing experience of the beholder."[10] Beauty is processed fluently; good-looking faces are easy on the eyes *because* they are easy on the mind.[11] There's plenty of evidence suggesting a universal agreement about which faces are attractive that predates the increasingly homogenized, Westernized, pervasive media landscape perpetually broadcasting the same faces du jour on magazine covers.[12]

People differing along gender, culture, and race lines agree who the hotties are—and so do babies. When shown two faces of wildly varied attractiveness ratings, six-month-old infants spend more time looking at faces—even those of other races and genders—rated as more attractive by adults.[13] Infants even prefer to look at other *infants* rated as highly attractive; even infants as young as two months old spent longer gazing at the ones Galton would have rated highly.[14] Unless everyone in the study spent their entire sixty days of existence staring at a copy of *Vogue for Infants,* the fact that babies are superficial bolsters the argument that our preference for beauty is hardwired and appears to stem from a deeply hardwired evolutionary advantage.[15]

We can't directly view the quality of someone else's genes, so we make assumptions about their fitness based on whatever information is available. People with mixed genetic ancestry are typically healthier because of their increased diversity of antibodies, as well as their decreased likelihood of carrying multiple copies of recessive genes that can be detrimental to offspring.[16] Physically attractive faces—all that symmetry and smooth skin—signify a lack of illness or parasites, an abundance of genes worth spreading.[17]

Whether you're comparing two apples or debating between going to a party or staying in for the night, your brain's reward circuitry calculates the values of those options.[18] Pretty faces activate this reward circuitry, including the striatum (the brain's motivational center) and the orbitofrontal cortex, or OFC.[19] Remember the OFC? It's the site where our brain collects marbles in favor of each option, weighing and comparing them on a scale. More OFC activation—more marbles—is seen when people view things of "hedonic interest" like appetizing food, pleasurable music, or attractive faces.[20] It's also receptive to momentary desires, becoming less active to food as we get our fill, indicating that we find it less appealing.[21] While the law of diminishing marginal returns applies to cheeseburgers—the first one is tastier than the tenth—doesn't every human want infinite bites out of a Javier Bardem and Penélope Cruz sandwich? Sí.

Jennifer Lawrence and Ryan Gosling walk through life with their faces bestowing a reward (a piece of cheese, a $100 bill, a lovely song) to all who look in their direction. They don't need to flaunt their yale.edu email address, demonstrate that they can hook you up with *Hamilton* tickets, or even give you a back rub to get you interested. We don't have to learn about rewards that foster survival, and simply *seeing* a beautiful face is an immediate reward symbolizing abundant, life-promoting resources.[22]

Our implicit, instinctual preference for physically attractive people influences how many cognitive resources we allocate to looking at them, as well as how we treat them and interpret everything they do.[23] Beauty, we assume, signifies other qualities we value in addition to truth. For example, subjects in Korea assume that the pleasingly faced, in addition to being smarter and socially well adjusted, possess an abundance of the traits they revere: more integrity and concern for others.[24] They get all the attention, all the love, and perpetual benefit of the doubt.

The Social Benefits of Beauty: How the Pretty Get Luckier

Beauty's benefits begin shortly after birth. Parents whose infants were deemed more attractive by third parties were more nurturing toward their three-month-olds than the parents of average-looking babies. Although the mothers of less attractive babies didn't report any difference in attitude toward their children—no one thinks that their own child is anything less than perfect—they paid less attention to their kids and were less playful when they *did* pay attention to them, all without being aware that they were doing so.[25] If you're protesting this by thinking, "There are no ugly babies!," please just be honest with yourself for a second. Seriously. No one is judging.

Remember the Trust Game from the last chapter, where subjects decide whether they trust someone enough to part with some of their hard-earned money in the hopes that they'll both wind up with more cash at the end? When subjects believe they're playing with someone attractive, they're more likely to extend trust, and offer the person more money when they do.[26]

In examining yearbook photos of attractive people, we automatically link them to descriptions of high-status students, assuming that if they have a particular jawline and set of cheekbones, they must be captain of the soccer team or the student council president.[27] Those with envy-inspiring cheekbones are even more likely to get their mail returned. In another classic study, experimenters left graduate school applications in phone booths— small glass cages that once restricted where people were allowed to have phone conversations in public—with photos of attractive or plain-looking applicants; applications accompanied by attractive photos were significantly more likely to be returned than the others.[28]

In addition to giving them extra points in social interactions, we grade their accomplishments on a curve.[29] Of poorly performing students, attractive students are less likely to be recommended for remedial classes.[30] Teacher expectations are robust predictors of academic success years later, and expecting a student to do well increases the quantity and quality of education; combined, these factors lead to a beauty bonus at school, where attractive students earn higher GPAs. The same research paper will get a higher grade when thought to be written by someone attractive than when written by a homelier student.[31] (If I were pretty, this book wouldn't get bad reviews: This is a scientific *fact*.)

Among poor kids, the cute ones manage to move up in the world by getting more education, enough to overcome their early socioeconomic disadvantages.[32] The wage gap between Sarah Palin and Mr. Bean is on par with race and gender differences, partly because attractive people have an easier time entering into more visible jobs that pay more, like upscale hotel clerk, newscaster, and governor of Alaska.[33] They're more successful as salespeople, get higher ratings as counselors, wind up in more prestigious occupations, and typically hang their hats quite high on the social totem pole—a bonus so robust and measurable that sociologists refer to it as "aesthetic capital."[34]

Life Is Easier in the Beauty Bubble

In one famous study, researchers told undergraduates they were examining the differences between initial encounters that included body language and those that didn't, like phone calls; like most decent psychology studies, it was built on a bed of lies. After both men and women completed questionnaires, the guys received a packet of information on their future conversation partner, including her photograph and questionnaire. On the basis of the picture and a few factoids, the men rated twenty-seven of the women's traits, like intelligence, friendliness, and warmth. Then the phone calls—ten minutes long—followed by answering more questions about their impression of the person they'd just spoken to. As is the case in every social psychology study known to humanity, good times were surely had by all.

Without knowing what anyone looked like, another group listened to one end of the conversation—either the female or the male—and rated them along a list of traits. Compared with the plain Janes, judges said that the attractive ladies enjoyed themselves more, were more confident and animated, and liked their partners more.[35] But the information packets they received included photos of *completely different women*—women whose appearances had been rated as either 8.1 or 2.6 in another study beforehand. The guys who thought they were going to be talking with more attractive women "expected to interact with comparatively sociable, poised, humorous, and socially adept women." Being motivated to bring your A-game makes you friendlier and assume better things about that person.

The first piece of information we get about something has a slew of downstream effects on how we view the rest of it because it frames our expectations. "Your first impressions . . . they're hard to overcome. When you get something that doesn't match your expectations, you tend to not learn from it. It's selective learning. It creates a confirmation bias, and can create a self-fulfilling prophecy," says Tor Wager, who has researched widely on the power of expectations.[36] In the case of other people, this first piece of information tends to be what they look like, which influences what we pay attention to, how we treat them, and how we interpret their actions. Because we expect pretty people to be awesome, we treat them better. The Sarah Palins of the world are simply lucky, all because people make the same assumption about their most prominent feature.[37]

Understanding an organism requires that we consider its proper ecological context; a fish makes no sense without water.[38] Humans have mastered the art of successfully living in every possible climate and landscape on earth—provided we're with other people. Our unique ecological niche that we've adapted to is the presence of others: social living, our average state of being, our baseline.[39] We choose our friends, jobs, lovers, hobbies, and environments, but a select few have better options. People like Palin, who have elicited such reliably positive responses from others since infancy, spend their lives in a unique environment: the Beauty Bubble.[40] Because our very survival depends on being accepted by others and having a fairly accurate view of how we fit into the world, feeling confident that you're included profoundly affects how you interact with the world.[41]

Other humans are big mysteries that unfold over time. But the one thing that's perpetually on display about them is their appearance. (And remember from the first chapter, we use the available information to judge.) Assuming that the unknown things will be as good as this piece of positive information is called the halo effect, leading us to expect that aesthetically pleasing people will be more awesome, intelligent, well adjusted, and mentally healthy than others.[42] This is just our lazy brain's way of learning about others: The obvious reward of their facial structure acts as a bright, shiny filter that makes everything else about them seem like puppies and rainbows, meaning that the exact same behavior is interpreted differently depending on how someone looks.[43]

After reading more about beauty than any sane person should simply because all of the effects seemed too bizarre to be true, I only found a few examples where beauty acts as a liability. When charged with crimes, attractive people usually receive more lenient sentences—except for crimes like fraud or deception, where they use their appearance as a weapon.[44] Good-looking women are expected to be more generous than average-faced gals, so even when they contribute as much as others, we interpret their behavior as selfish. (Attractive men don't pay this penalty because *life is simply not fair*.)[45]

Beauty's status can backfire when it's seen as a threat to someone's sense of self, which is why people with lower self-esteem are less likely to hire attractive people of the same gender, especially when they foresee lots of contact in the future. (Women, who can derive more of their self-worth from their appearance, are more prone to this sense of competition with one another.)[46] "If you're on a hiring committee and you're looking at job applicants, you may not even know that you have the goal of protecting yourself from a romantic rival, and you may not know why you're evaluating somebody negatively. It makes those biases hard to combat," says one study's author, Jon K. Maner.[47]

But Wait, There's More! (Status)

Cameron Anderson, a professor at the University of California, Berkeley, has been studying status and why some people rise to the top for decades. In one of his classic studies, Anderson examined how social networks developed in fraternities and sororities. When two people differing in status interact—be it a boss and an employee, or Sarah Palin and the bottom-feeders of the Wasilla city council—those below defer to the boss. Our brain constantly receives signals about where we are in the pecking order, and constantly being deferred to by others stamps in the idea that you have status.[48]

"Pretty much by all measures, it's better to be on the top of the totem pole," says Anderson.[49] "[If] you're on the bottom, there is more pressure for you to stay quiet. If you do speak up, you're going to get more looks. You're going to get more people giving you subtle or not-so-subtle signals, like, who do you think you are?" When coming from two different people, the exact same behavior is interpreted quite differently.[50] So yes, while I *could* wear my push-up bra to a Wasilla city council meeting, unless I pined to be awkwardly ignored, photographed, and turned into a meme symbolizing obliviousness, I would not get what I wanted that night.

Just as Francis Galton measured attractiveness by asking a bunch of people to rate faces, the sociologist Jacob Moreno devised a similar way to measure popularity in groups by asking each member to assess the other members, ranking who they were most attracted to and repelled by.[51] Those who garnered the most "attracted to" votes, the popular kids, were connected to everyone, and these leaders are typically good-looking.[52] Repeatedly winning popularity contests profoundly impacts how people see themselves.[53] It may never even dawn on you that you're unqualified for one of the most powerful positions in the free world, because, throughout your entire life, no one has ever told you *no*.[54]

Mark Leary is a social psychologist at Duke University, and one of the most preeminent researchers on identity and the self. In his model, self-esteem monitors our risk of social exclusion; because being ostracized is a death sentence for humans, self-esteem regulates our behavior.[55]

"It all gets centered around people's concerns with how they're viewed by other people."[56] *Everyone* wants to be friends with residents of the Beauty Bubble; when attractive people look at a crowd, they see more helpful, friendly, and flirty faces who perpetually give them the benefit of the doubt, an expanded sense of what they can do. Because we're so keen on getting close to the hotties, we manage to simultaneously get to know them better *and* focus on their bright spots. Getting more opportunities to practice flirting, clever one-liners, and fist bumps—and receiving more positive feedback in return—allows them to develop better social skills. "People do judge a book by its cover," write researchers, "but a beautiful cover prompts a closer reading, leading more physically attractive people to be seen both more positively and more accurately."[57]

Rose-Colored Glasses: Good for All, Easier for Some

We can often trace initial sparks back to stochastic events, but endurance takes more than randomness. Birth is luck, survival is a skill, and the persistence of cognitive biases is no different. In a comprehensive review of these so-called misbeliefs, the philosopher Daniel Dennett identified one family of mental quirks as adaptive: *positive illusions*. Seeing the world—ourselves, our future, and our ability to do what we set out to do—through rose-colored glasses is functional because it promotes survival by encouraging goal-directed action. Positive illusions (hooray, my life! my chances! my decisions!) form a large part of the psychological immune system that protects our mental health.[58] To maintain a sense of well-being and the motivation required to navigate the world, it's adaptive to see things as fair—we're less likely to play a rigged game that has constantly changing rules—so most of us focus on the parts we think are fair, or we adjust our attitudes to fit the situation.[59]

Our initial experiences with interacting with others—discovering who responds to our overtures, approaches us, and encourages us—help us internalize our sense of self-worth, which in turn informs who we pursue. To minimize ego-bruising, time-wasting rejection while maximizing the awesomeness in our lives, we need to calibrate our aspiration level well, so we aim as high as we think we can get.[60]

Humans can survive anywhere on earth, provided we're in the company of others, which makes the social rewards of being accepted, liked, or placed on a pedestal the most important rewards in the world. But a new pair of sneakers cannot object to being purchased, a pint of lager will never criticize your life choices, and cake won't suddenly stop returning your texts. Because we need other people to live, being rejected, ignored, or criticized activates the brain's WTF Just Happened signal, making us recalibrate and narrow our options.[61] So imagine if you felt like you could go anywhere or try anything with a greater chance of being accepted?

It behooves the survival of any social animal to know its place in the pecking order, and because appearance is such an obvious, inescapable status cue, beautiful people get an added boost to their psychological immune system by seeing themselves on top. Because they're used to envisioning life on that perch, they're also more likely to see the hierarchy itself as fair.[62] After all, they see the hard work they've done to get to where they are. They just don't see the impact of the lucky rewards, like parental affection, inclusion by schoolmates, flirtation, positive encouragement, and once-lost returned mail.

In the two-sided marketplace of dating, our sense of who's been interested in us romantically determines who we're willing to take the time to get to know—to be blunt, how high we aim and how quickly we settle. It will both depress and not surprise you that a woman's self-perceived mate value *depends entirely on her looks.*[63] It's as Joyce Carol Oates wrote: "Ugliness in a man doesn't matter, much. Ugliness in a woman is her life."[64] To calculate what they can fetch in the marketplace of mates, men get an overall sense of what they bring to the table, like their intelligence, attractiveness, income, and status. Women look in the mirror.

Beauty benefits people by bolstering their sense of self-worth. It gives them the confidence to pursue what they want and extra-wide hoops to jump through on their way to success. But beauty is anything *but* lucky when it forms an integral part of someone's self-worth. Because our self-concept depends on how well we seem to be doing in areas of life that matter to us, being overly appearance-concerned can lead people to objectify themselves, constantly thinking about how others judge their appearance. This, my friends, is *tiring*. Defining your sense of self-worth according to your rank in the Beauty Bubble becomes toxic when it's threatened and is all that you've got. But having a certain kind of face can be beneficial by making people feel more likely to be accepted, wherever they go.[65] It's all fun and games until the brain's That Did Not Pan Out signal is activated, and social rejection counts as a cost—one that some people simply don't have to pay as often as others.

We look out into the world and think about what to do.

I've been on the basketball team, a beauty queen, a news anchor, and a mayor. I've run a state so large that if it were an independent country, it would be the eighteenth largest in the world. No one has ever doubted me. I've gotten tons of social support and have succeeded at everything I've ever tried, so if anyone could lead the free world, well, why not me?

Notes for Those of Us Whose Invitations to Appear on the Cover of *Vanity Fair* Have Clearly Gotten Lost in the Mail

- The lesson of beauty that's adaptive for everyone is to internalize a sense of awesomeness and transform it into a very robust sense of self-worth that you can then use to conquer the world. Alas, for the lucky, beautiful people, it's easy.

- This chapter focused on facial attractiveness, but we rate appearance as a package deal that includes someone's personality: Being a jerk makes someone uglier; being kind and interesting makes him hotter. The longer people know each other before they start dating, the less likely they are to be as attractive to each other. Gathering more "this person is awesome!" marbles to add to the scale changes our overall impression of someone over time, including the big one: your perception of that person as a partner.[66] When it comes to relationships, "looks mean nothing in the grand scheme of things," says the matchmaker Lisa Clampitt.[67] Job, height, age, hair color, amount of facial symmetry—all of these shortcuts we use to filter out potential mates—don't influence the *quality* of a relationship.

- Physical attractiveness is both your face and how much you make the most of what you have. Performing the aesthetic labor of managing your appearance, also known as grooming, accounts for a large portion of the beauty premium. We have total control over our wardrobe, accessories, how well we take care of our body (being physically fit, height/weight proportionate, keeping fat to a minimum; for men, achieving some level of muscularity; for women, a low waist-to-hip ratio), hair, skin, teeth, and body odor.[68]

- Women who wear an amount of makeup deemed professionally acceptable make more money than those who go barefaced. In one study, grooming (everything you can control) accounted for the entire "beauty bonus" earned by women.[69]

- Appearance is a form of nonverbal communication we present to the world that others decode regardless of how much effort we've put into it, so it makes sense to make *something* of an effort. You don't have to stare at yourself all day, but other people do, which is why being well groomed signals agreeableness, or an interest in other people's perspectives and a desire to maintain good relationships with others.[70]

- Pursuing a beauty upgrade by trying to change your body (hitting the gym, eating healthier) and your wardrobe, or by getting cosmetic surgery can make people become hyper-focused on their perceived blemishes, causing self-esteem to plummet. Obsessing over what you dislike about yourself can make anyone feel bad, which is why being "objectively" beautiful is no guarantee of constant confidence.[71]

- How often do you defer to others because you think they're more attractive? How often do you perceive others to be higher on the totem pole because of their face? As *Star Wars* actress Carrie Fisher stated, "Youth and beauty are not accomplishments, they're the temporary happy by-products of time and/or DNA. Don't hold your breath for either."[72]

- Make yourself as hot as possible, and then stand up tall. Make the most of what you've got. You're a 10 to someone, so go out and conquer the world.

5

I Got This

The Lucky Art of Confidence and Approaching Rewards

t's April in New York and the heat is starting to swell, a pregnant belly of warmth jutting from spring's crisp shadows. Outside Grace Chapel downtown, trench coats and briefcases are slung over arms. Venture downstairs into the gymnasium and the density becomes cloyingly thick, with enough Burberry plaid, tweed, and sundry textured and lined clothes visible to upholster the seats in Carnegie Hall twice over. In one of the most diverse cities on earth, this gym is replete with hundreds of fit Caucasians in their thirties and forties who have unknowingly arrived in uniforms. Slim-cut suits and sleeveless, solid-color dresses are accessorized with French manicures, TAG Heuer watches, and pearl earrings. Shiny clips and pins and links anchor every scarf, tie, and cuff.

No one's hair looks out of place.

Not one hair.

This is the Kindergarten Admissions Fair hosted by the Parents League of New York, a nonprofit group that declared its guiding principle in an article in the *New York Sun*: "Let us make it fashionable to be sensible and unfashionable to be foolish."

Constituting the nation's rich and elegant, they are the type of people my grandmother would say are "doing quite well for themselves," all here clamoring for the one thing that cannot be purchased outright: a spot in one of New York City's most prestigious preschools.[1]

The middle and upper school admissions fair is much more diverse. By then, some families have enough positive report cards to consider their progeny scholarship-level bright. There's also more age diversity, because many parents bring their mini-me versions along for the ride, some of whom are actively driving the process. But at the Kindergarten Admissions Fair, only one generation is represented: the parents, who will go to great lengths to get their kids into the right school.

Back in 1999, an analyst named Jack Grubman who worked at Citigroup's investment-banking division reportedly wanted help getting his twins into the right nursery school. Grubman raised his stock rating of AT&T as a favor to his boss, Citigroup's Sanford "Sandy" Weill, who later donated $1 million to the 92nd Street Y, claiming that it was a part of that corporation's philanthropic program.[2] (The 92nd Street Y is a well-known institution that's been attended by plenty of celebrity progeny, including those of Woody Allen, a man with lavishly intimate knowledge of both New York and children.) A suspicious email in 2001 prompted an investigation. Ultimately, Grubman was fined $15 million and banned from the securities industry for life. The key line of Grubman's email: *"I used Sandy to get my kids in 92nd ST Y pre-school (which is harder than Harvard)."*

This is the world of the Parents League, in which people will risk a $15 million fine to get their kid into preschool.

Preschool.

Five long rows of folding tables fill the gymnasium. A dark, jewel-toned banner dangles off each table, sporting an upbeat Latinate motto. I wade throughout the bustle and stand in line with a bunch of parents, waiting my turn to talk to an admissions counselor. "People say you can't judge a four-year-old," jokes another admissions counselor. "But we can. We do."

A few years prior, the Independent Schools Admissions Association of

Greater New York recommended that schools stop using the Education Review Board's test as a part of the admissions process; too many three- and four-year-olds were being heavily tutored.[3]

"We don't think that standardized testing for four-year-olds is appropriate. It had become so corrupt because children were being prepped for it," states Nancy Schulman, co-author of *Practical Wisdom for Parents: Demystifying the Preschool Years.* Schulman gave those remarks at a panel discussion I attended on another aspect of the admissions process still in play for preschoolers: the Kindergarten Interview.[4]

The number of slots available in the most prestigious, storied schools (whether at the Ivy League or one of New York's top private institutions) remains constant,[5] but between natural population growth and an ever-increasing flood of international inquiries from the global 1 percent, more people apply each year, making it overwhelmingly easy to eliminate applicants.[6] There aren't enough spots for every straight-A-getting, student-council-leading, perfect-SAT-score-earning kind of person, so they pick a motley mix from that lot of perfect applicants. Ivy League schools are interested in a diverse set of high-achieving nerds of superhuman potential, an international mix of jocks, inventors, social entrepreneurs, mathematicians, and mavericks, echoing what the kindergarten admissions officers say: "We want a racially, ethnically, and socioeconomically diverse class. Diverse backgrounds, personalities, talents."

The room seems to be full of a homogeneous group of pearl-wearing effervescent yuppies. But then, while standing in line to talk to one of the admissions officers, I see someone striking a sharp contrast. It's a blonde in black jeans, a leather jacket, and booties. Her hair is bobbed and expertly tousled. By flaunting the norms, this woman might look out of place, but nowhere on earth would be unwelcoming for a star like Jane Krakowski, who made her Broadway debut at nineteen, played the singing secretary Elaine Vassal on *Ally McBeal,* and received four Emmy nominations for her role as the narcissistic actress Jenna Maroney on the sitcom *30 Rock.* Krakowski deftly defies the laws of physics, jumping ahead in line without actually cutting anyone.[7]

Jane Krakowski can wear jeans and part the sea; the rest of the room must wait their turn in Spanx.

This Is Your Brain on Confidence

How can people even apply to Harvard, knowing of its catastrophically low acceptance rate? For the same reason that Jane Krakowski can walk right up to the admissions counselor in expensive jeans and booties. In certain settings, the women in sleeveless dresses and French manicures would have the confidence to preside over the room. But in this ecosystem, Jane is the most confident one. Life's like Lotto—you have to be in it to win it—so need it even be said that having the confidence to pursue what you want makes it easier to *get* what you want? Confidence, in other words, makes it infinitely easier to be lucky.[8]

Your brain is an energy-efficient goal achiever whose default mode is "Netflix in sweatpants," which is why any sort of action requires us to view the potential rewards as outweighing the definite costs. You need enough "I got this" marbles to see a clearly tipping scale.[9] The brain's "go" system—known as the behavioral activation system, or BAS—handles our reactions to the good things in life, including how much potential rewards set our hearts aflutter, the speed and doggedness of our pursuit, and how we act once we get something good. As a neurotransmitter responsible for reward and motivation, dopamine is the main driver of the BAS. The renowned researcher John Salamone's series of seminal studies showed that injecting a dopamine blocker into rats' nucleus accumbens—reducing their baseline level of dopamine—made them less likely to pursue an effortful, rewarding option in favor of the less rewarding, easy way out.

Dopamine-depleted humans also demonstrate a similar behavioral shift, from working hard for their dreams to slacking for peanuts.[10] Genetic differences account for some of this luck, because some people have the right mix of dopamine levels and the right variations of dopamine receptors that make it easier for them to pursue things they perceive to be rewarding.[11]An energetic, reward-driven personality can boost people up the social ladder enough to compensate for early socioeconomic disadvantages; good things loom larger in the environment and feel closer to some.[12]

Confidence is the art of approaching rewards, of strutting right up to whatever we want, and in a simpler world, the entire story of confidence could be summarized thusly: *Approach rewards.* But if we want to do that, in addition to keeping one foot on the gas pedal, we've got to keep the other one off the brake, off the ACC, our brain's method of signaling errors. That's the behavioral inhibition system, or BIS, which uses stress and negative emotions like fear, anxiety, frustration, and hostility to help us avoid punishments or unrewarded behaviors; unchecked, it can lead to depression and general withdrawal from the world. For these and many other reasons, the behavioral inhibition system does not get invited to nearly as many parties as the behavioral activation system.

All things being equal, we'd act like the alpha and strut right up to whatever reward we wanted. But as ultrasocial, prediction-loving creatures, simply getting a hint that others might negatively evaluate us—a way of knocking us down the totem pole, which they'd never do to the alpha—can jump-start the BIS,[13] shifting our inner dialogue from *Cool, a reward!* to *Don't screw up! Be careful! Who do you think you are? No one ever loved you anyway! You are going to die alone!* Fewer rewards are more important than social acceptance, and fearing negative social evaluation (which can lead to ostracism, akin to a death sentence for humans) can make us collect enough "why bother" marbles to not act at all.

And *that's* why a sure sign of confidence is to walk up to the table wearing jeans in a sea of Spanx.

It's Good to Be King

The desire to be top dog is pervasive and universal in the animal kingdom. Being dominant, the queen bee, alpha, a high roller, the biggest, the brightest, the undisputed king, the best—the "baller"—allows for better and easier access to resources, resulting in a longer life and more opportunities to propagate your genes, whether you're a human in Canada, a chimpanzee in Uganda, a parakeet in France, or a honeybee in Thailand.[14] Alphas have abundant resources to protect themselves, and having a sense of power or status actually changes the way we process information, making us feel higher up, free from the tyranny of what others might say—safe, comfortable, and able to focus on going after what we want.[15]

Why can't everyone be a top dog? Although we may cherish the ideal of equality, cultures throughout time have demonstrated a surprisingly universal, implicit preference for a hierarchy.[16] "People believe in equality. They think, 'Let's just get rid of the hierarchy.' [But] if you do that, some other hierarchy will be created. You can't just opt out," says Professor Larissa Tiedens of Stanford Business School. "You will end up with a hierarchy of some sort."[17]

Hierarchies form on the smallest of scales. Tiedens's work has shown that people overwhelmingly like their conversation partners more when they exhibit complementary nonverbal behavior; when one person expands, the other person should contract. (Pro tip: On mixed-gender first dates, people feel more comfortable when the female steers the conversation.)[18] Smooth dances require one person to take the lead, and groups run more efficiently when *somebody* is driving the bus, preferably when we pick a driver as soon as possible. Attractive people internalize a sense of status because of how constantly they're treated, but others learn the kind of behaviors that help them rise in the ranks and elicit deferential behavior.[19]

Some people hail from families that help them internalize a sense of status, which creates the confidence required to throw your hat into the ring and get lucky. In his seminal work *Distinction,* the sociologist Pierre Bourdieu referred to this as "*habitus*," or habitual ways of interacting with the world that can reproduce socioeconomic class differences. Kids whose parents can afford to spend $50,000 a year on kindergarten grow up learning a specific set of norms, skills, and behaviors that give them a unique sense of where they stand in the world. They grow up with access to different information and resources that make it easier for them to get into Harvard (start practicing the SAT in middle school—and here's a great tutor who will make it fun).

While members of the working class are taught to submissively defer to authority figures, children of the Parents League learn different ways of interacting with institutions and their superiors, because they're effectively learning how to *be* authority figures. At home, they're versed in the art of respectful inquiry and engagement with higher-ups; by the time they enter kindergarten, kids from wealthier homes are more likely to interrupt others, ask for help, stand their ground, and argue. In classes with students hailing from diverse economic backgrounds, working-class kids are submissive, deferring to both teacher and bossy classmates—both of which help them internalize a sense of lower status. We learn behaviors that lead to status well before we even interact with our peers. The poor kids think the rich kids are entitled, the rich kids think the poor kids are wimps, but they're all just behaving as they've been told to.[20]

Knowledge of a student's background influences how teachers judge his or her behavior. When viewing tapes of a child taking a test, people give higher ratings to kids they believe hail from wealthier backgrounds than those they're told come from a working-class background—even though people are seeing and rating the same tapes. Teachers told that certain students are poised for an academic breakout give those kids more positive feedback and more chances to try throughout the year; the grades of those "future star" students *did* spike, even though those students were chosen completely at random. Coaches with greater expectations of certain athletes give them more "I got this" marbles over time by offering more instruction, positive reinforcement, higher-quality feedback, and more chances to practice—all of which ultimately improve performance.[21]

This Is Your Brain on Winning[22]

Traits like wealth and beauty that a culture values highly are called status characteristics, and they hint at who should be driving the bus. Though not a perfect proxy, they do offer a clue as to how that person has been treated and expects to be treated in the future. Confidence is acting with the certainty that your place on the totem pole and in the group is secure, which is why people who violate social norms—which activate our That Did Not Pan Out signal, instinctively evoking punishment from others—seem like such ballers. There are no hard, objective ways to measure confidence because our brain is constantly getting signals about where we are in the pecking order. People have baseline levels of chutzpah (ranging from Sarah Palin to Dobby, timid house elf), but these are also context dependent.

What *really* matters is how you feel in whatever pond you're in. Do you think making $25,000 a year is a lot of money? It depends on whether you live in Monaco or a trailer park. Think about something that you do better than anyone in your immediate family: Making your bed? Dancing? Baking? Calligraphy? Now imagine, say, making your bed/dancing/baking/ doing calligraphy in a huge stadium in front of everyone you've ever known, right next to the world champion bed maker/master baker. Not as confident now, are you?[23]

If experiences change the brain, then perhaps some magical tweak can increase my reward-approaching confidence and, by proxy, my BAS. A Google search reveals one quick way to improve confidence is the power pose: Standing in an expansive posture for a few minutes allegedly increases testosterone, making people act more boldly and assertively. The former Harvard professor Amy Cuddy delivered a TED talk inspired by the study, but after several failed replication attempts, one of the authors of the original power-posing study publicly refuted the findings. "When the risk-taking task was administered, participants were told immediately after whether they had 'won,'" wrote the co-author Dana Carney. "Research shows that winning increases testosterone. . . . [T]his testosterone effect—if it is even to be believed—may merely be a winning effect, not an expansive posture effect."[24]

Winning creates confidence. Stable hierarchies are less stressful for species, which the primatologist Robert Sapolsky documented in a well-known series of naturalistic studies examining real-world dominance in baboons.[25]

Do we like stress? No, we do not. Even small stressors can release the stress hormone cortisol and initiate the fight-or-flight response that rapidly deteriorates our higher cognitive abilities, hijacking our emotions to force us to pay attention to potential threats, which is why getting a sign that we're on the losing team forces us to be more sensitive to the opinions of others.[26] But because betas have been defeating alphas in every species throughout history, evolution has preserved the mechanisms for helping our brain make the shift from follower to leader, which is why the circulating levels of our hormones, including testosterone, can change so quickly.

Confidence leads to victory, and winning creates confidence; it's a chicken-and-egg scenario creating an upward spiral of increased awesomeness. Status and power are self-reinforcing because getting a sign that you're on the winning team changes how your brain works: Winning raises testosterone, the status-seeking hormone. The increased confidence in being rated highly by others makes you more willing to approach what you want yet again. Getting a signal that you're on top makes you feel more capable and impervious to negative feedback, giving you more confidence to go after what you want. Simply wearing formal clothing or being assigned to the role of a superior (rather than a subordinate) improves performance in tests.

I want more confidence, because the cumulative effect of going after what you want to do without dithering or fearing outside opinions adds up to a luckier, more successful life that's more fully lived. If I can get myself to instinctively put my foot on the gas pedal to approach rewards (and learn to ignore the brake), I'll get luckier, because winning contests, getting dates, and receiving promotions and raises all require you to throw your hat into the ring in the first place.

Because the constant signals we get about where we are in the pecking order influence our confidence, I apply these principles to my everyday life. I throw out old furnishings and ratty garments and redecorate my room. I buy new clothes. I start noticing how women's magazines ask celebrities like Mindy Kaling, "How did you get your confidence?" while *GQ* doesn't show the same level of interest in how Leonardo DiCaprio maintains a solid sense of self. I stop reading women's magazines and spend less time on social media. I focus on my bright spots and spend less time with negative, sarcastic people. After researching embodied cognition, I understand the appeal of power posing, because our body is a potent source of status signals.[27] A genuine sense of physical power can increase our sense of personal power. I start lifting weights. I have no problem curating my reading material, but the weights: They are difficult for me.

Why are the weights so hard to lift? Most people keep doing whatever they've been praised for in the past; when we do try new things, we stick to what we think we'd be good at. What gives some of us more confidence in unfamiliar arenas than others?

The Shape Game: When Things Go to Hell

One way to demonstrate how this plays out in the real world is to play the Shape Game—which, like all games, is completely made up. In the Shape Game, researchers give a bunch of four- and five-year-olds pieces of paper filled with the outlines of triangles, squares, circles, stars, and crosses; kids are told to draw a circle within each shape. This seems like (and is) an easy test for adults, but for children it requires a variety of still-developing motor control skills, adding lots of tongue biting and furrowed brows to the scene.[28] At any age, the kids want the reward of social approval and sense of personal mastery that comes from completing the task well.

So, what if a researcher casually remarked to a class of four- and five-year-olds that boys seem to get higher grades than girls at the Shape Game? Hinting that "boys are Shape Game naturals" in the kids' minds is enough to decrease motivation in *both genders*. Being told that you're not a natural makes it harder to justify putting in the effort, which we naturally avoid whenever possible. Doing well would isolate a girl from her female friends, placing her in a group with boys, brand her a tomboy, and sentence her to a life shunned by both groups, reinforced by parents with stringent gender norms.

A girl playing the Shape Game would be operating under the assumption that she'd have a harder time learning how to play and wouldn't do as well as a boy, even when working to the best of her abilities. Such information is especially sticky for kids' relatively simplistic understanding of how things work. By the time humans are a relatively seasoned six, hearing one little generic statement about their ability decreases their interest and motivation. Additional studies [29] have shown that merely linking one trait with superior performance at the Shape Game—*just once!*—impacts kids' performance, even after the dipshit who made that statement left and his replacement is clueless that anything was ever said at all.[30] Suggesting that an ability is innate can lead to what the psychologist Carol Dweck calls a "fixed mindset," a designation implying that some people have it—talent, strength, intelligence, self-control, ability to learn math—while others have a fundamentally lower ceiling on their abilities that makes trying not even worthwhile.[31]

Here's another way things can go to hell: What if 75 percent of kids who played the first few rounds of the Shape Game were boys? Or what if there was an even split between genders among the players, but their games were subsequently graded at random? In either of these scenarios, more boys would claim the top grades because of a difference in opportunity or sheer luck. The brain works via prediction and laziness, and as we saw in the studies examining bitches in glasses, when it comes to people, this means that we wind up making assumptions about them based on observed patterns (more boys claimed the top Shape Game grades!) and their nonvisible traits (boys are simply better at the Shape Game!).[32]

"It is only with the heart that one can see rightly; what is essential is invisible to the eye," wrote Antoine de Saint-Exupery, adding heft to my theory that many ideas argued in *Behavioral and Brain Sciences* first appeared in *The Little Prince*: We need to see the world as understandable and predictable, so seeing patterns often leads us to assume that something inherent and fundamental is causing them. When three- and four-year-olds see more examples of boys playing or excelling at the Shape Game—even because of some lucky, historical accident—they begin developing expectations for gender-specific behavior. As a species, humans survive by following social norms, and at this age, kids start punishing social norm violators: tomboys and sissies.[33]

What if someone told you when you were three that people who excel at the Shape Game don't look like you? And throughout your entire life, you hadn't seen anyone you could relate to getting a high score on the Shape Game? Our perception of where we are in the pecking order—either in general or when playing the Shape Game—depends on how others treat us, what they say about us or people just like us, by dint of indifference or deference.[34]

This is the age when girls start to learn that *girls don't compete,* a gender difference in self-selection into competitive situations that lasts for the rest of their lives.[35] Winning increases testosterone, and women who opt out of competing also opt out of experiencing that testosterone boost, that surge in confidence and satisfaction that accompanies the thrill of victory.

Competitive behaviors are regulated by a host of neurobiological processes including the status-seeking, social-approach-driving hormone, testosterone.[36] What's more, our predictive brains like things that predict, which is why the exact same behavior is interpreted quite differently when coming from two different people.[37] Because it saves time to decide in advance who will rule the hierarchy, most cultures adopt a pervasive and widespread social norm that frowns upon dominant, competitive, assertive, or bold behaviors when they come from women.

The social neuroendocrinologist Pranjal Mehta's studies have refined our understanding of who rises to the top by testing subjects' baseline levels of hormones before assigning them to be the leader or follower in tasks.[39] Yes, those who excel in stressful situations have high levels of status-seeking testosterone, but they also have low levels of cortisol, commonly referred to as the stress hormone. The cumulative effects of a lifetime of being told that you're not on top (and who do you think you are?), facing negative evaluation, or being high in the trait of "social concern" can cause a surge of cortisol that can create anxiety, blocking the benefits of power. Childhood poverty, current socioeconomic status, being nonwhite, and being female are all predictors of allostatic load, the accumulation of that lifetime of stress.[40] Remember the lesson of the Beauty Bubble: We're expected to defer to status.

This Is the Shape Game in Real Life

We can't all get perfect scores on every test. The distribution of scores, however, can make it hard to figure out where the line is between Shape Game natural and the effects of the Shape Game. In a large-scale meta-analysis examining the scores of almost nineteen thousand people, researchers compared the academic achievement of those in control conditions and under stereotype threat. Overall, this decreased women's math scores by 20 points and the SAT scores of blacks and Latinos by about 40 points. Another recent large-scale analysis on math performance by the economists Roland G. Fryer and Steven D. Levitt, co-author of *Freakonomics,* showed no mean difference between sexes or ethnicities at the beginning of school. Over the first six years, however, girls fell back by two-tenths of a standard deviation; black students fell behind nearly twice as much.[41]

Perhaps all brains can deal with simple math, but more difficult subject material reveals immutable biological differences? The idea that a white penis is mandatory for the highest levels of math makes it hard to explain the *total lack* of gender differences in math achievement and performance in countries like Norway, Sweden, and Iran. One tweak can change female performance. When women were told to imagine themselves as a "stereotypical male" before taking the test, the gender differences all but disappeared; the subjects' confidence in their abilities made the difference.[42]

Stereotype threat—the predicament of being told that you'll do poorly on the Shape Game, which not only kick-starts your BIS but makes others judge you more harshly, to boot—explains why Asian American women do well when they're told to report their ethnicity on tests but poorly when they mark their gender; why white guys do poorly when told they're taking a test of their natural athletic ability; why the senior members of our species can have a hard time with electronics; why women underperform when playing video games; why men underperform during tests of social sensitivity.

Stereotype threat explained why I still felt flustered two years after I started lifting weights, and why women don't feel as comfortable at the gym and have a harder time making progress there.[43] Because of a personal history with sports best described as "They Laughed at Me in Gym Class," my scale was already tilting to the "why bother" side when I joined the gym. Additional marbles were added whenever a newer member got special attention because of his or her age or gender, whenever I felt excluded, whenever I read online comments about how ugly "ripped" women looked, or whenever I endured a family member critiquing women lifting weights.[44] In specific arenas and the world in general, we're *constantly* getting signals about where we are in the pecking order, making it easier for some to develop confidence and others to doubt themselves; signs that we're not on the winning team (chronically devalued status characteristics, like being short, nonwhite, female, poor, unattractive, or older) make people more susceptible to stereotype threat and feel its effects more acutely.[45]

To Get Lucky, Fake It Until You Make It

The way that other people treat us matters because it infuses our day with signals: We're on the all-star team (wearing high-status clothes like a doctor's coat, in a location where we feel comfortable), so we go for it. We're on the losing team (reminded that no one else in our family went to college, we feel like an outsider), which decreases our confidence to act boldly and go after what we want.[46]

Readers will be happy to note that the brain's malleability goes both ways, because doing things that confident people do can increase your confidence. People who appear competent speak fluidly, assertively, and more often than others. Their posture and body language are more relaxed and expansive. They're more expressive and command more space. When speaking, they look at others; when listening, they don't. At the end, we remember the people who speak most in groups as having the best ideas, even when they didn't.[47] People who *look* like they own the place are the ones who end up owning places.

"They really just believe in what they're doing," says Cameron Anderson. "They believe that they have something to contribute, so they're contributing. They truly, genuinely believe that they're great, even though they're not. They're just genuinely confident."[48]

Genuine confidence! It enhances performance. Stacking your scale with "I got this" marbles also helps when times go bad, allowing us to conceptualize challenges as surmountable bumps in the road rather than a sign that it's time to bow out. Viewing things as uncontrollable threats to homeostasis and survival is what kick-starts the stress response, which is why athletes and spelling bee contestants can decrease their anxiety simply by interpreting the physical effects of cortisol and stress differently, labeling their pre-performance butterflies as excitement rather than a signal of impending doom. If we believe that our actions will lead to effort-worthy outcomes—and that there's no discrepancy between who we are and what it takes to get there—then we're more likely to persist. When we don't let the threat of disapproval knock us down and focus on the task at hand, we can stop the surge of cortisol.[49]

Redefining Merit

But as Cameron Anderson points out, it's not quite that simple.[50] "It's not just you can't think as clearly because you're on the bottom—there is more pressure for you to stay quiet. If you do speak up, you're going to get more looks. You're going to get more people giving you subtle or not-so-subtle signals, like, who do you think you are?" says Anderson.[51] Envisioning how others might evaluate us is influenced by how others *do* evaluate us, or have evaluated others in our in-group.

Microaggressions are ways of telling people they're on the losing team—only assigning reading by dead white male authors; telling athletes that they throw like a girl; telling certain patients that their symptoms are only in their head; praising someone as being "a credit" to their race; or attributing an achievement to a diversity measure.[52] Shape Game naturals, buffered by the status of their "I got this" marbles, typically don't see these subtle clues, and they *certainly* don't see what the big deal is in continuing to do what's always been done. The less frequently told side of the story is that passing out "I got this" marbles to one group means giving "who do you think you are?" marbles to the others.

Even for dogs used to getting their paws shocked, it's simply easier to change your attitude and accept the world as is; it's part of the well-documented bias for everyone to accept the status quo. People assigned to an all-star team aren't exposed to stereotype threat or chronic social stressors; it's easier to dismiss the cries of others as part of the "victimhood culture" than it is to feel compassion or admit to being on the winning side of an unfair system.[53]

People can't see the ways that they're biased. It's called the bias blind spot, meaning that we genuinely think *our* view of the world is accurate, just, and objective. Everyone who gets a 100 percent on a test concludes that the grades depend entirely on *merit*. In fact, some of the people who got to play the Shape Game first because of antiquated social norms have grown up in a world fully supportive of their Shape Game efforts, and haven't experienced the constant stress of being a beta or having their Shape Game victories questioned.[54] Being king means that you can focus on whatever you want to do; the betas are expected to constantly be sensitive to others, the very thing that interferes with confidence.

People are surprisingly nimble when it comes to redefining merit to give Shape Game naturals a boost. The predictive brain likes things that predict, and isn't it easier to already have an idea of who's going to drive the bus in certain situations? Doesn't it make life simpler to think of some people as naturals?[55]

Isn't life luckier for beautiful people? We've all seen them get more chances, more friends, and better treatment. Now what if we wanted to treat everyone like that?

Trying to level the playing field may look unfair to those on top, but they're missing the fact that they've been graded on a curve this entire time.[56] Attractive people probably don't realize that they're constantly treated better by others, or how this has shaped their perception of the world; the definition of privilege includes being oblivious of it. We only see what's been difficult for us.[57]

I know how being a woman has made me unlucky, but I can't see how being white has made me lucky. Bad information sticks with us more than the good, and a white woman has been at the center of every experience I've ever had. I can't point to specific instances of being the recipient of skin-color-based luck, but I know that it exists because the fact that I'm white rarely crosses my mind.[58] Having a valued status characteristic makes me feel free, liberated, bulletproof—confident.

The ability to forget or ignore transgressions may protect us from their long-term impact, but experience changes the brain. The cumulative impact of things that happen a thousand times a day, or just at one critical moment in the past—or to others who look like us—establishes expectations for how we're going to be treated. As the ultra-social species, we're highly attuned to signs of being excluded, criticized, rejected, or told that what we're doing is wrong. Our brain constantly gets signals about our place in the pecking order. In an effort to balance the need for accurately knowing where we stand in the world with the need to feel *good* about it, we're skilled at focusing on the options that allow us to escape criticism. Getting a sign that we're *not* the alpha forces us to think about others more because we increasingly depend on them for survival, which also makes us less responsive to being treated differently.[59]

But what if the world *isn't* fair—what if there doesn't seem to be any justification for how we're treated? The way we interpret people's opinions or actions depends on where we see them in the pecking order; those on the bottom who say the world isn't fair are seen as self-serving.[60] Sarah Palin can get away with being mean at a city council meeting, but an older, comelier newcomer? These lessons can tip the scale into "why bother" territory so early and sneakily that we don't even realize that we're choosing to avoid certain activities altogether; they simply do not exist in our world. An invisible death by a thousand cuts is death nonetheless.[61]

To Get Lucky, Ignore the Haters

On the subway, I notice someone who walks through the cars and expects others to move aside, the human version of one social stress test that places two mice in a tube, one on either end, to see who backs away from the other. When you're lower on the totem pole, you're expected to be more sensitive to the needs of others; underlings have to wait their turn to keep the dominant ones happy, who are free to focus on doing whatever they want to do.[62]

Using the areas of your brain associated with mentalizing—thinking about what others are thinking about—is associated with more metabolically taxing, recently evolved areas of the brain; there are real physical costs associated with the emotional labor of constantly being expected to think about what other people might do or say, especially when you're not sure which set of rules they're judging you by.

Being able to control your attention is key, if not *the* key, to confidence. Self-affirmation actions like thinking about your own bright spots and savoring past victories help you add more marbles to the "I got this" side of the scale.[63] I ask Cameron Anderson about gender differences, especially how status interactions in all species relate to humans' expecting women to be higher on the trait of social concern.[64]

"I'm aware of all of that, and I'm still doing it," he says. "We have a ten-year-old daughter, and I'm watching myself reward her every time she shows emotional sensitivity to other kids. And I'm not doing the same thing to my seven-year-old boy." Something can seem a little *off* when women confidently approach their own rewards by focusing on their personal projects or failing to put other people's needs first.

"A tendency to think too much about other people's perspectives can lead to heightened anxiety," says the researcher Jacob Hirsh.[65] Women are hit on multiple fronts, constantly being expected to consider others' perspectives while deriving more of our self-worth from relationships and body image, two omnipresent sources of social evaluative threat. "Women are exposed to more conflicting expectations," he says.[66]

The man approaches me on the subway. I don't move my arm. Attention flows up the status hierarchy, and not looking at someone sends the message that *you are irrelevant*. Not paying attention to people makes me look like a bitch, but ignoring the possibility of negative evaluation is precisely what's required to get stuff done. I don't see him because I'm lost in a book. In a simpler world, the entire story of confidence could be summarized thus: *Approach rewards*. The world tries to complicate that story, but it's up to us to keep it to that.

The guy on the subway gets in my face. Years after taking my first weight-lifting class, the gym hires a better coach, who teaches me confidence in my ability to improve. I feel strong and capable in my own body. Confidence isn't a zero-sum game. I don't have time to criticize people when I'm focused on improving myself and helping others. The power of not needing approval from those around me—and not deriving my self-worth from what other people say about my actions and appearance—builds an unshakeable confidence that can't be taken away by random strangers. You learn a lot about someone by how he tries to make you feel.[67]

"You have a real problem, you know that, missy?"[68]

I turn away. Thanks to five billion years of evolution, the brain of the baller has mastered the fine art of not giving a flying fuck.

Notes for Those of Us Interested in Approaching Rewards

- Perfect confidence is a scale weighing the pros and cons of doing something that's fully loaded with "I got this" marbles, which we get from both our generalized self-esteem and task-specific expectations. Imagine Sarah Palin as a Shape Game natural. One intervention is stereotype inoculation, or finding and identifying with role models who help internalize the idea that you can do that thing.

- Feeling like you don't belong is normal when entering a new situation; it doesn't mean that you don't belong, don't have what it takes, or will always feel uncomfortable. It just means you're still figuring out the lay of the land.

- Be aware of the people and places around you; your brain is constantly getting signals about where you are in the pecking order and what you're capable of. Our surroundings influence our confidence—how well we perform and what we aspire to—even when we're not aware of it. Women who viewed commercials of other women excited about the prospect of becoming homecoming queen were less likely to volunteer for leadership roles than women exposed to neutral commercials about cell phones.[69] Taking a math test in the presence of a man can decrease women's scores; seeing a *Star Trek* poster in a computer science class can decrease people's sense of ambient belonging, making them feel as if programming "isn't for them."

- Focus on your own bright spots. Just as the relationship between confidence and doing well is an upward spiral, the relationship between stereotype threat and performance is a downward spiral that can persist over time. One self-affirmation intervention that asked students to write about an important personal value for fifteen minutes—like creativity or independence—eliminated their GPA decline over the course of the year compared with a control group.[70]

- Find ways to reduce your stress and cortisol levels.[71] Meditate. Get enough sleep. Exercise.

- Go elsewhere. Onlookers can cripple your focus and performance by giving the overlooming threat of negative feedback a real, inescapable face, causing us to actively monitor our own performance and choke. Marbles get added to the "maybe not" side of the scale through fear of negative social evaluation by violating social norms.

- Do you feel slighted because you don't feel you're given as much praise as you deserve? Remember: Confidence is a positive evaluation of your *own* actions.

- Our brains are constantly getting signals about where we are in the pecking order and what we're capable of, so surround yourself with reminders that you're on the all-star team: Clean up your habitat. Take care of yourself. Pile the scale of your life with "I got this" marbles.

- Pay attention to how often you *feel* as if others might be judging you, your appearance, your actions. How often do you censor yourself because of what you think others *might* say, rather than what they *actually* say? And if what they're saying is because they're self-serving or following social norms, why would you let them get in the way of your luck?

- What would you do if you knew that everyone supported you? Set your behavioral activation system to "Do that thing." And then: *Go do that thing.*

6

Find Your Thing

Why Gold Medals Require Luck

I

n 2007, Donald Thomas became the world champion in the high jump. He'd started seriously training in that sport eight months earlier.[1]

Thomas's story began with a standard catalyst: peer pressure. While this often leads to felony charges, a trip to the emergency room, or 3 a.m. Amazon purchases that kind of make sense, Thomas's peers were his college basketball teammates. Unbelievably impressed with his vertical leap, they wanted to see how high he could jump. He cleared six feet six inches on his first try.

Properly executing a high jump requires a favorable strength-to-weight ratio, long and speedy legs, and a well-coordinated effort of the leg muscles, glutes, core, and momentum-supplying arms to initiate the style of high-jumping that allows athletes to clear intimidating heights. Here's what's typically omitted in Thomas's tale: He completed that first attempt Fosbury Flop–style.[2] This method was developed by Dick Fosbury, whose own coach at Oregon State University once called this style "a shortcut to mediocrity." (Fosbury went on to win the gold medal in the high jump.) His coach only began to take him seriously after recording the jump and realizing that Fosbury had cleared the bar by several inches. "Sometimes I see movies, and I really wonder how I do it," Fosbury told the *New York Times*.[3] Jumping with your side to the bar and arching your back over it allows for higher jumps because it shifts your center of gravity upward, toward that curvature in your spine.[4]

Thomas's world-class genetic endowment for the high jump wasn't obvious when he dabbled and trained in that sport in high school, where he first learned proper high jump form. By the time it was clear that he was "gifted with a large Achilles tendon" enabling him to quickly and powerfully propel his weight over the bar—akin to a naturally longer spring—he was playing basketball for Lindenwood University in Missouri, a competitive athlete in peak physical condition. He had remembered that motor skill so simple (it's just one jump!) yet so complex (*Seriously, how on earth is jumping so high even possible?*) that it perplexed Fosbury himself.

Thomas's lucky high jump victory relied on his immutable physical traits (spearheaded by his large Achilles tendon) being exposed to an activity that he was uniquely suited to. But it also required access to world-class coaches, training facilities, social support, motivation to engage in the countless daily chores that athletic expertise demands—skill work, strength and conditioning training, monitored nutrition, recovery, all at the expense of doing anything else with his time—as well as the desire to compete in high-stakes events, the confidence to do so mere months after taking up the sport, and the general belief that committing himself to these activities was, somehow, worthwhile.

We're used to seeing the kind of graph shown on page 90 when it comes to reaching our genetic potential.

Even for a singular skill like the high jump, world-class expertise requires a million things to come together, meaning that an individual's ultimate trajectory depends on "the ongoing interactions among the components." While the ability to jump over seven feet is *influenced* by height, no single gene is responsible for the rest of what it takes to win the world championship, like

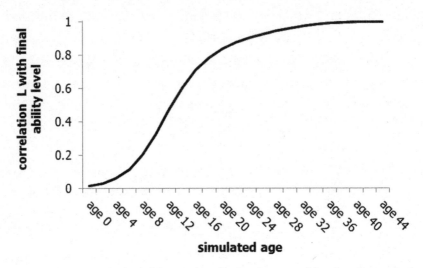

From "A Dynamic Network Model to Explain the Development of Excellent Human Performance," by R. J. R. Den Hartigh, M. W. G. Van Dijk, H. W. Steenbeek, and P. L. C. Van Geert, 2016, *Frontiers in Psychology*, 7th, ed., p. 9. Copyright 2016 by R. J. R. Den Hartigh. Reprinted with permission.

an amazing strength-to-weight ratio, coordination, explosive strength, running speed, ability to remain calm under pressure, leg length, flexibility, and mental toughness, meaning that the path to becoming a world-class high jumper looks a little more like the graph on page 91.[5]

The height of the bold black line measuring overall ability is constrained by the lines below, each of which constitutes one of those separable components. Thomas's trajectory likely resembled the graph on the bottom. What was he doing during the growth spurt of skills that allowed him to become a world champion high jumper in less than a year? Playing basketball.

In this chapter, we'll learn why, in order to reach the pinnacle of human performance, it's not enough for one thing to go right: *Everything* has to go right. You have to be lucky.

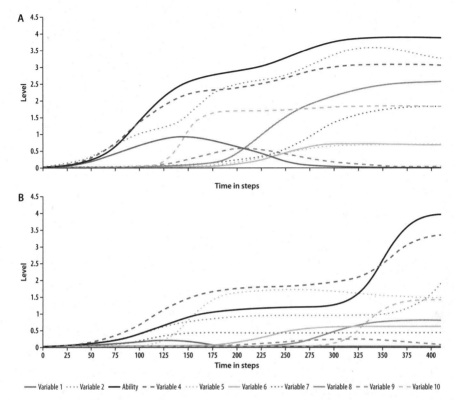

From "A Dynamic Network Model to Explain the Development of Excellent Human Performance," by R. J. R. Den Hartigh, M. W. G. Van Dijk, H. W. Steenbeek, and P. L. C. Van Geert, 2016, *Frontiers in Psychology*, 7th ed., p. 10. Copyright 2016 by R. J. R. Den Hartigh. Reprinted with permission.

First, You Need a Lucky Pair of Genes

"When it comes to skill, there are three components," states John Krakauer, a neuroscientist at Johns Hopkins University and one of the world's leading experts on expertise. His lab, BLAM—Brain, Learning, Animation, and Movement—uses a variety of methods to study motor-learning and neurological recovery from brain injuries. In doing so, he's become one of the world's leading experts in motor skill development—how we learn how to become an expert.[6]

"One is genetics." Roughly 99.5 percent of the human genetic code is universal, but that 0.5 percent differentiates Serena Williams from Stephen

Hawking.[7] Researchers typically compare the genetic code of elite athletes with us couch potatoes, reasoning that what's more common in athletes is there because it boosts performance. For example, researchers estimate that as much as 66 percent of the variance in sports participation *itself* is genetic. Complex physical abilities and traits are polygenic, or the result of several genetic variants working together, with each contributing slightly to overall skill. Because you might get a few lucky genes for hormonal metabolism but a few bad ones for oxygen capacity, genetic differences account for an astonishing amount of variation between athletes, with estimates ranging from 31 percent to 85 percent.[8]

A recent review found 155 genetic markers repeatedly linked to elite athlete performance, 93 influencing endurance and 62 implicated on that opposing end of muscular capability: power and strength.[9] Slow-twitch muscle fibers are like long-burning coals on a fire; they're less explosive. The two types of fast-twitch muscle fibers are like fireworks, carrying explosive, short-lived strength and power. Most of us have a fifty-fifty split between these types, but world-class sprinters and marathon runners have had the luck of falling in love with the sport best designed for their muscles.[10]

Even being a world-class pianist is subject to biological constraints. Larger, more dexterous hands make it easier to play complex chords and decrease the likelihood of injury from physical strain.[11] The composer Sergei Rachmaninoff could allegedly play a thirteenth on the piano—well more than an octave at once, requiring a hand span of at least twelve inches— meaning that his own arduous compositions were easier for him to play. Virtuoso performances require superhuman dexterity and speed that's easier for some. In one study, researchers asked Japanese pianists to repeatedly tap two keys at four different volumes to see who could tap loudest, longest, and fastest. There was no correlation between being one of the fastest tappers and the musician's age when they began training, hand span, or how many hours of intense practice they had logged, leading researchers to conclude that there is "a ceiling effect of extensive training." Practice improves everyone's performance, but genes constrain the upper limits of how much better we can get; just as some legs can only jump so high, some fingers can only move so fast.[12]

Why 10,000 Hours May Never Be Enough

The sociologist Dan Chambliss was a competitive swimmer in his youth—even placing second in a state meet—and a swimming coach in college. For his now-classic ethnographic study "The Mundanity of Excellence," Chambliss spent years interviewing over 120 national and world-class swimmers and coaches in Los Angeles training for the Olympics, comparing them with athletes at other levels of the sport.[13]

"It turns out what they think makes them good isn't really it. Coaches, the same way. . . . There's a thing: 'I work hard. I'm good. It must be because I work hard.' It's because you're focused on the stuff that's, in a sense, difficult for you, and you attribute your success to that. The fact is that millions of people work hard [but] that's not what separates the really successful from the unsuccessful. It's not the volume of work."[14] Like the rest of us, it's easier for world-class athletes to see the difficulties they've had to overcome than the things that have come easy.[15]

"It's very easy to say, 'If you can't do this, you just haven't practiced enough.' But sometimes there's a limit," says Miriam Mosing, a researcher at Karolinska Institutet in Sweden who has published widely on the influence of genes on expertise.[16] "Some people might feel like, 'If only I work hard enough, I can achieve anything,' and that may be a little bit the American dream. . . . [So] if you're not successful, that means you haven't been working hard; you have been lazy."

The idea that our actions alone are responsible for the fruits of our labor (like gold medals) is built into the cultural DNA of the United States, somewhere between the Protestant work ethic and our obsession with self-reliance, both of which motivate people to work hard while teaching them to expect nothing from a government. Early success manuals—precursors to this book—echoed this and "rested on the belief that in an open society anyone who was morally deserving might rise to social and economic prominence."[17]

Karl Anders Ericsson, famous for his studies on the acquisition of expertise, observed musicians of different levels and found that most elite had

practiced for an average of ten thousand hours, leading to the overly simpli-
fied idea that anyone can become an expert with ten thousand hours of
practice. While expert violinists had practiced for an *average* of more than
ten thousand hours, there was considerable variability; practice was neither
a necessary nor a sufficient factor for making it to Carnegie Hall.[18] Our
cultural obsession with self-reliance and the idea that you can become anything through hard work alone (specifically, the hard work of deliberate
practice) is one reason why the "10,000-hour rule" is so hard to extinguish.
Who doesn't secretly enjoy thinking that they could have been a world-class
contender, had they just stuck with those damn oboe/biathlon/C++ lessons?

In one study conducted by the front-runner of Sweden's next generation
of expert-experts, the behavioral geneticist Mosing collected data from
2,569 pairs of Swedish twins born between 1959 and 1985, many of whom
had music backgrounds. Regardless of how many hours they'd spent practicing overall, twins tended to get the *same scores* in overall music ability. In
the most extreme example, while one twin logged more than twenty thousand more hours of music practice than his genetic replicant, both received
the same score.[19]

That highest tier of athletes responsible for breaking world records is a
classic example of what researchers call *survivorship bias*: Because there are
so many things that can filter people out over time—lucky genes being just
one example—it's impossible to make fast, sweeping generalizations about
what it takes to become successful. Gold medalists just see their years of
hard work, not the fact that, say, they performed last in a competition at the
right age in a sport they were genetically suited to. What we do know is that
winning gold medals requires an athlete's trajectory to be the exact opposite
of my first marriage: *Everything* has to go right.

Professional musicians' fast fingers are a classic example of survivorship
bias, just like the abundant slow-twitch muscles found in the legs of champion marathon runners. Because early studies found no difference in the
percentage of fast-twitch and slow-twitch muscles in untrained muscles, Ericsson concluded that "the characteristics of muscle fibers can be changed,
namely from fast-twitch to slow-twitch and vice versa." We now know that

the ratio of our fast-twitch or slow-twitch muscle fibers is genetically deter-mined, finished developing by the time we're six, and set in stone for the rest of our life.[20]

Second, Have the Resources to Develop Your Genes

In addition to genetics, there's another component of greatness, says Krakauer. "The other one is being lucky enough—that you *can* practice. Nowadays, if you want to do any of these things, it requires a significant outlay of money and time on part of parents and everyone else to actually be able to do hours and hours of anything every day." Developing expertise is an investment. Substantial improvements require athletes and coaches to identify and address any limiting factors—working harder *and* smarter—which demands more attention to detail, the kinds of fine-grained improve-ments offered by resource-intensive coaches and facilities.

"I'd been in very close contact with every level of the sport over an extended period of time," says the sociologist Chambliss. One key difference between the Phelpses and the world's also-swams is the quality of their early training. "If you've got a lousy first teacher, if your first stroke technique when you're young is bad, that becomes ingrained. And you're screwed," he says.[21] "If you really practice a lot [and] you're practicing bad technique, you're going to be stuck with it for life. The basics are so important. If you're looking at a baby and saying, 'How do you make this baby to be good at certain things?' you want their first teacher to be really good. In a way, that's more important than their last teacher."

The trajectory of most people's experience with sports runs counter to what might yield world-class expertise. We start by dabbling in cheap classes for years, perhaps a once-weekly group swimming session at a crowded YMCA taught by a timid waterman. Eventually, when our parents are fi-nally convinced that "this whole swimming thing isn't just another phase," they may dig deep for a swimming suit that actually fits and twice-weekly classes. After Michael Phelps's coach identified him as having the physiological makeup of an ideal swimmer's body, he took a special interest in his athletic development when Phelps was still young.

An athlete's overall potential is limited by his resources, both his immutable genes and the facilities and coaches that maximize this genetic potential, and becoming the all-time winningest Olympian requires that this all begin as early as possible.

Quality coaching maximizes our potential, and brains are as varied as bodies. For example, there are actually two different classes of dopamine receptors; some people have more D1 receptors and are more reward-driven, while others have more D2 receptors and learn how to avoid punishments better. Just as muscle fibers vary, receptors for neurotransmitters come in different SNPs (single nucleotide polymorphisms) that process the neurotransmitters differently.[22] People's genetic variations and preferences mean that we can all respond differently to the same kind of training, environment, or motivation. The individual attention afforded by an experienced coach and better facilities in a more supportive atmosphere yield better results than another mindless hour at the gym.[23]

Just because someone didn't enjoy art class in third grade doesn't mean anything about his or her artistic potential. What about with a different teacher, in another, more supportive environment? What about working with clay instead of photography? Pencils instead of calligraphy? Yarn instead of glass? More individualized attention? Or what if you're naturally competitive and would have benefited more from group classes, in order for the others to spur you into action? What if you're naturally collaborative and need strict accountability—should you really be surprised that a free online class isn't doing it for you?

"One training hour might have a much larger effect in some people than in another," says Mosing. Our genes make some achievements easier to attain than others, but getting there still takes time and money. Because sports in particular require attention to every aspect of your physical life—nutrition, health care, sleep, recovery, stress management, social support—athletes are only as good as their weakest link.

Finding the sport you're best suited to and having the resources to develop your skills are easier when you have more money, which gives you more opportunities and possibilities en route to finding your thing. One glaringly obvious place where this gap resides is in the snow. Currently, the person with the world's best genetic makeup to set records as a skier may be living in a housing development in Mexico. Although the modern Summer Olympics began in 1896, winter sports were dubbed "the snobbish play of the rich" by the founder of the modern Olympics as late as 1921, who argued that the relatively small number of countries that could even seriously compete in activities like skiing, skating, and hockey ran counter to the utopian spirit of the games. In addition to being ecologically limited to wealthier countries, these sports require considerable infrastructural investments to merely exist in an area, compounded by hefty personal investments to seriously pursue—the antithesis of more democratic sports like running. To recap: Skiing was called "the snobbish play of the rich" by the founder of the modern Olympics, someone named *Baron Pierre de Coubertin*. Here, the playing field may not be level. (Lucky, rich people started getting snow-covered medals in 1924.)[24]

As Chambliss noted in his study of the most elite swimming teams, "We can, with a little effort, see what these factors are in swimming: geographical location, particularly living in southern California where the sun shines year round and everybody swims; fairly high family income, which allows for the travel to meets and payments of the fees entailed in the sport, not to mention sheer access to swimming pools when one is young."[25]

Gold medals aren't free. Remember the showdown between Tara Lipinski and Michelle Kwan at the 1998 Winter Olympics, either from 1998 itself or from the first chapter? When she was nine, Lipinski's father got a job in Sugar Land, Texas. Two years later, fearing that her skating was slipping because of the quality of the training facilities in Texas, she and her mother moved to Delaware to train at the University of Delaware's ice arena. Two years later, Lipinski and her mother opted for an even better coach and relocated to Michigan to train at the Detroit Skating Club with Richard Callaghan. Coaching, travel, costumes, equipment, and housing ran $50,000 a year, which the Lipinskis were able to afford by mortgaging their home. The Kwans paid for their daughter's training by selling theirs, a pattern once feared by Baron Pierre de Coubertin that also holds true today for many individual summer Olympic sports, like gymnastics, or even sports like the pole vault that require expensive equipment. Being exposed to more possibilities, including what and how to practice, makes it easier to find your sport and the environment you respond to best, and to become an expert.[26]

Having money also makes it easy to dabble in different activities and find what you love. The National Strength and Conditioning Association recently released a statement on long-term athletic development explaining its stance *against* early specialization, which is linked to significant *downsides* to developing talent. There's a greater chance of developing the kind of repetitive motion injuries that are most obvious in games like tennis or throwing-sports like football and baseball. Specializing can shortchange neuromuscular development, creating a blunted repertoire of motor skills— the physical equivalent of enforcing a "one language only" rule at home to provide a head start on a promising career as a lexicographer.[27] (While there is a 0.000001 percent chance that this will work, there is a 99.999999 percent chance that this strategy will merely teach your child to be insufferable.) According to the NSCA, "The assumption that earlier specialization will lead to enhanced sports performance has largely been driven by the incorrect extrapolation of data examining the development of expert musicians and the proposed '10,000-hour rule.'"[28] The *quality* of practice counts more than the quantity.

Current guidelines recommend a trajectory of athletic development not unlike that of Roger Federer—because, yes, one man can have it all—who played soccer, squash, badminton, and tennis before focusing on tennis when he was twelve. What of his occasional rival, that tennis-playing Spaniard Rafael Nadal? In what will surely come as a shock to anyone with passing familiarity of either Europe or the Spanish-speaking world, Nadal's first love was soccer (*fútbol*), which his uncle persuaded him to give up at fourteen to focus on *tenis*.[29]

How You Can Learn to Have Lucky Genes

One shortcut to becoming an expert is to find something you're already good at. Or at least something you pick up faster than others. Talent, after all, is relative—which is why our confidence in walking increases next to a baby, but decreases next to someone who takes that whole "left right" thing to a new damn level.

Olympians have spent years dedicating themselves to their skill, testing the human body's maximum potential against others at their lifetime physical peak. The Olympics represent the pinnacle of sporting achievement, and just like Carnegie Hall, getting there requires practice—and victory. Competing in rhythmic gymnastics requires more than uploading videos clearly showing one's ability to make pretty shapes out of ribbons while wearing a leotard; one must also demonstrate superior achievement in public. Despite the variation in how long Ericsson's elite violinists practiced before reaching Carnegie Hall, they all shared one thing: Starting at age eight, they won 67 percent of the competitions that they entered, while those in the lowest-ranking group won only 18 percent of the time. [30] Practice makes the greats even greater; while there was a time when Yo-Yo Ma couldn't even play an F scale, at some point early it became evident that he played better than his peers. Eight-year-old Stephen Hawking wasn't smarter than forty-year-old Stephen Hawking, but he was smarter than other eight-year-olds.

Discovering what you pick up easily gives you the *motivation* required to get through the practice. As we saw in the last chapter, winning increases testosterone, regardless of *whom* we beat or how skilled our opponents are. Winning provides a confidence boost by allowing us to evaluate ourselves favorably compared with our peers. Having the luck to find something you pick up quickly creates a positive, upward spiral in which confidence and performance bolster each other, making it easier to enjoy and stick with the necessary practice. [31]

When we set goals that we're genuinely interested in achieving, we're better able to find the energy and time to pursue them by ignoring temptations or obstacles. While the reinforcement learning signal (the That Did Not Go According to Plan sign) occurs when we get corrective feedback about our actions, it's *amplified* when we see a link between our behaviors and the outcomes, when we're *interested* in the outcomes, and when we get a sense that we can actually learn how to correctly modify our behavior to do better next time. Knowing that we can improve, and how to improve, at something that we care about actually makes it easier to learn.[32]

Experts seem crazy because they repeatedly run headfirst into their brain's aversive That Did Not Pan Out signal—the horrible, effortful tediousness of repeatedly confronting their weaknesses and errors known as deliberate practice—when it's well documented that what most of us really want in life is to be paid $1 million to eat a sandwich and take a nap. But this isn't the only method of learning: We can also improve through deliberate "play," a form of unstructured practice guided by the participants. Think of children playing soccer in the favelas of Rio de Janeiro, hockey on suburban streets in Minnesota, one-on-one basketball in a park, or surfers spending their weekends at the coast. Repeat after me: *Forging new neuromuscular connections can be fun.* Alas, our opportunities to do so depend on our surroundings.[33]

Vivienne Ming is a theoretical neuroscientist turned serial start-up founder whose work on maximizing human potential has helped reveal which traits predict who winds up on top.[34] A few years ago, Ming was invited to a Red Bull–sponsored conference in Santa Monica, where she happened to eat lunch next to Rodney Mullen, one of the greatest skateboarders of all time. The heel flip? The 360? The flat-ground ollie? He didn't just execute them while winning national championships: He *invented* them.

"I began to wonder what's in common between the best developers, the best everybody else, the best salespeople—and then, truly interestingly, the best skateboarders." Ming prodded him for details about the experience of preparing for and competing in a world championship. She got the expected answer about a superhuman focus until the competition. After the competition, most people would opt for that sandwich and nap; the skateboard greats Rodney Mullen and Tony Hawk are not most people.

"'Well, Tony [Hawk] and I would go back to the after party and drink a little champagne. And then twenty or thirty minutes later, *we would be out back practicing new moves.*' Which was exactly what I wanted to hear, because [of] what I found in the best developers and the best salespeople. Independent of their skill sets, independent of their grades, I could predict the best people by simply looking at what they did when they didn't have to do it.'"[35]

It's after a victory, competition, or completion of a project, Ming says, that most of us would say, "'*Take a break. No one cares.*' But *they* do. They are incentive insensitive. *They are fanatics.*" Being able to choose an activity you find genuinely interesting makes it easier to make an effort; as we saw in the first chapter, people will gladly participate in a demanding activity, just as long as it doesn't feel like work. Having the luck to find something that you love enough to practice a lot creates a positive, upward spiral that makes you want to stick with it.[36] Being forced to do something—even if it seems fun to others—dramatically increases the risk of disengagement and burnout.[37]

Experts Are Lucky Enough to Be Mentally Tough

No matter how physically capable you are, how hot your coach is, how much you love beating other nine-year-old oboists—or how long it's been since you've actually beaten anyone—your future as an expert depends on never saying two words: "I quit."

Even if you *do* happen to discover a hidden talent, exploiting that luck requires devotion. Competing, improving, and overcoming plateaus require an ever-increasing amount of dedication as you reach the limits determined by your resources, whether time, money, energy, or genetic potential. In addition to genetics and the ability to practice, Krakauer cites this mental quirk as the final component of developing world-class skill.

"I think it all boils down to how do you situate yourself in that space in your life based on all kinds of factors to allow you to stay motivated to practice this thing at the expense of everything else. It's kind of freakish. It's like when Freud said, 'Anyone with ambition is pathological.'"[38]

The region of the brain that's repeatedly shown to be the most predictive of decisions is the one that makes us human. When subjects are given multiple options, the decision value—the area of the brain most active when subjects see the option they ultimately choose—is the ventromedial prefrontal cortex.[39] The vmPFC, which casts the final vote in our decision making, is particularly active whenever you're thinking about yourself, imagining the future, and assigning value to something: It's the brain's official "I want to go to there" hub.[40]

"There are three schools of thought converging," says Joseph Kable of the University of Pennsylvania, "which make sense if you think about those things together: imagining possible futures, and deciding how to act, or what steps can I take to get to the awesome thing?"[41] We make decisions based on which future we want—specifically, which version of our future self we want to be, how much we actually expect that outcome to materialize, and whether its benefits outweigh its costs. *Is it worth it?* Goals shape our world, and increasing your level of expertise requires that more of your world centers around the goal of getting better.[42]

But first, you have to believe that you *can* get better. As elegantly stated by the researcher James E. Maddux, "The truth is that believing that you can accomplish what you want to accomplish is one of the most important ingredients—perhaps the most important ingredient—in the recipe for success." This magical belief in our ability to get better that influences our entire life has a name: self-efficacy. Becoming an expert—which is simply the process of learning something, taken to the extreme—requires a mix of genuine personal interest and a sense of self-efficacy, loving something, and enjoying getting better.[43]

Self-efficacy matters because along with death and taxes, there is another inevitability in life: failure. At some point, things go south. Even the best of us suck sometimes—to wit, those elite violinists *didn't* win 33 percent of the competitions they entered, but what they thought of themselves beforehand made a huge difference in how likely they were to persist.

We can develop our sense of self-efficacy by being encouraged for our efforts rather than the outcome. In a study by Andrei Cimpian, four-year-olds were given a drawing task; for the sake of simplicity, let's call it the Shape Game. None of the kids knew if they were good, or the type of kid who would usually do well at it. The kids completed four drawings. After each one, half were told, "You did a good job drawing." The other half heard, "You are a good drawer." They were given two more drawing tasks but were told that they made mistakes in both of them. Afterward, when asked, "If you had a chance to do something tomorrow, would you draw or would you do something else?" kids who had been told that they were good artists—only to have that blow up in their faces when they forgot to add wheels on the bus—gave up. When criticized, kids who thought they were naturals opted "to denigrate their skill, feel sad, avoid the unsuccessful drawings and even drawing in general, and fail to generate strategies to repair their mistake," exhibiting "helpless behavior." (According to science, offering the wrong kind of praise to four-year-olds can set them on a path leading to homelessness and heroin addiction. *No pressure.*)[44]

Even if we've found something that we're well suited to, enjoy, and can afford the resources needed to improve, we need something extra to keep us working toward our goal, despite any inevitable ups and downs. Athletic expertise in particular carries its share of downs, because sports have clear, unambiguous outcomes that repeatedly subject athletes to the possibility of suffering an agonizing defeat in front of everyone they've ever met *while wearing spandex.* A high, stable self-esteem is an invisible backpack of privilege that buffers against the threat of negative feedback and "facilitates persistence after failure." The Tom Bradys of the world keep whipping out their scale full of "I got this" marbles, getting up after repeated losses, framing defeats as learning experiences, acknowledging that sometimes fate favors the other team on game day, forever focused on improving, and generally doing everything right. People with a low self-esteem can't handle criticism as well, preferring self-protective feedback that temporarily protects the ego at the expense of improving; these people are typically not married to Giselle Bündchen.[45]

Coming from money makes it easier to get lucky, but this time, it's because of what people with money say. One study that tracked family interactions over four years found a depressingly large difference between the kind of reinforcement that children received, which depended on their parents' socioeconomic status. "In the first four years after birth, the average child from a professional family receives 560,000 more instances of encouraging feedback than discouraging feedback. A working-class child receives merely 100,000 more encouragements than discouragements; a welfare child receives 125,000 more discouragements than encouragements."[46] Researchers typically use socioeconomic status as a measure of people's place in the hierarchy; confidence to act or learn requires us to focus on rewards, and people unknowingly teach their children to focus on rewards or perceived punishments, internalizing reinforcement that's hard to shake after hearing it hundreds of thousands of times.

What people think they're capable of achieving is shaped by what other people say about them, and people whose coaches have higher expectations receive better feedback that's more instructional and encouraging and are given more opportunities to practice. In the short term, this makes people try a little harder and feel better about their ability to improve; over time, this extra motivation, guidance, and practice lead to better performance outcomes.[47] Telling people that they're doing better than others makes them learn faster and perform better—even when that feedback is false.[48]

As Chambliss wrote in his paper differentiating levels of swimmers, "The very features of the sport which the 'C' swimmer finds unpleasant, the top-level swimmer enjoys. What others see as boring—swimming back and forth over a black line for two hours, say—they find peaceful, even meditative, often challenging, or therapeutic. They enjoy hard practices, look forward to difficult competitions, try to set difficult goals. . . . It is incorrect to believe that top athletes suffer great sacrifices to achieve their goals. Often, they don't see what they do as sacrificial at all. They like it."

Enjoying the process of getting better—and wanting to improve because of a genuine internal drive—makes it easier to stick it out for the long term. When you want to do something, you jump out of bed; when you *have* to do something, you simply hit the snooze button until your life blows up.[49] Even though Donald Thomas had the good fortune of stumbling upon the high jump at just the right time, he was also lucky enough to want to improve enough for his skill to be noticed by others.

Experts are lucky because they found something they loved and could commit the resources required to becoming the best possible version of themselves in that area of life. They were lucky to have had the mental resources to believe in their ability to constantly reach the next step; "positive feeling results when an action system is making rapid progress in doing what it is organized to do."[50] Experts are people who have found the activity, environment, and kind of coaching that they're suited to. We mortals look at the path to becoming an Olympian as an impossible, Everest-worthy climb. Experts simply spend years focusing on taking that next step, doing whatever it takes to improve and win the very next competition, overcoming each plateau with an additional level of devotion. After years of consistently focusing their energy and time, they eventually emerge, miles ahead of the rest of the world.[51]

Notes for Those of Us Who Would Enjoy Kicking Ass Just Once in Our Lives

- Regularly learn and try new things. Getting the luck of Donald Thomas and stumbling upon a world-class talent requires trying something new. Revisit old activities. Remember how your high school debating coach/art teacher said you didn't have what it takes? Maybe you reminded him of a former bully; maybe he was just a depressed, soul-crushing asshole.

- What kinds of things do you do when you don't have to do anything?

- People willing to do anything to improve refuse to let obstacles stand in their way. But, come game day, you won't get extra points for having made the journey more difficult for yourself. Being in the kind of environment that you respond to best—which includes practicing something you actually like—makes it easier to improve. Exposure to more possibilities, including what and how to practice, makes it easier to find your niche, improve, and become an expert. Try new environments to see how you learn best and what motivates you.

- Invest in quality lessons as soon as possible. Increasing how much helpful, timely feedback you get will improve skill faster than cranking out a few more hours of practice.

- Experts have a constant belief in their ability to improve: They're confident that they can get better and refuse to accept ceilings on their own performance. (For tips on gaining confidence, see the last chapter.)

- It's never too late to improve or learn something new. For everyone reading this thinking, "It's too late for me to pick up tennis/photography/social skills/that new cheesecake recipe!" there is somebody older who wishes that she'd started when she was your age.

- "I can't because _____." Many people give up prematurely because of what they perceive to be insurmountable difficulties. We don't see others' good luck, only our bad luck.

- Gold medals are easiest to win if you fall in love with the right sport for your genes when you're young; are cute, and cocky and have rich parents; and *everything* goes right on game day.

- Don't compare your performance with others. Focus on how good it feels to improve.

7

Check Yourself Prior to Wrecking Yourself

How Self-Control Leads to Lucky Outcomes

When I first met Derek Sivers in the fall of 2007, he was beaming. One of his heroes, Chris Anderson—then the editor in chief of *Wired*—had just complimented Sivers's company, CD Baby. In the 1990s, listening to music required getting your hands on something tangible, like a CD or tape. CD Baby emerged as a reputable online storefront that would sell your music; its online store and shipping warehouse made independent music accessible to anyone. Anderson had just touted CD Baby as a perfect model of how the internet allowed niche markets to flourish.

"So I just shot him an email: 'Big fan, long-time subscriber! Thanks for the mention!'" Sivers said.

In all aspects of life, Sivers is unflinchingly optimistic and excited about whatever he happens to be doing. The only time he got embarrassed was when I asked if he had any connection to the nearby NE Win Sivers Drive, an artery running through the industrial and commercial warehouses near the airport in Portland, Oregon. It is, in fact, named after his grandfather.[1]

Sivers has another striking personality trait on top of his cheerfulness.

Derek's friends used to nickname him the Robot. "I don't hang out, don't party. If there's something I can't play, sing, or write, I shut the door and work on it for three to eight hours until it's finished," he explains. "I've got a *really* long attention span." Few people can block out the world for such long stretches in order to make progress on something that isn't binge-watching a TV series. Even if you *are* lucky enough to discover something you pick up quickly, you still have to *develop* that talent enough to get noticed or be useful to others. Eventually, you'll have to sit your ass down and get to work—which Derek has repeatedly proven that he's more than willing to do.

Why *do* some people seem to win more often than others? One of the simplest, Occam's razor–level answers is that they do what's needed to win. After graduating from the Berklee College of Music, Sivers found out (via a lucky break from a friend) that the musician Ryuichi Sakamoto was looking for a guitarist for his Japanese tour. Sivers stayed up all night, writing and recording new guitar arrangements. The next day, he layered on the tracks and handed Sakamoto the demo tape. He got the gig and toured Japan.

Later, in 1993, when Sivers's roommate—a multimedia studies major at New York University—mentioned the internet, Sivers's curiosity flared up yet again. "Right away I wanted to figure out how to make World Wide Web pages of my own," he says. "There wasn't much to it. Even though I had no computer experience at the time, making basic HTML tags was really no harder than making a Word document."

The internet spread throughout the world slowly, like a bucket of ink dumped into a swimming pool, a process the sociologist Everett M. Rogers dubbed the "*diffusion of innovations.*" The first to try something new are what Rogers termed the innovators, followed by early adopters; 68 percent of us fall into the early or late majority. Laggards, that final 16 percent, eventually come around when they're damn good and ready.[2] Sivers was a pioneer in the internet's early halcyon days, when its relative difficulty of use required you to be a genuine nerd to be online at all; there were no spambots or marketing Ponzi schemes to sully the entire notion of leaving links, just a bunch of well-intentioned dorks with stuff to share.

Sivers taught himself HTML in one afternoon, giving him an edge over nonprogrammers by allowing him to post things online. Driven by his new obsession, he became a fixture on early bulletin board systems, sharing technical and legal information with clueless musicians. He used his site to post photos, describe himself ("creator, entertainer, professional pest, hopeless heterosexual, optimist, flirt, learning addict, cat person"), interview music publicists, and turn their advice into blog posts. He wrote, recorded, and posted a "Song of the Week" and encouraged feedback. He frequented Usenet and other early 1990s online groups, leaving links to the pages on his site that had already covered the topic, signing off with his web address.

While most of us only chip away at learning a programming language like PHP when we feel like it, or update our blog when *forced* to—which has never actually happened—making a habit out of following through yields all sorts of lucky dividends over time. Sivers's reputation at the intersection of business, technology, and music flourished because he consistently set and accomplished new goals, including setting up a credit card merchant account and website to sell CDs for his own band, Hit Me.

After his less computer-savvy musician friend Marko Ahtisaari asked if he would set up something like that for other bands to sell their CDs online, Sivers built a website and put up $500 to start the company, including $100 for a web design program from Microsoft and $50 to get the domain name. He never advertised, and focused on independent musicians interested in selling a few CDs apiece. "I was just doing this as a favor," he recalls. Like the Ryuichi Sakamoto demo tape, CD Baby was something that he simply sat down and hammered out over the course of a weekend.

Ten years after starting CD Baby for $500 and a year after I met him, Derek Sivers cashed out for $22 million. Today the entrepreneur is based in New Zealand and Singapore, living a life we all dream about.

"I always say that I'm the luckiest person I know."

· · · · · · · · ·

Looking the part, being cute, and playing tennis aren't the only ways to get lucky: Sometimes we just have to put on our big-kid pants and finish our work. Being able to regulate your own behavior allows you to build and capitalize on lucky opportunities. Even people with dream jobs like actors, musicians, and professional athletes have to spend large chunks of their lives traveling, rehearsing, exercising, eating this, wearing that, attending press conferences, and waking up at ungodly hours in order to spend the rest of their time doing what they love. Add in the fact that *everyone* has weaknesses that tempt them, and you can see how self-control is like confidence, another skill in the tool belt of life that will only add to your luck.[3] But there's a plot twist: How easily we can learn the fine art of mastering ourselves has a lot to do with things beyond our control; getting lucky depends on luck.

Self-Discipline Is More than Wind in Your Sails: It's the Sail Itself

Many of your defining personality traits are situational. Just as the quietest among us can morph into an extrovert when seeing a long-lost friend, everyone can turn into a paragon of self-control under the right circumstances. Think about the last time you rushed to get something done: In those moments spent running to a meeting, cleaning before company arrived, speeding to a store before closing time, or writing a paper/email/book before its deadline, you were an efficiency *machine.* Minus the sense of impending doom, this is the essence of self-control: focusing your energy on doing whatever most effectively gets you closer to completing things that matter.[4]

To discuss our relatively stable personality traits, psychologists use the acronym OCEAN: openness to experience, conscientiousness, extroversion, agreeableness, and neuroticism. Conscientiousness includes facets like self-discipline, order, and perseverance that facilitate achievement.[5] These are all components of self-regulation, "the process of purposefully directing one's actions, thoughts, and feelings toward a goal," or the ability to plan, adjust your behavioral activation system to "complete this thing," and ignore everything else—anxiety, lack of motivation, Netflix, friends, failing marriages, Facebook—all while monitoring your progress until reaching the desired end.[6]

While intelligence is a valuable asset that can increase your luck, it only accounts for half of what distinguishes academic high achievers, in part because it merely suggests what you *can* do while working to the fullest extent of your abilities.[7] Stable behavior patterns predict real-world outcomes so well because they determine what we're *likely* to do when the pressure is off—and one of those times we follow through efficiently may lead to the thing that hits the jackpot. That's why half of what determines who makes the honor roll is aspects of self-regulation like self-control and *grit*, the term popularized by Angela Duckworth. (Both of these measure the ability to stay the course; grit measures perseverance, or self-control on a longer timescale.)[8]

Self-control determines how much larger, future rewards guide our actions, so how much we're motivated to get some goodies influences how we act in certain contexts.[9] Becoming a world-class expert requires world-class self-control in *one* area of life, which is why the sociologist Dan Chambliss noted of Olympic-level swimmers that "their energy is carefully channeled."[10] The cumulative effect of working toward larger, future rewards in all areas is why self-regulation is one of the biggest predictors of success.[11]

What we've repeatedly done when the pressure is off hints at what we're likely to do in the future, which is why self-control can also be a shortcut to earning trust. People like Sivers who demonstrate a history of following through develop reputations that make it easier for others to trust them and extend opportunities. Marko Ahtisaari contacted Sivers for a reason; we may judge ourselves by our intentions, but the world only sees what we've actually done.[12]

If Champagne Comes from France, Where Does Self-Control Come From?

Is self-regulation a skill you can learn or something you're born with? Research suggests it's like the high jump: easier for a lucky few, but something everyone can improve.[13]

Many moons ago, the Stanford psychologist Walter Mischel started researching children's ability to delay immediate gratification in favor of a larger, future reward. In his seminal study, four-year-olds were told that if they could wait until the researcher returned—roughly fifteen minutes—they'd get something great, like two pieces of candy, such as marshmallows. (This study was conducted several decades ago, possibly during wartime, when decent candy didn't exist.) If they couldn't stand to wait that long, all they had to do was signal to the researchers, who would end the study by giving the kid a smaller treat. Being able to wait predicted a host of beneficial outcomes years later, like higher SAT scores.[14]

Our ability to act on behalf of the distant future is influenced by biological components. Different brains process dopamine differently; variations in dopamine receptors render some people less sensitive to punishing outcomes and are linked to obesity and pathological gambling. Genetic differences in serotonin receptors predispose people to developing issues with impulse-control in social settings, like aggression and anger. Staying on task, steering clear of less beneficial options, and avoiding the temptation to bludgeon co-workers are all possibilities for anyone with a brain, but getting lucky depends on how well we can play whatever hand we were dealt.[15]

Four decades later, some of Mischel's subjects were retested. Kids with better self-control grew into adults with better self-control whose decisions recruited more activity from the prefrontal cortex, the brain's executive center, to override the basal ganglia, where reward and motivation meet to initiate our actions.[16] Consistently focusing on getting those bigger treats in the future creates a positive domino effect.[17]

In one longitudinal study, Dan Belsky, a behavioral geneticist at Duke

University, found that genetic components influencing self-control had a wide range of positive outcomes. Less impulsive three-year-olds with high reading scores became upwardly mobile, financially successful thirty-eight-year-olds.[18] Constantly orienting your thoughts and actions toward the service of future goals adds up.

"They end up doing so well and capitalizing on these opportunities because when they do arise, they're less likely to fumble the ball," says Belsky.[19]

Just imagine that after creating a website for your band to sell its music online, another band wanted to get in on that service. Would you say, "Sorry, I've got band practice this weekend"? Or, because self-control also leads to successful group living by allowing us to consider the needs of others, would you imagine that others might have that same need? Would you add it to your lengthy to-do list, only to see, in a few months, that someone else created an online store selling CDs by independent bands?

Walter Mischel, the marshmallow guy, also found that prior success increased how likely kids were to wait for that larger reward.[20] Another study published in 1970, examining the choices of young kids in West Virginia, found that children from disadvantaged homes—if they qualified for free school lunches or their parents were on welfare—were less likely to wait.[21] Simply showing the impulsive, grabby kids three candies and explaining that they would have had them, had they exercised patience, was enough to make them change course and wait for the larger reward later on.

Years later, Laura Michaelson stumbled across Mischel's early research—before he focused on kids from higher socioeconomic classes—while at the University of Colorado Boulder. Her study was set up just like Mischel's, with one key difference: Beforehand, the subjects were given reason to doubt that the experimenters would actually follow through on their promises. The kids who doubted them didn't wait.[22] In other words, if you don't trust the system—if you've heard too many stories about editorial assistants only reading their friends' manuscripts, are convinced you'll get a C for handing in even the most amazing science project, or suspect that the end of net neutrality will doom your new start-up—you won't write that book, add glitter to your diorama, or launch that start-up.

"Most of the other people who have prominent theories about self-control and delaying gratification don't acknowledge the social factors at all," states Michaelson.[23] Being motivated to pursue a certain goal depends on how much we actually *expect* it to happen as well as how much we value it, a combination of expectancy and value first written about by the seventeenth-century French philosopher Blaise Pascal that remains a staple of behavioral analysis by psychologists and economists. Doubting that future awesomeness will actually come to pass can erase people's motivation to do the work required to get there.[24]

In 2014, the Italian economists Paola Giuliano and Antonio Spilimbergo published "Growing Up in a Recession," which chronicled the long-term impact of facing a severe macroeconomic shock when young or first entering the job market. People who appear to be acting in ways that run counter to their own interests may in fact be doing so because of the uncertain reward history that accompanies a chaotic, uncontrollable environment. We know that the early stuff sticks because it can also happen to entire generations.[25]

Experiencing a large-scale economic downturn while impressionable—like the Great Recession—makes people more likely to attribute success to factors beyond their control, like luck. Just as it's adaptive for everyone to assume that they'll be included and treated well (but easier for attractive people), it's adaptive to work hard for larger, distant rewards—but easier when you grow up in a stable environment. Baby boomers' careers were built on the idea that sacrifice would yield large returns over time, like pensions and employer loyalty. Millennials grew up in a different environment, where playing by those rules doesn't guarantee a second marshmallow or a pension, let alone a full-time job with benefits. Their grandparents and parents were losing houses and retirement funds. When you can't trust that long-term rewards will materialize, your focus shifts to immediate rewards: a good work environment for a company with a mission that resonates.[26]

Self-Improvement Is Always Hard

Our brain reveals its ultimate choices in the ventromedial prefrontal cortex, which arises as a feeling—the value of our future self, or the brain's I Want to Go to There bat signal—but something can override *that*: the dorsolateral prefrontal cortex. As the most responsible, mature adult in the adult part of our brain, it offers top-down control over the rest of the prefrontal cortex.[27] Like any expert, it knows what it's doing but doesn't work for cheap.[28]

"What [the neurons] do is create persistence firing when they excite each other, and that is very metabolically intensive," says Yale's Amy Arnsten, a pioneer in neurobiology. "These have many, many more connections than other neurons in the brain. It's the number of connections that increases exponentially, over evolution, and each of those connections is excitatory, so it's related to the requirement for energy to keep it going."[29] The brain is the master of accomplishing tasks while using as little energy as possible, obeying the law of least effort, and the cognitive effort of running this machine is, itself, work. The brain effectively decides how much of itself to use, at any given time; mental fatigue is our brain's way of saying, "This isn't worth it."[30] Just as we feel physically tired even when we still have some energy in the tank to prevent catastrophic system shutdown, our mind can prematurely start to fade because of motivation and physiological limitations.[31]

Doing things that don't feel automatic—ordering a salad when you crave a burger, building a website when you just want to relax and have a drink—requires us to use the most metabolically costly part of our brain (the prefrontal cortex) to guide the center of motor control, the basal ganglia. Repetition makes actions feel easier because our brain downshifts over time, using less of the prefrontal cortex's plan-and-plot abilities; eventually, fully automated habits initiate in the basal ganglia, where motivation and reward meet up to control our movements.[32] Self-improvement is difficult because we have to overcome many taxing, trying things. We have to put the brakes on our habitual responses by using the taxing Adult part of our brain. We may have to recruit the brain's That Did Not Pan Out signal and correct *ourselves* from doing what we want right now in favor of doing something that feels more difficult, just to get a less tangible reward. We have to put our big-kid pants on, over and over again. We have to be our own adult.[33]

And damn it, we are tired.

What Others Really Witness When They Witness Our Fitness

I'm in Samantha von Sperling's penthouse apartment. Von Sperling, who has served as an image consultant for the Miss Universe pageant, greets me in her office in New York's Financial District, the ceilings of its lobby painted like the Bellagio.[34] Other people make snap decisions based on whatever information is available, and the qualities about us that others see as controllable broadcast strong signals about our self-control. Clothes, accessories, hair, skin, and bodies send messages about our inner selves.[35] Von Sperling has made a career out of helping people calibrate their appearance to how they want to be perceived by the outside world.

Von Sperling wears a slightly large 6-carat ring on her left ring finger, a gift from her grandmother that hints at her wealthy roots. She speaks not in full sentences or paragraphs but in short stories that inevitably circle back to her family's wealth, the phrase "joie de vivre," her clients, and her recent, brutal divorce. She is, in fact, the only person I've ever met who earnestly pronounces the word "to-*mah*-toes." On one wall hangs the office requisite smattering of press clippings, including a full-page story in the *New York Times* that ran several years ago. "That changed everything," she admits. The article "Long Christmas List? You Can Outsource It" focused on von Sperling's personal shopping service but also mentioned her lessons on "etiquette, dance, speech and overall style." Today, von Sperling consults with the elite and the would-be elite, offering, for example, an $8,000 intensive weekend course for young women seeking a polish to prepare for pledging a sorority.

She's wearing a clingy red dress with animal-print sandals and explains that she's lost fifteen of the thirty pounds she recently gained during her excruciating divorce but soon shifts into professional mode by examining how I'm presenting myself.

"I like the cut of that dress, the V-neck, but it's bare," she says, looking me over. "What about scarves?" she asks.

"I have one," I say. "It's hot pink."

She wrinkles her nose and cocks her head to the side. "That's it?" she gasps. "You don't have a great-aunt who has a nice collection of Hermès scarves to give you?"

"My aunt works at Target."

Von Sperling offers me more advice. "Go gluten-free. You need to spend an hour on your body every day—exercising for an hour, or even just a morning and evening walk." After coaching me on the perks of a low-carb Mediterranean diet, she advises that in addition to exercising, I spend an hour each day on spa activities like lotions, creams, self-massage, manicures; these were the things that would help me get my mojo back and prep me for life as a working woman. "No one should see your knees. I think you could lose ten pounds and you'd be much happier," she says. "If you could lose fifteen, even better."

During times of economic scarcity, we envy the voluptuous; excess adipose tissue suggests that someone has access to great resources, like cookies. Yet in times of plenty, when cookies are abundant, self-control is especially attractive. People can't choose their genetic tendency to become obese; regardless of what genetic mechanisms are at play, people who are obese and overweight suffer from discrimination based on the assumptions we make about their character and self-control.[36] (Arguing, perhaps, that we can choose how frequently we place ourselves in front of food.) Bad assumptions about your self-control can create a negative domino effect for your economic future that starts when you're young.

Parents are less likely to help their children pay for college if they're obese. In hiring scenarios, people assume that those with a higher body mass index have less education, and are less likely to recommend them; this effect is especially strong for hiring managers who are faster at linking *"weight"* to words like *"ineffective," "incompetent," "slow,"* and *"lazy."* (While those studied used résumés with photos, we can assume that the findings are relevant in situations where hiring managers can look up photos of applicants online.)[37]

Regardless of whether I'd actually be happier if I lost weight, as von Sperling predicted, research indicates I might be richer. If I, an average-weight woman, lost twenty-five pounds, I'd make an additional $389,300 over a twenty-five-year span.[38] A man who weighs twenty-five pounds less than what's typical for his height can expect to earn $210,925 less across a twenty-five-year career than a man of average weight; it's the opposite for men, who are actually rewarded for gaining weight up to a certain point—obesity—at which point their income suffers.

We view the obese as belonging to a lower social and economic class, and perceiving yourself to be lower on the totem pole leads to cumulative health disadvantages that can impact your stress and body weight.[39] We all want more self-control, but self-improvement is hard for everyone, which is one reason why *looking* as if we have loads of it by becoming more physically fit can make us more desirable as partners and employees.[40] Potential employees, partners, and friends who have their acts together are implicitly more trustworthy and more desirable because they can help us get to where we need to go.[41]

Self-Regulation Is That One Neat Trick, and It Has a Few Neat Tricks of Its Own

Using the parts of our brain needed to control our impulses is hard for everyone. One trick to being a superior self-regulator is to arrange your environment so that you don't even *need* self-control. Remember how Sivers described himself:[42] "I don't hang out, don't party. *If there's something I can't play, sing, or write, I shut the door and work on it for three to eight hours until it's finished."* Dopamine neurons respond to reward cues, not just the rewards themselves, and simply looking at something makes us ponder its good traits—collecting marbles that correspond to its values—which is why marketers pay more for product placement, manipulating preference through proximity. In Mischel's original marshmallow study, kids who were exposed to candy waited less than six minutes, but in the real world those with superior self-control wouldn't have even put themselves in that situation. They would choose a stark office to get more work done, go to the quiet library to finish a paper, eat at a restaurant that only serves healthy food, and shop at stores where they're not afraid to look at the price tags. Not putting yourself in situations where you have to sit on your hands and bite your tongue frees up your mental energy to do what you actually *need* to do.[43]

Self-control can even make people happier when they act like another successful segment of Mischel's kids, who waited when looking at a photo of two pieces of candy, directing their attention to the larger reward worth waiting for. We're sensitive to rewards and energized by them, but we can't control everything in our environment. Changing your values shifts how you habitually deploy your attention, and successful dieters change what kinds of marbles they add to the scale when looking at food: Instead of comparing "tasty" marbles when deciding what to eat, they weigh its "healthy" marbles.[44]

Focusing on the benefits of what you're approaching and finding enjoyment in the forward-thinking smart habits make people happier and more likely to adhere to long-term goals. You don't need to trick yourself into exercising when you find a physical activity you actually enjoy. Focusing on the serenity of having a healthy bank balance is a smarter, saner way to save money than obsessing over what you're not choosing and the fun you think you're missing out on.[45] There seems to be a limit to how many times we can say *no* before it gets annoying, but because rewards energize us, there's no limit to how often people can say, "Yes, I want that thing." People who successfully save money decide with the picture of two marshmallows in front of them, asking themselves, "Do I want an iPod or a house? Do I want a latte or a house?"[46]

Another benefit of focusing on the positive daily habits that lead to being physically, financially, mentally, and socially fit is that they provide increased buffers from bad luck. Even if you're genetically inclined to develop diabetes or cancer, years of making smart health decisions build a strong immune system that can prevent chronic illnesses. The safety net provided by a savings account can prevent bad luck from snowballing in the event of being laid off, stop a cascade of financial nightmares, and maximize lifetime earnings by giving people time to wait for better job offers. Just as hanging out with a crowd that favors shortsighted rewards in high school can have a negative domino effect, preventing bad luck from snowballing is just as important as maximizing your good luck.[47]

People with high self-control are viewed as more appealing partners, friends, and co-workers because we instinctively trust them more, knowing they're not the types to fly off the handle or make our lives more difficult. But people who emphasize their future when making decisions or constructing their environments tend to stick together because they share values: Both collect "healthy" marbles when viewing food. Befriending future-oriented people in high school and college changes our life trajectory, and choosing a similarly forward-thinking life partner has the added benefit of giving us a sane, stable home life. Couples with high self-control who help each other achieve their goals have happier relationships that are less likely to lead to divorce.[48] Dan Chambliss, the sociologist who studied Olympic-level swimmers, observes that conformity is more efficient than self-discipline. "If you join a great team, you're not constantly saying, 'I've gotta drag my ass out of bed at four in the morning' . . . because *everybody* is getting up at four. You just think, 'Oh, we get up at four.'"[49]

Focusing on the benefits of what you're working toward and constructing your environment to benefit those big, future plans can also help keep negative emotions and stress from snowballing, giving people more stable relationships and smoother progress toward their goals. Champion athletes excel at regulating their emotions, either upstream by minimizing daily stressors or by redefining their anxiety as excitement. Minimizing the time spent wallowing in defeat, disappointment, or nervousness by kindly getting yourself back on track as soon as possible acts as a buffer against stress, making it easier to keep your health, finances, and relationships in check.[50] Provided they don't stress themselves out along the way during life's inevitable hiccups, people with high standards are actually happier in the long run because they experience the profound satisfaction of accomplishing their lofty goals.[51]

I ask Dan Belsky, the behavioral geneticist whose work examines the genetics of success, how we can circumvent early life woes. "Intelligence helps you get order out of chaos," he says. "The brighter a person is, the better able they are to order the chaos of the world, the more effectively they can learn from it. Developing self-control depends on being able to regulate these regularities in the environment."[52] People who believe that life is controlled by chance factors beyond their control are more realistic, but they're also more likely to suffer from depression, which is partly characterized by a lack of motivation. People whose behavior focuses on long-term benefits have more favorable life outcomes, but they're also slightly delusional and optimistic.[53]

We can go to a better school than our parents, buy nicer clothes than they wore, take better care of ourselves, befriend a different breed of human, travel to collect experiences and stories, learn how to navigate different institutions from the ones they inhabited, and learn things like French and horseback riding and JavaScript that would act as investments in our future income. But aiming higher than everyone around you requires a value shift from your social class of origin, effectively abandoning the culture where you grew up. Just as all Olympians once made the decision to stop taking group classes, we have to flee the nest of the habits of our family and friends if we want to level up.[54]

Doing all of the things that von Sperling suggests *would* decrease my overall stress levels, which in turn would promote healthier brain functioning and develop my capacity for self-regulation, which would allow me to sit down like Sivers and Beyoncé, keep my emotions in check, and take care of whatever came my way with calm authority. But I don't have the time or money, and just thinking about how I'd find it is stressing me out. Even if getting an M.B.A. guaranteed that you'd make a comfortable living for the rest of your life, you can't go to grad school unless you currently have the money to go to grad school. Because we can't use those future earnings to pay for the next semester of business school, our ability to level up is constrained by whatever resources we currently have, be they financial (loans and applications to colleges aren't free), environmental (an understanding family who gives you quiet time to finish your work), or mental (perseverance and focus to work in the situation you're in).

Even when you're given a "make a $22 million website in a weekend" kind of idea, at some point you have to start where you are and do the work. Later, you have to choose to wisely invest a family gift in your growing company instead of a short-term reward like a trip or a car. Sometimes when we see luck like Sivers's building CD Baby or Donald Thomas's high jump, we're so focused on one moment that we miss the lifetime of habits before and after that made it possible at all.

Notes for Those of Us Who Want to Get Our Shit Together

- It doesn't matter that you *know* better unless you *do* better. As the comparative psychologist Michael Tomasello says, "In evolution, being smart counts for nothing if it does not lead to *acting* smart."[55]

- Mental fatigue is our brain's way of saying, "This isn't worth it," so find ways to decrease the perceived effort. Exercise doesn't have to be a chore—it can be a physical activity you enjoy with friends. Focus on what you have to do *today* to get closer to your preferred future.

- Arrange your life so that the smart choice is the *default* choice. Want to save more money? Have your bank automatically transfer money to your savings account on payday. Want to become an early riser? Join the army.

- Choices feel "worth it" when we see how our decisions directly lead us to the big rewards we're working toward. Envision how turning down that snack will help you fit into your jeans or achieve a fitness goal. If you're tempted to divert money from a retirement account to upgrade your TV, visualize the size of your future retirement home. Ice cream or pull-ups? TV or Palm Springs?

- Organizing your life to focus on long-term rewards may put you at odds with your loved ones; you want to study for the MCAT, but they want to get high and watch *Game of Thrones* all weekend. Rather than let them bring you down, simply find a new family—they can find someone to replace you easily. (It is, after all, *Game of Thrones*.) Better yet, find a like-minded group of friends. Surround yourself with others who share or respect your values.

- Because of differing brains, situations, and goals, there is no one-size-fits-all approach to developing conscientiousness. There's no magic number of days needed to build a new habit, no magic productivity app, no secret manual, and no special system that would equally improve everyone's ability to regulate their own behavior. Superior self-regulators are experts on themselves: They know how they function best, what motivates them, and hold themselves accountable.[56]

- We're tempted when we overvalue a small, immediate reward. Get perspective by playing the tape forward and imagining which version of your future self this decision is bringing you closer to. Consider how you'd advise someone in an identical situation.

- Mischel's original study noted that "disadvantaged children cannot categorically be termed 'nondelayers.'" If you want to teach your kids self-control and patience, make sure they trust that the larger, future benefits will materialize.

- Find joy in the process. Celebrate your efforts. Practice kindness to your future self. That person will be old, tired, and frustrated that you didn't try a little harder.

8

. . . .

You Had Me at Hello

The Lucky Art of Conquering the Interpersonal Frontier

Today is one of those days when events in the sporting world can legitimately be found on the front page of any newspaper. The NBA draft is starting in four hours. A few hours earlier, Germany defeated the United States 1–0 in the World Cup. *Things are happening.*

Leigh Steinberg, the sports superagent best known as the inspiration and technical consultant of the film *Jerry Maguire,* reaches into the minifridge next to his oak-colored desk for a can of diet Dr Pepper, his third in two hours; he's too distracted by preparations for his weekly podcast to shut the fridge door all the way.

To my left, Don West Jr., the self-described "lion tamer" of Steinberg Sports and Entertainment, sets up a camera; Diego Escutia stands over Steinberg, giving him a run-through of highlighted articles from *Bloomberg* and *Business Insider* that will serve as talking points for his weekly podcast, *Leigh Steinberg Radio Show,* one marketing arm of Steinberg Sports and Entertainment.

"They want to retain Carmelo and LeBron. They want to put shooters in the perimeter," says Escutia, pointing to the articles to explain the logic behind the anticipated draft picks. "Wiggins should be first," he says of the nineteen-year-old superstar guard from Kansas.

"Who?" asks Steinberg, staring at the articles.

Escutia informs him about basketball and the World Cup.

"These are not my sports," Steinberg says, taking a swig of soda. "What I know about soccer could fit into a thimble." Steinberg runs off to use the restroom.

He returns.

It begins.

But the story really begins when Leigh was a kid—he was the student body president of his elementary school, junior high, high school, college, and law school. When he was a senior at the University of California, Berkeley, he served as the counselor in a dorm that happened to be housing the football team. Three years later, Steinberg had graduated from the Berkeley School of Law; one of his residents, Steve Bartkowski, had become one of college football's premier passers and was the Atlanta Falcons' first-round draft pick. Back in 1975, prospective NFL players' parents usually sat in on these discussions, serving as makeshift legal proxies who kept the athletes' best interests in mind, but Bartkowski turned to his old resident adviser, Steinberg, for legal help.

With nothing to lose, the accidental twenty-five-year-old sports agent fought for his friend, securing a four-year contract with the Atlanta Falcons that was the largest contract an NFL rookie had ever signed at the time. Although Steinberg originally dreamed of becoming a "defense lawyer like Perry Mason," he's since pioneered the field of sports representation, made millions, and inspired the only movie with Cuba Gooding Jr. worth mentioning.

The most astute podcast listeners might never guess that Steinberg couldn't even pronounce some of the names of the NBA predicted first-round draft picks until a few minutes ago, nor that that day marks Leigh Steinberg's 1,558th day of sobriety, nor what the man has been through over the past few years. "Cancer. Blindness. Divorce. Lost a home to a flood," he says, marking each point with an X-filled circle. Podcast listeners would never guess that the superstar agent, who sold his agency years ago with his former business partner for $124 million and has represented the number one draft pick of the NFL a record eight times throughout his career, now resembles his fictional alter ego, Jerry Maguire, in one crucial way: After a string of personal and professional setbacks, including multiple arrests for public intoxication and filing for bankruptcy protection, Steinberg is back down to representing a single client.[1]

And yet his office walls are lined with non-Photoshopped photos of him alongside Barack Obama, Julia Roberts, and Tom Cruise. Yet he's still going. I don't care about the potbelly, the bankruptcy, the public drunkenness, or even the fact that he has a very public connection to Tom Cruise—and not just because I'm also guilty of some of these—but because, contrary to my expectations, after spending a few hours at Steinberg's office, I find myself actively rooting for him.[2]

Why do some people seem to win more than others? They may have more people in their lives who can give them lucky winning opportunities. Other people provide our luck: They're how Charlie Brewer became the quarterback, how Kristen Paladino chose her actors, how John McCain picked Sarah Palin, how Yale fills its freshman class, how Donald Thomas tried the high jump, and how Derek Sivers got a $22 million business idea. It's how Steinberg was given the opportunity to pioneer a field within law and then gathered the chutzpah to try once again.

Life is a random, luck-filled crapshoot; you never know who you're going to meet or where they're going to be three years later. Constantly being motivated to bond with other people and make the most of our face-to-face encounters—dates, auditions, job interviews, parties, sitting next to someone at a bus stop in Bangkok at 3:00 a.m.—can only increase your luck. Also, in order for said social interaction to occur at all, you have to be wearing a novelty propeller hat that constantly invites friendly commentary from outsiders. But what if it's being cleaned and we're on our own? Then, at some point, we must be masters of our own fate and start that conversation ourselves. *Wanting* to talk is a good place to start.

We Need People for Life (and Luck)

Automatically pairing pleasure with things that promote survival—calories, sugar, sex, pretty faces—"may be seen as evolution's boldest trick," an elegant solution for enabling organisms with adaptive behaviors. Social rewards—positive interactions with others—fall under this category.[3] Because we need others to live, the unique ecological niche that we've adapted to—our baseline—is group living.[4] Knowing that we can count on others for help in the group project that is life makes us feel like we have more resources to handle whatever comes our way.[5]

"Social rewards are primary rewards," reports the researcher Alice Lin. "You don't have to teach a child that getting a hug is rewarding." It's pretty universal to look at an attractive face smiling in our direction and dump several "this person is worth getting to know" marbles on the scale, but the path from looking at a stranger to declaring "a future friend worth talking to" is less clear-cut.

Being motivated to bond with others like Steinberg is easier for lucky people who had a stable childhood, the same way that it's easier for some kids to hold out for the second marshmallow because they were more confident that it would even materialize.[6]

Feeling pleasure from positive social interactions is partly genetic. Opioid receptors, concentrated in a few areas of the brain, determine our response to pain and pleasure, and the number and density of them continue developing during the first few years of life. Positive early social interactions with our caregivers foster the development of oxytocin and opioid receptors; in addition to having a higher ceiling of potential pleasure from positive interactions with others, the brains of some people can more easily reduce the distress associated with isolation or rejection.[7] Subjects with a specific genetic variation of the μ-opioid receptor known as OPRM1, located on chromosome 6q25.2, needed *less* pain medication following surgery and reported being significantly less distressed after being socially excluded.[8] Why? Because life is not fair.

Early peer interactions help set the stage for how people see themselves within the social world. Rewarding social experiences—like being elected the student body president of your elementary, junior high, high school, college, and law school—calibrate expectations about that second social marshmallow appearing; one lucky vote can change someone's social trajectory. We smile and give more attention to the class president, increasing how easily the Leigh Steinbergs of the world associate "people" with "good things." Belonging to a socially skilled peer group helps the rich get richer, the equivalent of joining an elite swimming team whose members exponentially develop one another's comfort and abilities in the social subtleties of reading body language, interacting with peers and strangers, and being able to accomplish what they set out to. This comfort with others allows them to enter unfamiliar situations more easily, expanding their behavioral tool kit over time.[9]

How We Can Talk Our Way Out of Luck

There are three sides to every story—his, hers, and the truth—and it's hard to argue with the objective lens of the camera. In the late 1970s, the researchers Robert E. Kleck and Angelo Strenta wanted to examine how medical conditions influenced day-to-day social interactions. They randomly assigned subjects to play the role of someone with a facial scar, epilepsy, or allergy, even though none of them had these conditions. For those in the scar condition, researchers applied a special kind of makeup to their faces that you've probably seen in a horror movie; when dried, it looked just like a prominently visible scar. After the subjects with the fake scars looked at themselves in a mirror to verify their newly disfigured faces—but just before they left to interact with others—the researchers applied a cream to prevent the makeup from cracking and breaking off. Then, they were told not to discuss their fictional maladies with the other person (researchers wanted to study how these stigmatized health conditions would affect conversations on irrelevant topics). Finally, subjects entered a room with two chairs and spoke freely with the other, non-diseased student for six minutes.

After good times were surely had by all, they parted ways and answered a questionnaire about the other person that included questions comparing what that interaction was like with other ones they'd had when they didn't appear to have a giant scar on their face: How much did that person talk or make eye contact? Did she seem tense or patronizing? Did he seem to like them?[10]

"It's the only study I've ever done in which every subject behaved the same way," says Kleck, who still vividly remembers conducting this study more than three decades later. "They all said, 'Oh, my God. It had such an impact on the other person.'" Subjects reported plenty of negative side effects that they usually didn't have to deal with when people found them blemish-, epilepsy-, and allergy-free.[11]

Then, the tape.

"We said, 'Hey, we [made] a videotape of that other person. We didn't tell either of you ahead of time because we felt that would make you uncomfortable, but I want you to go through that videotape and point out the behaviors that gave you the clue that they were responding to that facial scar.'" Subjects then watched the video, which only showed the *other* person they'd been speaking with, and were asked to point out anything unusual in the interaction like a gesture, sideways glance, weird vocal inflection, or a look of discomfort, pity, or concern.

"Turn on the tape, and they stop it almost immediately. 'Did you see them just shift in their chair? They are very nervous.' Turn the tape back on? Bang and I stop it. 'They're staring at me. They're afraid if they look away I'll be aware that they're upset by my scar.'

"Start the tape again, bang: 'They're looking away. They can't stand to look at my face anymore.'"

They can't stand to look at my face anymore.

I can empathize with that: *No one should see your knees. I would like you to lose ten pounds. I think you could lose ten pounds and you'd be much happier. If you could lose fifteen, even better.*

But like most decent psychology studies, this one was built on a bed of lies. The subjects with the fake scars didn't know that the researchers had lied about lotion; the cream didn't keep the scar in place: It *removed* it.

They were flawless and scar-free throughout the conversation.

"Some of these reports were forty-five minutes in length," remembers Kleck, "going on [with] great specifics about how the other person's behavior was affected by the scar they didn't have."

To Get Lucky, Pay Attention

Our ability to navigate and find pleasure in social exchanges depends largely on how we interpret them. In the Charlie Brewer principle, we learned that when our scale starts to tip in one direction—even when we don't realize that it is—those hunches influence what we pay attention to and how we interpret what we see, creating a positive feedback loop that gives us more ammunition to present our hunches as fact.

Is anything more ambiguous than the social world? Entering a conversation with our scale tipping toward "This isn't worth it" or "I'm not worthy" makes it easier to pick up those corresponding marbles: We interpret someone's look as "I can't believe you said that" when it was simply "I have something in my eye." We see a pair of crossed arms as "stay away," rather than "damn, I forgot my sweater again." We see a wink as a cheesy gesture or lazy attempt to flirt; we don't see the amount of courage it took for that typically shy person to wink at all.

If expressions are as ambiguous as modern art, we can think of conversations as interactive works of modern art. Because motivation is a combination of expectancy and value, fundamental differences in how often we expect interactions to pan out well, or even value them in the first place, shape how we habitually orient ourselves to others from the get-go. The individual quirks of beliefs and baggage that emerge in individual conversations can create wildly different social paths over time. Downplaying the value of social rewards makes us more likely to avoid them.

Craving a connection but being uncertain about it even happening—anticipating or fearing rejection—turns us into the people with fake scars, making us downplay positive behavior, interpreting behavior negatively (he just texted back because he feels sorry for me!), and zoom in on bad things, all of which destabilize the very connections we crave. These negative patterns can continue ad infinitum because of what happens in any self-fulfilling prophecy: Our hunches are confirmed. The world continues as predicted. At no point in this process do we learn that we're the ones keeping others at a distance or driving them away by making them feel uneasy. Because our WTF Just Happened signal never goes off, we never learn.[12]

Developing any skill requires quality feedback. After a stint as a child actor morphed into teaching psychology for a number of years, Blake Eastman put his moxie and independence to work by opening up a consultancy and body language school called the Nonverbal Group, and he has since appeared on *The Daily Show* and CNN.[13] One weekend I spent over sixteen hours learning about body language with a surprisingly young, good-looking group of professionals, a motley mix of marketing managers, graphic designers, and police officers turned physical therapists; to my left was a biracial medical executive; to my right, a Korean artist.

We break off into pairs, and Eastman instructs one of us to speak for a few minutes while maintaining the other's interest. Eastman stands at the periphery, leaning forward, darting in and out to make observations.

I've partnered up with Joe, who claims to have single-handedly turned around the 2008 Obama campaign by successfully canvassing rural Virginia. He begins talking about his new job—which is the most amazing thing that I should be deeply impressed with, don't get me wrong—but that look in his eye suggests that, perhaps, his heart still belongs to Obama. I notice his boomingly loud voice and self-assured posture as well as the way he steps well into my personal space and wonder if he's curious why pickup tips he's apparently gleaned from *The Game* aren't working for him. I develop various theories about his childhood, love life, and wardrobe selection as I notice how he always looks up and to the left for no reason whatsoever.[14] I can't figure out if this braggadocio is compensating for deep insecurity or reflects a genuine self-love. I contemplate sandwiches and the afterlife. I, too, pine for Obama.

I have time to do all of this within the span of a few minutes because Joe is so knee-deep in his own beloved story that he never even bothers to see if I am listening. He just won't. Stop. Talking.

Eastman approaches and turns to Joe. "Did you even notice that she checked out?"

No, he did not. Not one bit. But Leigh Steinberg had me at hello and kept me there for hours.

Feeling anxious around someone (typically because you see them as being of a slightly higher status, or fear rejection) means you've got marbles stacked on the "I'm not worthy" side, but you can't simply course correct by dumping "I got this" marbles prior to delivering your first-date soliloquy, or looking at the mirror while wearing rose-colored glasses. Conversations are like sex: Loving your own story or penis doesn't matter if the other side leaves unhappy. Getting others on our side requires looking at people and plunking an "interesting person worth knowing" marble on the scale. As with any skill, building the social skills that constitute *mutually* rewarding interactions requires getting real-time feedback about how much others actually enjoy our company.[15] People like Leigh Steinberg get lucky because they're fundamentally motivated to get *along,* which requires easing up on the walls of self-protection (shyness due to anxiety or fear of rejection) or self-enhancement (monologue delivery due to overconfidence or overcompensation).[16]

To Get Lucky, Make Others Feel Good

In a now-classic study, researchers gave subjects the neuropeptide oxytocin and found that it increased how much people trusted others, leading to its nickname "the love drug." Yes, there was a TED talk that's now understood to be oversimplified, especially because subsequent studies have demonstrated that oxytocin makes racists even more racist. Oxytocin, as it turns out, acts like a zoom lens on other people, promoting in-group survival by making us more sensitive to social information. Different variations of oxytocin receptor genes vary our baseline sensitivity to social information; people with autism, for example, seem to have a perfect storm of genes, finding nothing rewarding in a smile and nothing special in a face.[17]

We can maximize our likelihood of connecting in social interactions by putting our big-kid-plays-nice pants on and displaying expressive interest in others. Even when you're worried what someone else thinks about your big thighs, small bank account balance, facial scar—or the fact that it's been several years since you've had any clue what you're doing—it's important to recognize others as equally complex individuals equally worthy of regard with an unknown mix of interesting traits and to focus on the connection itself.[18] Creating positive social interactions depends on how much others find us pleasurable to be around, but to get the ball rolling, people need to feel safe about how we're going to judge them.[19]

"It's listening to other people, not judging them on the surface," says Steinberg. "It's quality compassion. It's understanding how life could be challenging, lonely. . . . It's having compassion for them and looking beyond the surface at the fact 'that may be a really interesting person.'" Luck-expanding emotional intelligence stems from genuine humility—seeing others as complex individuals, equally worthy of regard.

The best way to start a conversation is by sending signals that can only be interpreted as friendly, clear signs that the other person won't have to break out their opioid receptors to endure the blow of rejection. People who anticipate acceptance are more likely to let their guard down and display warm, expressive nonverbal behavior, undeniable signals of benevolent interest like smiles, open gestures, and forward leans. Unmistakable signs of interest allow others to let their guard down. One of the most important non-beauty factors influencing attraction is whether someone else likes *us*.[20]

To Make Others Feel Good, Be Enthusiastic

After two decades of performing, Chia-Jung Tsay, a Juilliard-trained concert pianist, started becoming intrigued by what she considered a quirk in the judging process.

"I realized depending on what type of evaluation process was involved—whether the competitions require audio recordings or video re-cordings or just coming in person—there could be very different results for the same performers," she says.[21] "That led me to just wondering what ex-actly influences the judges. It could be something that we're not even really aware of." In Tsay's study, subjects with no background or training in classical music were given three performances to evaluate—"the top three finalists in each of 10 prestigious international classical music competi-tions"—before being asked to guess the actual winner.

Some of the subjects were given audio recordings, others were shown video clips of the performances, and a third subset was shown silent video clips of the musicians performing. Novices correctly guessed the winners based on silent video clips 46.4 percent of the time.[22] When working musi-cians who had studied their instrument for an average of sixteen and a half years were asked to predict who won out of three audio clips, they only suc-ceeded 20.5 percent of the time.

Let that sink in for a second: Even though 96.3 percent of the experts said that sound mattered most when determining the winner, 100 percent of them were wrong. Compared with their performance judging entries based on sound alone, the experts were two and a half times better at choos-ing the winner of a music competition when they only had access to the visual cues.[23] We've seen that these rewarding visual cues can take the form of attire (formal concert attire gets better scores because it more closely aligns with our mental image of what that person should look like) or an attractive face.

Novices came to the same conclusions as experts after looking at short video clips that were subjected to a Photoshop-like treatment that elimi-nated all visual information aside from black outlines, leaving only the mu-sicians' movement and gesture. In six seconds, an untrained heathen with no background in classical music staring at some lines can guess the winner of a legitimately impressive competition as well as experts, a judgment that's two and a half times more accurate than relying on sound alone.

In this type of "thin slicing" study made famous by the researcher

Nalini Ambady, listening to the tone of a surgeon's voice for a few seconds was a good predictor of her likelihood of getting sued for malpractice. Watching thirty seconds of a lecture—also without the sound—is a good indicator of that professor's end-of-semester evaluations.[24]

I asked Jim Uleman, a social psychologist at New York University who has researched first impressions for decades, about these studies. "They're influenced by responsiveness; it's all about engagement." (If you needed another existential dilemma to ponder today, he also reports, "I don't trust first impressions the way I used to.")[25] Genuine passion, engagement, and interest are building blocks of charisma, which emanate through expressive and vivid language, gesturing fluidly, showing empathy, and using inclusive, "we"-based language, all of which help sync up the brains of others, giving them an energizing, happiness-promoting social reward.

Conversations are two-way streets; we influence others just as much as they influence us. The emotions of genuinely enthusiastic, positive people garner social support because they manifest as warm nonverbal behaviors and vocal inflections. Even in one-sided communication from music, movies, storytellers, professors, or leaders, positivity generates happiness in others; our mirror neurons become active when we see and understand someone else's emotions and intentions. Being able to make others feel good and comfortable is a key component of charisma; we can move others when we're genuinely moved and passionate ourselves, which is why emotional intelligence is such a strong predictor of leadership.[26]

Disagreements between judges while rating others typically come from personal baggage: the woman with short hair and glasses; the invisible scar on our face that people wouldn't stop looking at. What's captured by the thin-slicing studies are unmistakable rewards right in front of their faces; just as seeing an attractive face plunks a big "yes" marble on the scale, things that get high ratings fall under this category: fluent rewards like beauty, sugar, easily understood works of art, and pleasing motion. The undeniably pleasant evokes positive emotions in all, putting people on the same page by syncing up our brain waves. The speed of these emotions makes it easier for everyone to agree: YES.[27]

Be Enthusiastic about New People

Stable traits like self-control and confidence offer a window into our future outcomes because they predict what we're likely to do when no one's looking and the pressure is off, those seemingly transitional periods that end up constituting our lives.[28] Just as being genuinely moved by music wins competitions, being genuinely moved by people can help you win social support. Sociability, usually measured as a component of extroversion, is a genuine interest in others that fills your world with potentially beautiful, interesting friends.[29]

Responsiveness distinguishes the animate from the inanimate—even single-celled amoebas respond to light—and is the core trait of a relationship. (Until James Franco actually responds to my letters, it's not technically a "relationship." Technically.) Responsiveness starts on a microlevel, paying attention to the subtle details of how others respond to you.[30]

Developing a trait called self-monitoring makes it easier to develop a diverse set of social connections. This ability is simply taking the time to test the social waters before jumping in: identifying what the group deems appropriate by detecting social cues and presenting the version of ourselves that best fits into the situation, avoiding the faux pas of being seen as someone standing in the way of what the group wants to do. Those with more social tact than adopting a "love me or leave me" approach get promoted faster, are liked by more people, and occupy better positions in social networks.[31]

Striking up benign chats with strangers is a good way to develop social skills and learn how to read people, the same way that learning how to sight-read can improve a musician's confidence and ability to play diverse genres of music. Because people are designed for coordinated behaviors, we automatically influence the body language and speech patterns of others we interact with; interactions feel more effortless when both parties speak and move similarly, meaning that they don't have as much work to do before syncing up. When the entire office agrees that someone is a chore to interact with, it's usually because Jerry never budges from his usual style of speaking.

Clicking with someone is a state of mutual responsiveness, synchronization, and interest, the conversational equivalent of flow. Paying attention to how others communicate and being the more flexible one makes the conversation feel easier for others.[32] When they enter a new social situation, the agreeable excel at taking the group's perspective, integrating it into their own, and adjusting their behavior accordingly. They can be assertive without diverting the group from its goals. They use their time to help others accomplish what they want to do.[33]

As the author and financial planner Carl Richards once wrote in the *New York Times,* "I have a lucky friend. Chances are you know him. He has written several *New York Times* best sellers. By any outward appearance, he has officially made it. I wanted to know what role he thought luck played in his career. Without batting an eye, he said, 'Oh, luck has been everything. I can point to at least 10 occasions where pure, dumb luck landed me a huge break in my career.'

"I was skeptical. 'O.K., maybe you've had some luck,' I said. 'But you've been working hard and "playing in traffic," right?'

"'No,' he told me. 'I'm talking about flat-out luck. A guy I met on a plane, a random stranger, an introduction to a friend of a friend who happened to know a great book agent—that kind of luck.'"[34] Lucky encounters magically emerge from well-designed public squares or open offices just as well-designed gyms generate visible abdominal muscles: They do not. It's what we actually do there that counts.[35] In order to have more lucky social interactions, you need to have more interactions overall and take responsibility for how many you initiate. But real luck happens when we develop those entry skills even further and dive deep when we meet people.

I asked Carol Dweck, author of *Mindset,* how we can overcome social inertia. "You never know who the person you're sitting next to really is," she told me. Moreover, you never know who that person next to you is going to be. "Everyone has something to teach us," she says.[36] While I can offer no generic methods of flattery or pickup lines because everyone is uniquely sensitive and damaged, we all want to feel understood and accepted for who we are, both accurately and positively understood. Imagine that everyone you meet is beautiful and fascinating; then make it your job to discover how.

People who can get others to open up and offer the social reward of acceptance can make fast friends wherever they go.[37] Self-disclosure isn't just rewarding to the people doing the disclosing; it's rewarding to the people *hearing* it. Feeling nervous or anxious about a new social encounter—to the point of saying little about yourself—is understandable, but typically has an unintended effect. Acting in a "pleasant but non-self-revealing way," dubbed innocuous sociability—think Stepford—creates a feeling of "discomfort, boredom, and less liking" in conversation partners.[38]

When we don't reveal anything about ourselves out of a fear of alienating others with our likes (what if she doesn't like Harry Potter?), pasts (the two-week marriage at age nineteen), hopes (to colonize Mars, to learn Danish), we fail to fully reveal ourselves as human, giving our conversation partner nothing genuine to respond to or connect with, no unique or interesting marbles about us for them to add to their scale. One way to disarm someone is by offering information about yourself. Increasingly personal mutual self-disclosure (taking turns peeling away the onion of what makes you tick) creates intimacy, which is why those lists of "forty questions that lead to love!" can turn strangers into fast friends.[39]

The unlucky may mistakenly assume that fascinating people give out life-changing opportunities to strangers at random. Turns out that we're more likely to offer life-changing opportunities to strangers when they no longer feel like strangers because they've made a personal connection. One shortcut is called "Fast Acceptance by Common Experience." Normally, you may not care about someone from the other side of the country, but when you're both in Australia, you can instantly bond over traveling across the world at the same time. Perceived similarity draws us closer and attracts us to others. Remember those marbles, that scale that helps us decide which way to go? Each thing we learn about people (if they're good, cute, enjoy our company, have good taste in music or similar priorities) is a marble. Provided that it's something you actually like about yourself, finding a "we have this thing in common!" marble helps tip the scales in your favor, with more important qualities adding even bigger marbles to the lot. The more we feel as if our identities overlap with other people's, the happier we feel when something goes well for them.[40]

To Get Lucky, Keep Diverse Connections

In 1989, the sociologist Katherine Giuffre wanted to examine the ebb and flow of the success of photographers in New York City. "How do people figure out a way in the art world of advancing their career, when it's not really obvious on the surface of it what it means to advance?" she asks. "It occurred to me that probably social connections mattered."[41]

To find out who successfully climbed the hierarchy of the fine art world, Giuffre focused on fine art photographers. Using industry directories like *Art in America*'s annual gallery guide and the Association of International Photography Art Dealers' membership guide, she cataloged every fine art photographer represented by a major gallery in 1979.

In the sublime, OCD-like fashion required of a completed dissertation, Giuffre then examined every *issue* of those same guides for the next decade, tracking careers, exhibits, galleries, and other photographers represented by that same gallery. (Artists enter into agreements with galleries to market and sell their work in exchange for a percentage of the sales, so being represented by the same gallery is one of the closest things these photographers have to a co-worker, someone whose financial livelihood relies upon the same source.)

After Giuffre charted the social connections of photographers in the 1980s, three distinct career trajectories emerged. Many photographers were in stable collectives that she dubbed "invisible colleges," lasting connections with mutual friends and artistic collaborators who knew the same curators and gallery owners. While some managed to support themselves with their art, their careers never really took off.

"They didn't get the same kind of attention from the art world journals, they didn't get the number of reviews, and the amount of notice, and the amount of discussion that some of their peers did," says Giuffre.

Giuffre dubbed those in another career trajectory "strugglers," who were probably most noteworthy for the grand total amount of art school loans left in permanent deferment.

But some artists got lucky by getting more attention from high-caliber art journals like *ARTnews, Art in America,* and *Artforum.* "People who had lots of wide-ranging weak ties," she found, "had bridge ties to other groups [and] a very dispersed social network. Not so much *more* people, but very *different* people in their network." Yes, they knew people, but more important their *connections* knew lots of people.

"In this filtering process, lots of great art gets filtered out. It may be incredible art, mind-blowing art, soul-expanding art, but what those people lack are those social connections," says Giuffre.

"Trust is developed from social networks," she says. "When we say someone has a good reputation, what does that mean? It means many of the people in my network have interacted with this person, and you can verify trust. I don't have to reinvent the wheel all the time, I can trust."

Maintaining diverse connections exponentially grows your luck over time.[42] Giuffre's most successful artists had more diverse groups of influences, leading critics to classify their work under multiple genres. People whose social roots grasp several kinds of soil reap dividends, because the divergent trajectories of their contacts bridge them to exponentially more people. These sets of wide-ranging, unpredictable, and non-overlapping clusters help bring a cascade of attention to their work by organically spreading news of their art throughout different networks. People inhabiting different social worlds bridge various networks and get access to unique knowledge that they can leverage and use creatively. If it seems as if most of your friends know each other, you're not maximizing your luck.[43]

"It is hardly possible to overrate the value . . . of placing human beings in contact with persons dissimilar to themselves, and with modes of thought and action unlike those with which they are familiar," said John Stuart Mill.[44] The people we stay in touch with can connect us to entirely new social circles, industries, geographic areas, and information, which is why constant curiosity and interest in others increase your luck over time. Maintaining bonds is a long-term investment in your social capital.[45]

"It should not be assumed that the ultimate elite career is one that hooks together all the perfect elite trajectories," wrote the sociologist Andrew Abbott. "The most elite individual may be that person who maintains the largest number of possible future trajectories that s/he could jump onto."[46]

Having many options lets you pick the best, which is what happened to our *Jerry Maguire* inspiration, Leigh Steinberg: He was the only lawyer-ish person that his acquaintance Steve Bartkowski knew, so he was Bartkowski's go-to guy for legal assistance. It's what happened to Derek Sivers, who sat between the worlds of programming and independent music: He was the first one his musician friend called when he needed help navigating the internet.

After all, there are plenty of things about Steinberg that even the most astute listeners of his podcast will never know: that he had been chewing Skoal tobacco and spitting the juice into the garbage can all day; that empty cans of diet Dr Pepper were strewn about his office; that the left breast pocket of his light-blue button-down oxford shirt had a noticeable black ink stain, which, while smaller than a dime, from afar could be mistaken for the signature silhouette of a Ralph Lauren pony; that he managed to keep his cool when three girls on paddleboards went by in plain view of his office, which overlooks Newport Bay, but was quick to point out the group of kids jumping from the nearby bridge; that a box of chocolate-flavored Premier Protein shake sat unopened next to the current can of diet Dr Pepper; that he had a sizable potbelly not visible in any recent photos; that a dog-eared copy of *Grain Brain* sat on his desk, his place held not by a bookmark or a pen but by a small packet of original-strength Alka-Seltzer tablets. Despite plentiful reasons to be distracted, arrogant, or self-conscious, he focused on making sure I felt good about the interview and left with what I needed.

"I was brought up by a father who had two core values. One was treasure relationships, especially family. The second was to try to make a difference in the world. He would look at me and he would say, 'When there's a problem, when there's something that's discordant and wrong, and you're looking for the "they" to fix it, they'll fix it, the amorphous "they" will fix it, someone will take care of this.' He'd look at me and he'd say, 'There is no "they." The "they" is *you.*'"

Treating everyone like an acquaintance and every interaction like a pleasantry—that barista *could* be your friend's friend, after all—makes everyone happier. We're attracted to people who make us feel good, and because we're responsible for 50 percent of the variance in our social interactions, each of us has an "affective presence," or a way that we reliably leave a unique mark on others. And you could be that person, bringing smiles and help to others and accumulating more social support along the way, creating your own upward spiral of positivity. You could be one of those people who know everyone, the ones who get lots of opportunities handed to them because of their social ties, the ones who have us at hello.[47]

Notes for Those Who Would Fancy Being Propped Up by Seven Billion Friends

- Social skills can be developed just like any other skill. And like any other skill, stacking our side of the scale with "why bother" marbles can make people choke.

- Developing any skill requires timely, quality feedback. Social skills can stagnate if we're only open to listening to feedback from people who are similar to us. You and your friends may love one another without realizing that the rest of the world sees you as overly sarcastic, arrogant, or nosy.

- To maximize the lucky opportunities you get from others *and* improve your social skills, befriend people of many ages, backgrounds, and interests. Think about which values are lacking in your inner circle: Do you pine for a sense of charity? Volunteer.

Logic? Take a programming class. Adventure? Join that bouldering gym. Travel.

- If depression is a failure to see the future through rose-colored glasses, social anxiety is a failure to look at the mirror with rose-colored glasses.[48]

- Instead of obsessing over your nonexistent facial scar, focus on being responsive to others. Look at people through rose-colored glasses.

- People who are overly concerned with the way that others view them think their mistakes are obvious to all. They are not. As the saying goes, "You wouldn't worry so much about what others think of you if you realized how seldom they do."[49]

- When you see other people, add some "future friend who deserves compassion" marbles to the scale. Imagine that others are beautiful and make it your job to figure out *how*.

- Things that are undeniably, universally pleasant—unmistakable rewards right in front of our faces that are fluently processed, like smiling babies, sugar, and elegant motion—evoke positive emotions that put people on the same page by syncing their brain waves.[50] The essence of charisma is emotional intelligence, or sensitivity to the well-being of others. Be expressive. Smile. Genuine emotion is contagious.

- Leave the house. "Good luck does not happen to those in a vacuum," Dweck explained. "You have to leave the house for it."[51]

- Stay on good terms with others and stay in touch. Ask if they need help. We reach out to people if we view them as having the capacity and the willingness to help us.[52]

9

My Future's So Bright,
I Gotta Wear Shades

*The Luck-enhancing Mind-set of Embracing
Your Inner Kanye West*

t's Monday morning, nine o'clock, and we're at the New York University Poly Incubator project on a brick street that was lightly vacant ten years ago. Inside a room scarcely larger than a freight elevator with overly polished floors—its walls, all whiteboards covered with words like *"CUs"* and *"Design + Technol"* and mock-ups of wire frames—the entrepreneur Sian-Pierre Regis sits across from the venture capitalist Charlie O'Donnell at a tiny table.

"We were just talking about money and interestingness."

The impeccably named Regis is leaning forward with his hands clasped. Regis's father is a Haitian engineer who he says taught him a work ethic befitting the American dream; his British mother is a longtime worker in the hospitality industry who helped foster his love of creativity. Regis—who, like Steinberg, was elected president of his class—graduated from Colgate University in 2006 with a degree in sociology. As the editor in chief of *Swagger,* a hip online content provider boasting a few million Facebook likes, he just looks the part: effortlessly well dressed, a smattering of bracelets on his right wrist, and a lapel-less black blazer. He's trying to persuade O'Donnell to invest hundreds of thousands of dollars in *Swagger*—and, by proxy, him.

A graduate of St. John's and Fordham, Charlie O'Donnell worked as an investment analyst and then at the venture capital firm Union Square Ventures before branching out on his own. After raising $8.3 million, he opened Brooklyn Bridge Ventures. ("I'm a start-up, too," he later tells me, adding that his own experience raising capital gave him insight into what founders actually need.)[1] A seasoned marathoner and triathlete, he always looks ready to exercise, which today means a gray Nike Dri-FIT shirt, dark jeans, and black Nikes. He leans back. He continues discussing the business of online content.

"What's interesting now is that there's this new policy . . . this layer of success. Investors think this is interesting, but they're not a hundred percent sure what the model is supposed to look like. And then there's some media-savvy folks, like Advancit, that's Les Moonves's daughter, serious media who really know the business."

"Yeah, yeah," says Regis, leaning in.

"To have people invest in you, you already have to invest in yourself," says O'Donnell. "Content, how can we scale? Looking at *HuffPo, BuzzFeed,* what they're doing."

"Just getting this advice is worth $300,000 to me," exclaims Regis, nodding his head, looking excited just to be there.

"You need a plan," says O'Donnell. Regis takes notes. He's into it.

O'Donnell's next meeting is with Todd Berger, about whom I will say nothing, save for the fact that calling his pitch "dry" would be an affront to moisture.[2] After five minutes, I'm not sure what this guy's business even is. He leaves, and O'Donnell and I get to talking about his impressions of the two pitches.

"I like that first guy," he says. "I felt like he's more into the process of wanting to learn what it's like to build a real business, and he was admittedly like, 'There are things I need to know. I've had conversations with people; I've learned from them.'"

About the second guy, we're less certain. "Then there's the likeability aspect," he says. "I mean, would I want to have a beer with him? I mean, you can have a good plan . . . but do you want to work with him?" In addition to the "wanting to grab a beer with someone" thing, investors want to work with someone giving off the same set of signals as Regis.

Venture capitalists making decisions about which start-ups to fund don't really back projects. According to the über-optimistic language of internet culture, start-ups never fail. Like a baby left on the side of the road or wedding vows after several shots of Jägermeister, a start-up only loses when completely abandoned, so the way to never fail is to pivot, or simply change course. And because a start-up might pivot at any time, venture capitalists fund what remains constant: They don't fund projects, they fund *people.* They don't just want to fund what someone is doing now, but the next thing that person is going to be a part of. Venture capitalists buy low, sell high; they invest in people who are going places.

Who hasn't dreamed of placing their MVP trophy in the corner office as their assistant enters to say, "The president's on the line . . . again"? Sure, we've all had dreams like this, but some people actually go for it.[3] Continuously leveling up to achieve such great heights requires you to be insanely optimistic and tolerate the inevitable bumps and failures along the way. You have to have a high overall sense of your self-worth, believe that you deserve and can achieve great things. You need, essentially, to be like Kanye West.

The comedian Dave Chappelle explained how he knew that Kanye West was going to be famous before he was a known public entity: "He answers the phone, he goes, 'Hello. Huh? What? Uh-uh, I can't. I can't. 'Cause, I'm at Dave Chappelle's show watching sketches that nobody's ever seen before.' And then he says, ''Cause my life is dope, and I do dope shit,' and then he hung up the phone."[4]

Having the confidence to focus on the rewards in front of us leads to luckier outcomes, because constantly pursuing good things (rather than avoiding bad ones) translates to taking more shots at life's targets. A subset of these people dream of rosier futures, keep setting the bar higher, keep swimming in bigger ponds, and are willing to do what it takes to get there. They have the mental resources to be their own biggest advocates and tolerate setbacks. While the rest of us can learn from them, mastering this fine art requires a few lucky things that are easier for a lucky few.[5]

If You Want People to Invest in You, You Have to Believe in Yourself

Thinking that you deserve to be on top depends, in part, on how frequently you wind up there. Over time, these moments of rising to the top of whatever group you happen to be in can stamp in where you see yourself on life's totem pole, adding marbles to the "I got this" side of your scale. In social groups, we typically follow the leader: a mixture of who has the qualities we generally associate with status and who has the specific, status-relevant traits needed for a particular task, or who we can easily imagine winning that variation of the Shape Game.

That is, a group automatically defers to its members on the basis of how closely they resemble Elon Musk—tall, attractive, intelligent, white, male, famous, billionaire—unless the group has another, specific goal best served by someone with different qualities. (A situation that requires someone to discuss growing up poor, having ovaries, and never reaching the top shelf is the only plausible scenario in which I would ever triumph over Musk.) Should it come down to myself and a similar-looking short, scrappy, ovary-brandishing human, the two of us would duke it out by flaunting the human equivalent of peacock tail feathers—demonstrating competence by way of confidence, dominance by way of assertive behavior and subtle physical cues—until the other backed down.[6]

A particular subset of optimistic go-getters choose to become their own bosses.

Entrepreneurs who fit the mold of our stereotypical image of what start-up founders typically look like—Musk, Zuckerberg, Steve Jobs, Jack

Dorsey—are lucky. They have had an expanded sense of options in life, guided by role models who look like them. It's easier to feel as if you belong at a tech conference in the Bay Area when you're a straight white guy, which influences not only how likely you are to throw your hat into the ring but how others rate your efforts: Thanks to the Charlie Brewer principle, they see you as a Shape Game natural. And when you get graded on a curve, you're more likely to be buffered from stress and rejection.[7]

What other people have said about us and how they've treated us shape our future aspirations, but some things end up getting in the way.[8] To avoid this anxiety, we change whatever is easiest to change. Constraints become preferences.[9] "If you're able to change your attitude and get all of your attitudes in line to support that decision, then you're going to function better with it," says the researcher Cindy Harmon-Jones.[10] So the world tells us that we're good at certain Shape Games and hands us a menu of possible life routes, ones that everyone will cheer us on for. Once we form a stable belief about who we might be—what our possible, future self consists of—we go with it.

While some see these as foolish dreams, some people who aim high luck out because rewards loom larger and seem more attainable. Some people get lucky because they have enough D2 receptors, and when your brain's "no go" switch works well, you're able to maintain a stiff upper lip in the face of brownies. Individual genetic differences play a role in our willingness to make more of an effort to get a bigger potential reward. Variations in the dopamine system influence our ability to keep approaching good things; for example, differences in people's D1 receptors—the brain's "Go" system— influence baseline activity in the behavioral activation system. Some people are more sensitive to the good things: Variations in one protein in the brain's motivational circuitry, DARPP-32, make it easier for some to learn from positive outcomes; higher DARPP-32 levels in the nucleus accumbens—the brain's "talking stick"—make some more inclined to choose high-energy, high-reward options.[11]

Leveling up Requires the Resources to Get There

Life is largely random (you didn't choose your parents, to start) but it's actually in our best interest to *overestimate* how much we control, because believing that you can't handle something is precisely what makes it stressful. Over time, stress degrades our health, relationships, ability to think, act, and reach our full potential. Stress is a threat to homeostasis, the perception that we don't have enough resources to deal with whatever's upcoming. Reframing hardships as opportunities to rise (rather than threats) is easier when we put a positive spin on our ability to handle things. Perceived social support, how frequently we experience positive emotions, and sensing a purpose in life make us feel like we have more resources to actively cope with stressors, adding "I got this" marbles to our scale.[12]

It's key behind ideas like mental toughness, resilience, hardiness, and grit, all of which refer to our capacity to bounce back and keep moving forward to what we want.[13]

When our actions directly influence outcomes (studying for a test will reliably increase your grade), tokens of a so-called irrational mind like superstitions, good-luck charms, prayers, and other religious rituals actually improve performance by reducing anxiety and increasing confidence in our ability to accomplish whatever we set out to do. Believing that you are lucky or destined for great things can be maladaptive if you think that all you have to do is wait by the phone for a great job offer or start thinking that games of chance are the way to go. Believing that good things will happen to you becomes a positive, self-fulfilling prophecy only to the extent that it promotes motivation, a belief in your capacity to improve, and confidence during a performance.[14]

The underlying theme here is adopting an approach-oriented mindset—using your strengths to address and conquer your weaknesses, rather than ignoring them. Think, "I got this. Why not me?" People with a high internal locus of control—who fully believe that they are masters of their destiny—have better life outcomes.[15] While that positivity illusion known as the status quo bias protects our view of the present—that things are cool as is—the better way to be delusional is to be like Kanye West and believe that as long as we do everything in our power to make it happen, eventually, the future will belong to us.[16]

On January 26, 2013, the billionaire CEO of Twitter and Square, Jack Dorsey, tweeted, "Success is never accidental." That's the ultimate "I got this. This was meant to happen." It's easy to say that becoming a billionaire can give anyone a huge ego, but having an ego and being willing to put in the work to back it up are just as much causes for success as effects.[17]

Aiming higher than we think we're capable of makes us anxious because of a perceived identity conflict between our current and our future selves, between "me" and "the person who knows how to do this sort of thing." It's easier to aim high when we don't see the ideal "want to" version of our future self in conflict with the "ought to/should" self that we feel obligated to pursue. Long-term goal compatibility is one of the best predictors of how long a relationship will last, and the same can be said about how long we remain committed to our ideal futures.[18]

Perceiving incompatibility between future career and family goals is one reason why women lean out, foreseeing trade-offs and inconveniences down the road. We make predictions about our own futures by watching others answer the question of work-life balance and envisioning ourselves on that path. Men don't typically see these as incompatible goals, often viewing the corner office as the best way to provide for their family.[19] The magic happens when we can focus our energy and time on attaining that idealized version of our own future self without feeling as though we're being pulled in a million directions or disappointing others by not following the expected life trajectory.

Believing that we're unlucky resembles a lack of confidence, causes anxiety (thinking that we don't have what it takes, that we're on the losing team), and actually impairs performance.[20]

Can you learn to be lucky? Greatness requires you to aim high and set lofty goals by embracing your inner Kanye West. Remaining self-employed depends on your tolerance for risk and how strongly you identify with the goal you're pursuing.[21] Ultimately, it's impossible to know when to throw in the towel. People who get their books published, start-ups funded, movies produced, or time in the spotlight are merely crazed holdouts. Remember the other inevitability in life alongside death and taxes: failure. At some point, things go south for everyone. Failure sucks, but less so for people who respond well to this inevitability by keeping their emotions and frustrations in check. Aiming high is most adaptive when you can be kind to yourself when you fail, rather than being overly concerned with how others see you, focusing on your imperfections, fearing mistakes, and always perceiving a gap between "where you are" and "where you should be."

Sound familiar? Our default is "Cool, a reward!" but whenever we're made aware of the fact that we're not high on the totem pole and given reason to see the possible downfalls of a situation, our brain makes the subtle shift to "BE CAREFUL WHAT ARE YOU DOING," focusing on possible mistakes and punishments. Being overly critical toward ourselves doesn't make us perform any better; it just increases stress and the possibility of burnout, depression, and anxiety.[22]

Alas, it's easier to be confident and optimistic about your professional future when you haven't been told to be humble your entire life and your confidence isn't described by others as bossy or uppity. If everyone tells you that you're incapable of doing something, eventually you believe them, because it's easier to start believing than it is to die rebelling and crazy.[23]

It's easier for us to think of white men as leaders and start-up founders; here, they got to the Shape Game first. The University of California, Berkeley economists Ross Levine and Rona Rubenstein analyzed the shared traits of entrepreneurs in a 2013 paper and found that most were white, male, and highly educated.[24] If we're told that we're on the team that's not great at the Shape Game, we get anxious and have a harder time believing that our future is unlimited, and others judge our efforts more harshly.[25] If everyone tells you that you're incapable of doing something, eventually you believe them, because it's easier to change your mind than it is to ignore every message from the rest of the world.

Even if you're around lots of other people who look like you, feeling as though you don't belong or aren't accepted interferes with how well you think.[26] It's easy to see who feels out of place and has faced more bumps along the way—just look at who's actually there: How many stay-at-home dads belong to the PTA? How many women are in graduate school for math or in the weight room? How many people of color are in the Senate?[27] Count the black start-up founders, female scientists, male kindergarten teachers, transgender leaders, people who take up tennis at age sixty, and entrepreneurs like Regis. These counterstereotypes who don't fit the mold have had their Shape Game efforts graded differently, their wins marked with asterisks calling their merit into question as they're scrutinized and held to different standards; to reach the same level as the Charlie Brewers of the world, they've already survived more naysayers and obstacles than others.[28] When you don't fit the mold, you have to ignore everybody else in the world, meaning that people like Regis have already shown how mentally tough they are—precisely the trait that would-be investors should look for.

To Be Lucky, Be the Next Big Thing

Gatekeepers want to buy low and sell high. They value potential; they want the Next Big Thing. In one study, subjects were told the five-year stats of an NBA player alongside the five-year performance projections of a rookie, before coming up with an estimate of what salary that player could command in the sixth season. Subjects were willing to give the rookie $1 million more per year, $5.25 million compared with a lowly $4.26 million.

This effect extended to the art world, where subjects were shown two paintings—one by an artist who had the potential to win a major art award, and one by someone who had actually won it. In that situation, 65 percent of subjects preferred the budding artist's painting. (These paintings were randomized to control for the possibility that some of them simply sucked more.) Even when asked about their preferences between the paintings of an up-and-comer and those of an artist who had already won the award four times, people preferred potential 57 percent of the time. After shown Facebook ads for a comedian who, critics say, "could become the next big thing," we like that comedian considerably more than the one that critics say "has become the next big thing." We like restaurants, chefs, Ph.D. applicants, and comedians more when framed in terms of their possible future selves.[29]

Chia-Jung Tsay, one of those Juilliard- and Harvard-trained underachievers, noticed this curiosity in how we evaluate others. In one of her most compelling studies, 103 professionally trained musicians read a biographical snippet of a musician said to have great promise before listening to twenty seconds of a performance of Stravinsky's *Trois mouvements de Petrouchka*; then they read about an accomplished musician before listening to another twenty seconds of that same piece. Experts considered the promising pianist more talented, destined for success, and attractive as a member of a musical group. The catch—because of course there is one—is that the subjects listened to clips of the pianist Gwhyneth Chen's recording of Stravinsky's *Trois mouvements de Petrouchka*. They listened to two clips of the same damn performance that were packaged differently.[30]

"It makes sense that people will just assume, 'Well, if they've already done so much just with natural talents, they may be able to just achieve even more,'" says Tsay.[31] When trying to get lucky and have others evaluate us positively, we should remember that minds automatically use whatever information is on hand to fill in the blanks. People are possibilities, our futures ultimately unknowable, and because others can't know our work ethic or future sight unseen, we can present ourselves as someone who doesn't even have to try. We give people the "Shape Game natural" treatment when we think of their potential, making us assume better things about their future and innate talents, leading to the same kind of status bias in evaluation that happens before we drink wine with a $90 label or talk to someone with a pretty face.[32]

To Get Lucky, Invest in Yourself

"If one does not have money in the form of a family with money, the chances of becoming an entrepreneur drop quite a bit," Levine, the economist, told *Quartz*. Risks aren't quite risky when you can afford them.[33]

No successful person feels as if he's had it easy; the road bumps and headwinds we face stick out, while the privileges we've had remain invisible. Privilege, by definition, doesn't feel like anything, because individual worlds are designed for the dominant group, making it impossible for them to understand how others might feel uncomfortable. We don't see the world, just our world. Being right-handed allows you to float through life using cars, electronics, writing utensils, kitchen gadgets, guns, and sporting equipment more easily than the southpaws, who encounter little hassles on a daily basis. Privilege is the ability to be blind to the number of times we've been graded on a curve.[34]

Those without direct access to money can increase their luck by investing in their social capital, like Regis, whose network can help him access other resources.[35] That's easiest, as we saw in the last chapter, when you're not a jerk. Broadening our smile builds our world, and focusing on how good it feels to be making progress toward becoming the version of yourself you've always dreamed of being—staying positive—is what allows you to build the mental resources required to get there in the first place: the optimism, confidence, grit, hope, resilience, and belief in your ability to get better and constantly level up.[36]

When I met Sian-Pierre, I sensed that his happiness would get him through, because happy, optimistic people excel at focusing on and being energized by rewards around them. Obsessing over the feeling of being on the losing team can impair performance and decrease our resilience; even when life grants us misfortune beyond our control—bad luck—it's in our best interest to ignore this.[37] When combined with focused determination and a belief in their ability to improve and learn what they need to learn along the way, they're able to supply their own energy. Extroversion, like entrepreneurship, is highly correlated to the behavioral activation system, and the facet of extroversion most predictive of who rises to the top of a hierarchy is dominance: the mouse who doesn't back down.

People like Charlie O'Donnell figure out who's going places by seeing who's willing to invest in themselves and get to their next level. A few years ago, Xiao-Ping Chen at the University of Washington noticed that the methods that universities use to evaluate professors bore a striking resemblance to start-up founders during competitions like *Dragons' Den,* where would-be entrepreneurs present their business plans to potential investors.[38] "One of the things we use is, how passionate is this person? Is this person really into that? You can tell from not only their talk but from other cues," she says.[39] "It's always important that you reveal that sort of passion. Then, no matter how difficult it might be in the process, you will stick to it and continue."

Chen and her colleagues studied how much venture capitalists' ultimate decisions were influenced by passion, which they measured in feelings and actions. We learned in the last chapter that enthusiasm generates charisma. Like the blood of a novice woodworker who hits the bourbon before the circular saw, genuine excitement—when not muffled by nervousness or the disenchanted freeze of being too cool for school—simply cannot be contained. Having a burning, genuine rage to do something manifests in our behaviors, thoughts, and emotions. Regis's passion spills over in his nonverbal behavior, generating the kind of charisma that motivates others. But interestingly, Chen's study found that a different aspect of passion influenced venture capitalists' even more.

"I would call 'preparedness' cognitive passion," explains Chen. *Preparedness* positively influenced decisions to fund ventures, which belies something more fundamental: that someone believes so strongly in this vision of their future, possible self that they're actively writing a road map for it. Being convinced enough in your bright future that you're willing to make Excel spreadsheets offers investors insight into how prepared and confident you are of your future. VCs, investors, and business decisions live and die on projections—we all thrive on certainty—yet their ability to envision someone's growth is often based on the Charlie Brewer principle: See this thing that turned out really well? Because this other, unknown thing is just like it, its future will probably be just like it, too.

On May 19, less than two hours after the venture capitalist Charlie O'Donnell sent out his weekly roundup of New York tech events, "This Week in the NYC Innovation Community," Sian-Pierre Regis's friend forwarded it to him along with the message "This VC guy is kind of 'intense,' but is well connected. His number four in 'people he wants to meet' describes you pretty perfectly."

4) Killer content professionals—not people who write, but editors, UX strategists, content designers, content marketers, media ad sales, etc. I've been seeing a lot of interesting new media businesses lately—along the lines of the next generation of Thrillist, Vice, HuffPo, etc. These new companies have strong brands and need to grow. They need to optimize their site experience for sharability, marketability, interesting branded experiences, fostering audience development through social, e-mail etc. If you built a growth machine around content, I'd love to talk with you.

Regis read the email and knew that it described him and the venture he had started a few years earlier while wandering around Paris during his "early quarter-life crisis." A longtime fan of the street-style website the Sartorialist, he began photographing random people walking around that city and asking them questions about their clothes. But he wasn't satisfied to keep asking about their philosophy on mixing fabrics and patterns. He wanted to know more: What music were they listening to? What movies were they excited about? What celebrities did they follow? So Regis made an appointment to meet and pitch O'Donnell. I sensed his inner drive.

A few days after the pitch meeting, I meet Regis at Paradis to Go in the East Village, an artisanal coffee shop wedged between a beauty store and a shoe repair seemingly constructed entirely from wood reclaimed by salvaged boats. He's wearing a Rolling Stones T-shirt (expertly ripped; revealing a surprising amount of chest hair), blue surf shorts, and black strappy leather sandals. He greets me with an oversized smile and a firm hug.

"I've been talking to investors for a while now, and I go into these meetings now, and I'm like, 'I don't fucking care. You can give me money or not, but I don't care. I'm gonna have a jet anyway,'" he says with a laugh, stabbing a spear of pineapple with a fork. "For me, there's something about me from my core that I'm going to be successful, so it's like, 'Whether it's now and I want to accelerate it now, or it's a year from now, it's gonna happen.' Everything in my life just has.

"Really, my thing was sociology of pop culture. I'd always wanted to be a veejay, which was sort of a shortsighted life goal," he says, laughing.

A few months later, I'm on Facebook when a photo of Sian-Pierre Regis pops up on my feed.

He's interviewing someone on TV.

Yep, I recognize that person he's interviewing. It's Jennifer goddamn Lopez.

A few years after that, Regis's mother was suddenly laid off. Because she was unemployed for the first time in decades and uncertain how to make ends meet, he decided to help her complete a bucket list of things she hadn't been able to do as a working single mother of two. Regis, ever the resourceful journalist, recognized the value in her story and used his own money to start making a documentary.

"To have people invest in you, you already have to invest in yourself," said O'Donnell.

Regis was going to go big or go home, as always. He compiled a professional trailer, contacted his social network, and hustled until his Kickstarter campaign for *Duty Free* reached its goal. And then he kept going.

The next time I saw him on *ABC News,* he was the one being interviewed.

Notes for Those of Us Who Want to Level Up

- It's easiest for others to support the perpetual motion machines of the world who demonstrate that they're willing to invest in themselves and make sacrifices to benefit their future.

- To get people to invest in you and your future ventures, take a step back and look at your *overall* improvement. Get them thinking about your potential.[40]

- Visualizing your best possible self and writing about it for twenty minutes increases optimism, or the perceived rosiness of your future. Imagine how good you'll feel and what your life will be like if everything turns out as well as you could possibly hope for. Savoring this future joy can increase how vigorously you pursue your goal, and unstoppable motivation is precisely what it takes.[41]

- After imagining a rosy future, the second part of the fine art of being Kanye West is resourcefulness. Yes, it's easier if you come from a family with money, but mental resourcefulness is even more important. Keep your emotions and attention in check. Actively deal with problems as soon as possible.[42]

- Don't confuse resilience with blind, stubborn persistence. Successfully recovering from setbacks and failures includes the ability to learn from mistakes. "Real life isn't so much about doing the same things over and over again, like sports are," says David Aldous, a statistics professor at UC Berkeley. He says that trying the same thing over and over and failing "isn't like three coin tosses coming up tails. You're supposed to be learning from your failures and doing better next time. Real life is not a coin toss."[43]

- The perceived highs motivate us, but the lows are what make people quit. Aim high and don't beat yourself up along the way. Self-compassion is key.[44]

- Are you really doing everything in your power? (Hint: no.)

- Believe in your ability to perform at the next level and swim in a bigger pond. Believe in your ability to recover from setbacks. Why *not* you?

10

Yes, and

Curiosity, Flexibility, Open-Mindedness, and the Law of Increasing the Surface Area of Your Luck[1]

Tony Hsieh, CEO of Zappos, was born in Illinois to Taiwanese immigrants, a social worker named Judy and a chemical engineer named Richard. "My parents were your typical Asian American parents," he writes in his memoir, *Delivering Happiness*. "They had high expectations in terms of academic performance for myself as well as for my two younger brothers."[2]

Hsieh managed to get good grades while soaking in a wide variety of subjects. "I tried to expose myself to as many interesting things in high school as possible. My thought was that the more perspectives I could gain, the better."[3] He learned BASIC computer programming in middle school and read Pascal in high school, studied foreign languages, fencing, and jazz piano, and dabbled in figure drawing to complete his art credit. The one constant in his life is curiosity and a willingness to engage with new ideas.

Hsieh's first entrepreneurial failure came at the age of nine, when he made his parents buy him a giant box of worms. He constructed a giant worm box in his backyard ("a sandbox with chicken wire on the bottom") and dumped them in there, waiting until they reproduced and he could sell the extras at a profit. Because they all escaped through the gaping holes in the wire, this did not come to pass. He held garage sales, sold lemonade, sold ads for his own newsletter named *The Gobbler*, and ran a mail-order button-making business. Not even a stint at Harvard could curtail his willingness to try new things. He joined the movie society, learned how to milk cows at a farm, learned how to bartend, got catering jobs, and worked as a programmer. During his junior and senior years, he took over an eating and gathering area in a dorm known as the Quincy House Grille, buying hamburgers at McDonald's for $1 and selling them for $3.

Years later he started and sold a company, LinkExchange, for millions, which he then used to seed Venture Frogs, a venture capital fund and incubator that capitalized on his love of exploring new ideas, and wove it into his life. An entrepreneur named Nick Swinmurn pitched an idea to sell shoes online. Despite having two feet, Hsieh was never particularly passionate about adorning them, but he decided to invest after hearing about the market's potential growth. Hsieh later hopped onboard as the CEO and poured all of his LinkExchange money into growing Zappos, overseeing its cultural shift and move to Las Vegas. Ten years later, Amazon acquired it in a deal valued at $1.2 billion.[4]

Hsieh's proven to be quite adept at making money. But his drive toward wealth came from the deeper value of the liberty it affords: "To me, money meant that later on in life I would have the freedom to do whatever I wanted."[5]

Yes, Hsieh is confident and persistent, aims high, and plays well with others. But most important, he's insatiably curious about what lies around the corner and willing to go there, exemplifying what the neurologist James Austin calls the Kettering Principle: "Chance favors those in motion. Events are brought together to form 'happy accidents' when you diffusely apply your energies in motions that are typically nonspecific."[6] In this chapter, we'll learn why those who make a habit of walking boldly into the dark maw of uncertainty get luckier over the course of their lives.

How the Curious Get Luckier

In the 1940s, the researcher Donald Hebb—who coined the phrase "neurons that fire together, wire together"—started noticing that the lab rats he took home were developing differently from those who stayed behind in cages.[7] After he brought some to an enriched environment for a few weeks before returning them to the land of mazes and lab coats, Hebb's lucky rats learned faster than their counterparts who never left the lab.

The impact of those few weeks was so long lasting that Hebb later wrote, "The richer experience of the pet group during development made them better able to profit by new experience at maturity—one of the characteristics of the 'intelligent' human being."[8] Engaging with new things *actually made the rats smarter.*

"Curiosity is the core of Openness/Intellect," states Colin DeYoung, a personality neuroscientist.[9] Stable traits influence our lives, luck, and future outcomes because they predict what we're likely to do when no one's looking and the pressure is off, and the cumulative effect of engaging with the unknown opens us up to new opportunities and creates wildly different trajectories over time. Combined with a decent working memory, curiosity and a general enjoyment of entertaining new thoughts positively influence intelligence, up to 24 percent of individual differences, according to one estimate.[10] A genuine interest in learning can improve your grades by making studying feel less like work (making you more attractive to prospective employers and schools), and accumulating more knowledge over time—or being interested in what others can teach us—increases our ability to connect with others.[11]

Curiosity is a *willingness* to engage with the new and unknown.[12] Constantly exposing yourself to new ideas and people leads to the virtuous, curious loop we first saw in the Charlie Brewer principle: Exploring and learning expand our mental tool kit, allowing us to make even more connections between things in the environment. When you have spent the entirety of your existence in Des Moines, the next city you visit will inevitably be compared with Des Moines, but eventually you'll start to see similarities in all of the world's cities and find joy in their commonalities. We like things that we can understand and associate with other things we know. The more we learn, the more we can learn that there is little to fear in the unknown.[13]

Making connections between things actually makes us *happy*. Broadening our smile builds our world, and building our world can also broaden our smile.[14] Indeed, making associations between things—the simple act of connecting dots in the universe—can improve people's moods. Just as it's easier to become an expert if you find something you actually enjoy (making the process of improving feel less like work), it's easier to thrive in the unknown if we trust that it will be rewarding.

As the behavioral geneticist Dan Belsky notes, "Over time, we become more like ourselves." People like Tony Hsieh become luckier over time because of their willingness to engage with what they don't know. And we have no idea how little we really know.

Life: A Game of Choose Your Own Adventure

Approaching the unknown isn't always easy. "The unknown is innately both threatening and promising," states the personality neuroscientist Colin De-Young. "The balance between those two responses, as they play out in competition with each other, explains a lot about human behavior and about individual differences."[15]

We don't always realize how much *we* influence our situations, assuming that we see the world as it is. But as our lives unfold, we actively select and create our environments, and small initial differences can create wildly different life trajectories. We put ourselves into arenas where we expect to be accepted and engaged; we interpret other people's behavior in a way that confirms our hunches. Our life trajectories—and luck!—are influenced by these reciprocal, dynamic interactions: We influence our surroundings, and they influence us right back, shaping us along the way, creating forking paths that solidify our sense of self and the world.

Being overly sensitive to rejection can make people shy, scared to jump into social interactions.[16] Those with aggressive tendencies may lash out at minor transgressions, causing others to scream, balk, and respond to anger with anger. They might conclude that others are aggressive without realizing that they're the cause. Convinced that the world is out to get them, they repeat these patterns—because they just feel *right*—and act in destructive, antisocial ways, ultimately moving against the world.

People with a slight temperamental aversion to novelty might be slower to warm up to unfamiliar environments when they're young. If this perceived inability to handle new things is reinforced by the adults in their lives—who may also be shy, familiarity fanatics—they could fail to develop an active approach toward the unknown. Because of a decreased sense of self-efficacy in being able to handle new things, they might prefer to deal with it by saying no: no to that dish, that restaurant, that day trip. Each "no" represents a lost chance to learn how to cope with change, a lost opportunity to expand their sense of the world.

Unlike male egos or my grandmother's knees, behavior patterns are hard to break. We end up in social circles of like-minded people who treat us the way we expect to be treated and value what we do. When plotting our life, we act like tattoo judges at the end of the night, overemphasizing the options in front of us without realizing how big the world really is.

Because it behooves living beings to see the world as understandable and manageable, a fear of the unknown may underlie all others—the one fear to rule them all.[17] Learned helplessness was originally thought to be an abnormal response to prolonged shitty situations, but we now know that passively accepting the status quo is the default response; even when you're stuck in jail, staying put is easier than trying to break free. The adaptive, active approach to improving our lives must be learned and drilled into our heads, because the rules always vary from one situation to another and the escape doors can open at any time.

Immediately assigning "why bother" marbles to uncertainty is also a default response that leads to fewer lucky outcomes. Because there's no way of knowing if we'll have the resources to successfully deal with the unknown thing, we usually err on the side of avoiding what may pose a threat to our safety.[18] So let's look at the unknown external factors that can influence our luck—things beyond our control.

Bad luck can look like losing when the deciding factor has nothing to do with merit: the order effect (last Olympian gets the gold!), the Bitches in Glasses/Everyone Has Baggage effect, the I Don't Like His Résumé effect, or even the He Has a Face Like a General effect. There's the You're Too Pretty for This Job effect, She Saw Your Profile on Tinder at the Wrong Time effect, the You Had to Indicate Your Ethnicity Before That Test effect. This mere sampling can help us understand why setbacks or rejections aren't objective statements of our overall abilities and learn to not take them personally, which can foster resilience and emotional stability. We can take cues from gold medalists, who focus on getting better by putting their ego aside and focusing on how good it feels to improve and work toward a goal.

We can focus on our bright spots, clean up how we look, and become more physically fit. We can save money for a rainy day, develop confidence to throw our hat into the ring, learn that we can learn anything, and reduce our stress levels. We can consistently reach out to and help more people so that our social roots grasp more soil, knowing that social support is a key protective measure in every aspect of life. We can get others to support our projects by demonstrating a resourcefulness and willingness to invest in ourselves.

In other words, we can become more confident when facing the unknown by developing the personal resources needed to actively approach the unknown, setting our behavioral activation system to "find rewards," and telling ourselves, "I got this." Making accurate predictions about how to get around in the world allows us to anticipate and plan, and feeling unprepared about our ability to handle the future makes us anxious. No wonder I felt so nervous leaving home for months after my accident: I felt as if everything could go to hell in a second. Indeed, it just had. But *really,* I felt this way because I didn't feel capable of handling anything remotely surprising.

I had suddenly lost many personal resources. I had just declared bank-ruptcy from my medical bills and had no money or credit. I couldn't con-centrate or think clearly for months after having brain surgery, erasing any confidence in my ability to learn or even do simple things. I was living in a place where I knew no one and didn't have access to any transportation. I felt broken. Believing that bad outcomes are inevitable makes any effort seem futile, stacks your scale with "why bother" marbles, and decreases your motivation to engage with the world.

Angrily obsessing over what we *thought* was supposed to happen reflects an inability to shift our perspective and learn from what is actually happen-ing. Ruminating and fixating keep us down. It's "the opposite of broad as-sociative thinking," explains researcher Moshe Bar. "You're stuck on the same topic over and over and over and over. You grind your neurons until you're depressed."[19] Mishaps need not bring us down forever. The ability to recover from them—post-traumatic growth—depends on our ability to find meaning, enabling us to grow from these experiences.[20]

Curiosity→Flexibility and Open-Mindedness

People like Hsieh respond to new forks in the road with nonjudgmental interest, an impulse that constantly expands their perception of what the future might entail.[21] The real magic starts when you allow new information to meaningfully impact your life and lead you down a new trajectory.[22] It's a core component of adaptability, a measure of people's ability to manage and use new encounters, information, events, and transitions to their advan-tage. Did Derek Sivers want to launch a website selling independent music when he was young? Did Sarah Palin set out to be the Republican nominee for vice president? Did Leigh Steinberg intend to become a sports agent? No, but they were all receptive when those paths opened up.[23]

"Part of the art of expertise is finding things you're good at," says the sociologist Dan Chambliss. "That's the problem with the Duckworth stuff on grit, is she emphasizes just hammer away at the thing for a while. Well, the problem with that is you might be hammering away at the wrong thing. As they say, try, try again—that's a mistake. Try once more, and then look around; make sure you're doing the right stuff."[24]

We might not even consider alternative paths, jobs, relationships, and opportunities, because we're committed to one *specific* path. We can unknowingly cut ourselves off from potential luck because we're married to a single idea of who we are, what we're supposed to do, and what kind of plan we're supposed to follow. But what if we're applying the fallacy of sunken costs to our own future, refusing to deviate from our initial trajectory because of the time we've already invested? Our perspective is neither the only one nor the best one, just what we're most familiar with. Taking a fork in the road doesn't mean that the time we've already spent on the path has been wasted; maybe its purpose was to introduce us to something or someone even better than we knew about before.

Pack Light

Capitalizing on the opportunities that arise is easier when we keep our lives agile and flexible. What kind of luck do you want to maximize? You can't plan accidental, serendipitous collisions (between you and your future soul mate, perfect job, financial windfall, new living situation, that ticket stub you lost years ago), but you can increase their likelihood by going to hot spots where they're more *likely* to happen. Trust-based networks and markets help people manage information overload; your paintings are more likely to be discovered at an art fair than online. Cultural events—film festivals, conventions, and forums like TechCrunch, SXSW, and Cannes—won't be replaced by the internet, because they're also a chance for major players to network and share information. Going to conferences or a city that actually has jobs in your industry requires actual motion that's easier when we have few things weighing us down.[25]

Adapting to life's upgrades, a phenomenon known as the hedonic tread-mill, means that while every little income raise feels negligible, by the time we're in our fifties, most scoff at the idea of spending months backpacking in hostels around Europe, the very thing our twenty-year-old self would have loved. It's easiest to break your addiction to hotels, Whole Foods, and Lululemon when you've never had one. Better opportunities can only enter the picture if you carve out room for them by relaxing your grip on your current life's structure. The less you pack, the more you can travel; the less you need, the more you can do.[26]

Moving to a city with nothing but a suitcase and a dream is the archetype of the American dream, as when "a young apprentice named Benjamin Franklin awkwardly entered colonial Philadelphia with two large bread rolls tucked under his arms and a third fast disappearing down his throat."[27] There is no age limit on the ability to hope for a bright future, and no deadline for starting something new.

Flexibility also helps your love life. I met with Cristina Morara, a high-end matchmaker with Stellar Hitch, at the Hotel Casa del Mar in Santa Monica for a drink. She told me about how much work she'd done for one client, how she'd scoured the earth to find a match. Finally, she found a man who wanted the same kind of life as her client, had the same values, and was generally everything she'd ever been looking for. Alas, there was a hitch.

"He was an inch too short," says Morara, shaking her head. "I said, 'He might be the love of your life! You'd turn down the chance to meet someone who would make you happy because of one inch?' She said he needed to be taller than her when she wears heels because she goes out a lot and likes to have her picture taken. 'Just think of the photos,' she said. 'It just wouldn't look right.'"[28] Daniel Kahneman called this bias the focusing illusion: We see the world through a fish-eye lens, distorting whatever is momentarily capturing our attention. When something is right in front of our face, the perspective we have is that it *seems* like it is the most important thing in the world—because, at that moment, *it is*.

"In real life, consensus is far from perfect about who is desirable and who is not," says the relationship researcher Paul Eastwick. "We have a poor appreciation for the amount of time that people typically know each other before they form a relationship," he states. "When people get together the first time, they've known each other for a year on average; it's friends and acquaintances who do most of the hooking up."

I ask him for advice. "Cultivate a lot of long-term friends and acquaintances of people of the sex you're attracted to, and just let them simmer and see what happens."[29]

Everything You Think You Know

Certainty is comforting, a crackling fireplace and a cup of hot chocolate on a cold autumn night. It's soothing to know who we are, what we've been through, what we like. We know what's what in the world. We *might* be willing to entertain the idea that in order to have more chance meetings and unplanned opportunities, we need to be more curious and flexible, but luck will never come out of them if we refuse to let these new things have any meaningful impact on our lives.[30]

Believing that your identity and whatever makes you "you" are complex and malleable is a key component of psychological health.[31] Truly maximizing the luck in your life requires open-mindedness and flexibility about whatever life presents you, and in order to do this, all you need to do is accept one tiny fact: Everything you think you know about yourself and the world is wrong.[32]

As Gloria Steinem wrote, "Old patterns, no matter how negative and painful they may be, have an incredible magnetic power—because they *do* feel *like home*."[33] You have, throughout your life, taken yourself with you wherever you've been. What you pay attention to and how you interpret everything has influenced what you think your choices are, how you think the world works, what you think you're capable of, and what you think will happen in the future. You can choose to be guided by rewards in the environment and how persistent to be when chasing them. You can whittle down your options, unknowingly constrained by fear. These ingrained habits of interacting with the world have influenced where you are. You are the only true source of your life's patterns.[34]

Selectively picking up marbles helps us quickly navigate the world, but also translates to a stubborn refusal to entertain new ideas that can prevent us from learning when even better things—people, opportunities, and ways of interacting with the world—show up. Rethinking our lives and worldviews feels threatening because we're tossing the marbles off the scale we've been using to gather information about ourselves and how the world works.

"Discrepant feedback can sometimes even induce disintegration anxiety—a fear that the self is disintegrating," notes the researcher William Swann, who has published some of the most important work on the self over the last few decades.[35]

Exploit but Don't Stop Exploring

Just like kids dreaming of the Olympics while learning how to ski, it's easier to envision that "we could be the next Dropbox/Twitter/self-employment gold" when we're young. The expert-experts warned about the self-fulfilling prophecy that accompanies aging: Getting older makes too many people assume that their "time is past," or "if I would have been great at something, I'd have known it by now," or "I think it's a little late for me to learn how to do that."[36]

Over time, it becomes easier to stop exploring. Our brain's That Did Not Pan Out signal, in fact, may also signal choice *difficulty*; who wants to feel as if they might be making the wrong choice? So we avoid the possibility of even feeling wrong by focusing our efforts on what we feel to be certain. Our goals shift from exploring potential futures to maintaining our life's status quo and being content with what we've already achieved.[37] When we *know* that our family will appreciate TV time, it gets harder to justify taking a class after work.[38] We unknowingly become collectors of "why bother" marbles over the course of our lives by seeing what's worked for other people and where they've failed and ignoring certain paths. Believing that bad outcomes are inevitable kills our motivation; from the outside, this looks like depression.

But there *is* hope, you see: There's plenty of time to branch out and start something new.

"Anyone who practices a lot will become quite phenomenal, even late in life," says John Krakauer. Even if we do find something that we enjoy and seem to pick up easily, we might mistakenly dismiss new loves as hobbies and tell ourselves to act our age. What if you don't find something that you're really passionate about until you're seventy? Be grateful, embrace it, and get to work. It's never too late to become a badass.

We come to life's beach with nothing but a backpack. We explore and discover what we like, slowly gathering marbles and learning about the world and ourselves. Our lives magically fill up with habits, preferences, responsibilities, goals, activities, and people, automatically piling up like driftwood, making it harder to leave that little section of the beach. Developing a fixed identity and staying married to our narrative of who we are is why we crystallize over time and why we can feel so much discomfort when we get the sense that we're somehow wrong about how the world really works. The key is humility—an openness to contrary ideas, opposing viewpoints, and accepting that our lack of omniscience includes an inability to predict the future.[39]

Our perspective is just one source of information, and in high school Hsieh knew the value of constantly expanding his: *"My thought was that the more perspectives I could gain, the better."*[40]

Stay Hungry; Stay Humble (Trust Me, I Didn't See This Coming)

The best way to account for the inevitable unpredictability of the future is by developing our flexibility.[41] Adapting to changing circumstances is a survival mechanism for all species; why should we think of ourselves any differently? Faster-changing species have a huge advantage in fluctuating environments, and even random changes can be better than none by allowing us to cultivate comfort in the ability to thrive amid transitions. Corporations that skimp on research and development or keep overly rigid business models are the most susceptible to breaking rather than bending amid change. Exploiting what's worked is par for the course; constantly exploring the unknown helps us learn to associate it with something vital to survival—the absence of bad things. Developing comfort with the unknown needs to be actively cultivated. External change is inevitable; the ability or willingness to adapt is not.

What if you started researching a book while trying to make sense of the world's randomness as a depressed and angry atheist, only to emerge as an optimistic believer? What if you realized that you really needed faith, the steadfast belief that things would turn out well? That, as long as you did what you could by working on yourself—maximizing what you brought to the table by developing qualities like optimism, resilience, compassion, self-control, self-efficacy, the ability to check your ego, and open-mindedness—you would feel confident in your ability to handle whatever arose?[42]

Having faith may be the most adaptive positivity illusion. Sensing something larger and transcendent at work inspires awe, binding us to fellow humans by pointing out our common smaller size. Seeing everyone as a fellow in-group member promotes compassion and humility, kindness-promoting emotions that connect us to others and benefit the very survival of our species. The divine makes us more human.

Believing that a larger narrative is at work also makes us happier and more resilient. Habitually reframing difficulties as obstacles that we can surmount by trusting that additional forces are helping us—provided we make use of our own resources, exercise patience, and keep a flexible, accepting view of the outcome—is a recipe for happiness.[43] It offers a sense of joy in the journey that sees life itself as the reward.[44] A narrow definition of luck (this trophy! that specific outcome! that one person's approval!), by definition, eliminates potential sources of good, life-changing things. The ability to find meaning in the outcome and practicing gratitude make you happier, and happiness makes everything easier.

Thinking of yourself as being happy-go-lucky may be life's great self-fulfilling prophecy. That's why people like Hsieh who constantly keep an open mind about where the path will lead exponentially increase the surface area of their luck over time, constantly exposing themselves to more possibilities.

Being lucky depends on saying yes to life.

I started researching luck after a few years in Argentina, when I moved back to the United States right at the height of the Great Recession, couldn't find a job, and got depressed while living on my mother's couch. After years of researching and applying what I learned, I take a shot of Fernet with a billionaire for work.

I almost died so I could tell people how lucky we all are just to be alive: I am lucky because I am alive and life is good.

It's easy to see that people choose whatever is good and in front of them when they're tired and decide to make up their minds in settings like the Olympics or *American Idol*, where we know precisely how many options we have. It's not simply that we find people *more* attractive at closing time, or a tattoo more artful at the end of the day, or a figure skater more skilled than everyone else who performed beforehand, or a programmer you know is willing to go that extra mile (and has a reputation for making things happen and gets an evaluative boost by virtue of being connected and trusted) but that so many factors influencing our luck are arbitrary. Too many people give up and sell themselves short because they mistake other people's decisions—guided by laziness and fear—for an objective assessment of their worth, rather than being resilient and using negative feedback as an opportunity to improve. Life, after all, is a crapshoot, but it's in our best interest not to think so. When you want to get lucky and be chosen, you simply have to figure out which avenue would offer you the best chances, present yourself as an ally to what someone fundamentally wants to do, and be open to whatever comes along so that you magically appear as the answer—right at the moment they have to decide.

Notes for Those of Us Who Might Enjoy Meeting Luck Where It Happens

- We're quick to assume that easy-to-process information is true, including information about our identity and life trajectory. Defining ourselves in complex terms is a protective buffer against depression and anxiety. It also helps open us up to more possibilities and more luck.

- Extinction is a fact of life for 99 percent of all animal species. The lucky ones who survive require fewer resources and are more adaptable to change. Adapt or die.

- You can't control how or when luck will arise. Prepare to capitalize on whatever opportunities arise by making your life as agile as possible: Minimize financial overhead. Save money for a rainy day. Maximize control over your own schedule. Spend more time in a hot spot.

- Being choosy about which marbles we pick up makes the world faster to navigate, but it also means that we might be leaving gems on the floor and failing to incorporate new information into our worldview. Stubbornness prevents learning, which we can overcome by practicing humility (you are intelligent, but not all-knowing) and self-compassion (forgive yourself, learn, and move on; life is short). If you can equate being wrong or making mistakes with learning instead of a lack of intelligence, you can do anything.

- We have complete control over what we pay attention to and how we interpret it. How you see things on a small scale influences how you see the big picture. Focusing on the positive aspects of the environment, interpreting neutral things in a positive light, and downplaying the negative by ignoring or quickly learning and recovering from them. Positively appraising your environment is a key element of resilience.

- Why *not* assume good things about others and your future? That things will turn out well? That someone has your back? Isn't it more illogical to deny yourself the benefits of simply shifting your attitude?

- Make it your mission to approach the unknown and find its rewards.

- Stay curious. Stay hungry. Stay humble.

- Say yes.

ACKNOWLEDGMENTS

To every acquaintance, friend, and family member who has been asking me, "So, how's the book going?" for the past eleven-billion years: Although this may very well be the first book to contain more mistakes than words, it is finished. And, as such, I am currently taking a nap.

To my agent, Laurie Abkmeier, for remaining a spirited cheerleader during the seventy years that it took me to complete this book. To my editor, Leah Trouwborst, for being the most patient and wonderful editor to have ever walked the earth.

To everyone who was kind enough to offer their time, expertise, and support, including Scott Allison, George Anders, Cameron Anderson, Amy Arnsten, Maria Avgitidis, Emily Balcetis, Moshe Bar, Jennifer Bartz, Kent Berridge, Olivier Berton, Matthew Botvinick, Ethan Bromberg-Martin, Elliot Brown, Wändi Bruine de Bruin, Gary Burns, Susan Busch, Dana Carney, Hank Carter, Dan Chambliss, Luke Chang, Tanya Chartrand, Xiao-Ping Chen, Kimberly Chiew, Mina Cikara, Lisa Clampitt, James Coan, Anne Collins, Jeff Cooper, Matt Cooper, Nicole Cooper, Bernard Crespi, Molly Crockett, Farokh Daruwala, Nilanjana Dasgupta, Nathaniel

Daw, Jan De Houwer, Mauricio Delgado, Hanneke den Ouden, Colin De-Young, Gül Dölen, Bradley Doll, Carol Dweck, Blake Eastman, Paul Eastwick, Scott Eidelman, K. Anders Ericsson, Emily Falk, Eric Fine, Gráinne Fitzsimons, Stan Floresco, Alison Fragale, Michael Frank, Nick Franklin, Jon Freeman, Adam Galinsky, Bertram Gawronski, Judith Gerberg, Bonnie Gillespie, Claire Gillian, Kathy Giuffre, Emily Glickman, Jackie Gottlieb, Leor Hackel, Greg Hajcak, Cindy Harmon-Jones, Barry Hirsch, Jacob B. Hirsh, Bobby Horton, Mickey Inzlicht, Joseph Kable, Tony Kiewel, Robert Kleck, John Krakauer, Kristine Kuhn, Nathan Kuncel, Robert Kurzban, Mark Leary, Tracy Lee, Alice Lin, Jon Maner, Antonia Mantonakis, Mike Maxim, Elizabeth McClintock, Ashley Mears, Pranjal Mehta, Laura Michaelson, Vivienne Ming, Daniel Molden, Richard Moreland, Miriam Mosing, Nolan Myers, Matt Nassar, Michael Norton, Charlie O'Donnell, Kristina Olson, Kristen Paladino, Keith Payne, Luiz Pessoa, Michael Platt, Robert Plomin, Sara Pollan, Vinnie Potestivo, Dennis Proffitt, Lena Quilty, Antonio Rangel, Sian-Pierre Regis, Cecilia Ridgeway, Lauren Rivera, Christian Rudder, Scott Russo, John Salamone, Norbert Schwarz, Amitai Shenhav, Derek Sivers, Ned Smith, Leigh Steinberg, Tina Strombach, William Swann, Warren Thorngate, Steven Tipper, Peter Todd, Alex Todorov, Zak Tormala, Stan Treger, Chia-Jung Tsay, Jim Uleman, Kathleen Utecht, Jay Van Bavel, Tor Wager, Dylan Wagner, Andrew Westbrook, Robert Withers, Paul Zak, and Jamil Zaki. Special thanks to Adam Kepecs for setting me straight early.

To everyone who offered writing support: Adam Alter, Oliver Burkeman, Susan Cain, Meehan Crist, Jay Dixit, David Epstein, Heidi Galvorson, Adam Grant, Chris Guillebeau, Jon Haidt, Chip Heath, Huan Hsu, Matt Hutson, Maria Konnikova, Brendan Koerner, David Lavin, Maggie Mertens, Dan Pink, Mary Roach, Kathryn Schulz, Rebecca Skloot, Clive Thompson, and Lori Zimmer. To the New York Public Library MaRLI program, the Science of Psychology Writers group, the Society for Neuroscience, the Association for Psychological Science, the Social and Affective Neuroscience Society, and the National Association of Science Writers for institutional help of varying magnitudes.

To all my friends in New York, Portland, and various parts around the globe: It brings me great joy to see you all doing so well on Facebook. Let's grab lunch so you can tell me what's really going on.

Thank you to my fit fam at CrossFit Queens for keeping me sane and fit by pushing me and giving me a place to talk about CrossFit for four years, especially my amazing coach David Charbonneau (forged-by-zeus.triib.com).

To Nick Jaina for fighting the good fight.

To you, dear reader.

To Erik Schultz for being the best brother a sister could ever hope to have.

To my mom, Sandy Starr, for being the best human ever.

NOTES

INTRODUCTION

1 Hugh Barclay, *The Journal of Jurisprudence,* vol. 29. T.&T. Clark, Law Booksellers, George Street (Edinburgh, 1885); Stanley A. Sidmon. "Act of God." *St. Louis Law Review* 8, no. 2 (1923): 124–28; Hermann Loimer and Michael Guarnieri, "Accidents and Acts of God: A History of the Terms," *American Journal of Public Health* 86, no. 1 (1996): 101–7.

2 Andy Clark, "Whatever Next? Predictive Brains, Situated Agents, and the Future of Cognitive Science," *Behavioral and Brain Sciences* 36 (2013): 181–253.

3 Jacob B. Hirsh, Raymond A. Mar, and Jordan B. Peterson, "Psychological Entropy: A Framework for Understanding Uncertainty-Related Anxiety," *Psychological Review* 119, no. 2 (2012): 304–20; Aaron C. Kay et al., "Compensatory Control: Achieving Order Through the Mind, Our Institutions, and the Heavens," *Current Directions in Psychological Science* 18, no. 5 (2009): 264–68; Eva Jonas et al., "Threat and Defense: From Anxiety to Approach," *Advances in Experimental Social Psychology* 49 (2014): 219–86; Martin Lang et al., "Effects of Anxiety on Spontaneous Ritualized Behavior," *Current Biology* 25, no. 14 (2015): 1,892–97; Alexa M. Tullett, Aaron C. Kay, and Michael Inzlicht, "Randomness Increases Self-Reported Anxiety and Neurophysiological Correlates of Performance Monitoring," *Social Cognitive and Affective Neuroscience* 10, no. 5 (2015): 628–35.

4 Andreas Wilke and Peter M. Todd, "The Evolved Foundations of Decision Making," in *Judgment and Decision Making as a Skill: Learning, Development, and*

Evolution, ed. Mandeep K. Dhami, Anne Schlottmann, and Michael R. Wald-mann (Cambridge, U.K.: Cambridge University Press, 2012), 3–27.

5 Quoted in Martin E. Seligman and Steven F. Maier, "Failure to Escape Traumatic Shock," *Journal of Experimental Psychology* 74, no. 1 (1967): 1–9. Recap of the original learned helplessness studies taken from Vincent M. LoLordo and J. Bruce Overmier, "Trauma, Learned Helplessness, Its Neuroscience, and Implications for Posttraumatic Stress Disorder," in *Associative Learning and Conditioning Theory: Human and Non-human Applications,* ed. Todd R. Schachtman and Steve Reilly (New York: Oxford University Press, 2011), 121–51. See also Steven F. Maier and Martin E. P. Seligman, "Learned Helplessness at Fifty: Insights from Neuroscience," *Psychological Review* 123, no. 4 (2016): 349–67.

6 Harry Smit, *The Social Evolution of Human Nature: From Biology to Language* (New York: Cambridge University Press, 2014), 31.

7 Michael Tomasello, *A Natural History of Human Thinking* (Cambridge, MA: Harvard University Press, 2014), 34–36; Andrew Whiten, "Culture and the Evolution of Interconnected Minds," in *Understanding Other Minds: Perspectives from Developmental Social Neuroscience,* ed. Simon Baron-Cohen, Helen Tager Flusberg, and Michael V. Lombardo (New York: Oxford University Press, 2013), 432; Daniel Sol, "The Cognitive-Buffer Hypothesis for the Evolution of Large Brains," in *Cognitive Ecology II,* ed. Reuven Dukas and John M. Ratcliffe (Chicago: University of Chicago Press, 2009), 114–15; Michael Tomasello et al., "Understanding and Sharing Intentions: The Origins of Cultural Cognition," *Behavioral and Brain Sciences* 28, no. 5 (2005): 675–91.

8 Jennifer E. Stellar et al., "Self-Transcendent Emotions and Their Social Functions: Compassion, Gratitude, and Awe Bind Us to Others Through Prosociality," *Emotion Review* 9, no. 3 (2017): 200–7; Kenneth I. Pargament and Annette Mahoney, "Spirituality: The Search for the Sacred," in *The Oxford Handbook of Positive Psychology,* ed. C. R. Snyder and Shane J. Lopez (New York: Oxford University Press, 2009), 616; Kenneth I. Pargament and Annette Mahoney, "Spirituality: Discovering and Conserving the Sacred," in *Handbook of Positive Psychology,* ed. C. R. Snyder and Shane J. Lopez (New York: Oxford University Press, 2002), 646–59; Scott Atran and Joseph Henrich, "The Evolution of Religion: How Cognitive By-Products, Adaptive Learning Heuristics, Ritual Displays, and Group Competition Generate Deep Commitments to Prosocial Religions," *Biological Theory* 5, no. 1 (2010): 18–30. It's the culture I was raised in: Claude S. Fischer, *Made in America: A Social History of American Culture and Character* (Chicago: University of Chicago Press, 2010): 210–14.

9 Richard Donkin, *The History of Work* (New York: Palgrave Macmillan, 2010), 46–47. Redemptive community: Jack P. Greene, *The Intellectual Construction of America: Exceptionalism and Identity from 1492 to 1800* (Chapel Hill: University of North Carolina, 1993), 55; Mary K. Geiter and W. A. Speck, *Colonial America: From Jamestown to Yorktown* (New York: Palgrave Macmillan, 2002), 12–13; Avihu Zakai, *Exile and Kingdom: History and Apocalypse in the Puritan Migration to*

America (Cambridge, U.K.: Cambridge University Press, 1992); Eric Luis Uhl-mann and Jeffrey Sanchez-Burks, "The Implicit Legacy of American Protestant-ism," *Journal of Cross-Cultural Psychology* 45, no. 6 (2014): 992–1,006; Fischer, *Made in America.*

10 Karen Halttunen, *Confidence Men and Painted Women* (New Haven, Conn.: Yale University Press, 1982), 201–2; Geiter and Speck, *Colonial America,* 12–13.

11 *The Laws and Liberties of Massachusetts, Reprinted from the Copy of the 1648 Edition in the Henry G. Huntington Library* (1929). Quotation taken from Lawrence Meir Friedman, *A History of American Law,* 2nd ed. (New York: Touchstone, 1985), 81.

12 Richard Weiss, *The American Myth of Success: From Horatio Alger to Norman Vincent Peale* (New York: Basic Books, 1969; repr., Illini Books, 1988); Lawrence Stone, *The Family, Sex, and Marriage in England, 1500–1800* (New York: Harper & Row, 1977), 260; David M. Potter, *People of Plenty: Economic Abundance and the Ameri-can Character* (Chicago: University of Chicago Press, 1954), 86–90; Matthew Hutson, "Still Puritan After All These Years," *New York Times,* Aug. 3, 2012.

13 Stephen J. McNamee and Robert K. Miller, *The Meritocracy Myth,* 2nd ed. (Lan-ham, MD.: Rowman & Littlefield, 2009), 160.

14 Halttunen, *Confidence Men and Painted Women,* 206.

15 Stephanie Coontz, *The Way We Never Were: American Families and the Nostalgia Trap* (New York: Basic Books, 1992), 70–71.

16 George W. Pierson, "The M-Factor in American History," *American Quarterly* 14 (Summer 1962): 275–89. Quotation on p. 286.

17 Weiss, *American Myth of Success,* 101.

18 Cf. Brian Roberts, *American Alchemy: The California Gold Rush and Middle-Class Culture* (Chapel Hill: University of North Carolina Press, 2000), 45–47.

19 Warren Susman, *Culture as History: The Transformation of American Society in the 20th Century* (1973; repr., Washington, D.C.: Smithsonian Institution Press, 2003); Fischer, *Made in America.*

20 Jackson Lears, *Something for Nothing: Luck in America* (New York: Viking, 2003); Janette Thomas Greenwood, *The Gilded Age: A History in Documents* (New York: Oxford University Press, 2000).

21 The idea of external vs. internal locus of control was introduced by Julian B. Rotter; for an introduction to Rotter's work, see David F. Barone, James E. Maddux, and C. R. Snyder, *Social Cognitive Psychology: History and Current Domains* (New York: Springer Science + Business Media New York, 1997), 52–54. See also Julian B. Rotter, *Social Learning and Clinical Psychology* (New York: Prentice-Hall, 1954); Julian B. Rotter, "Generalized Expectancies for Internal Versus External Control of Reinforcement," *Psychological Monographs: General and Applied* 80, no. 1 (1966): 1–28. Money quote from that paper: "In its simplest form, our basic hypothesis is that if a person perceives a reinforcement as contingent upon his own behavior, then the occurrence of either a positive or negative reinforcement will strengthen or weaken potential for that behavior to recur in the same or similar situation. If he sees the reinforcement as being outside his own control or not contingent, that is

depending upon chance, fate, powerful others, or unpredictable, then the preceding behavior is less likely to be strengthened or weakened." Julian B. Rotter, "Some Problems and Misconceptions Related to the Construct of Internal Versus External Control of Reinforcement," *Journal of Consulting and Clinical Psychology* 43 (1975): 56–67; Julian B. Rotter, "Internal Versus External Control of Reinforcement: A Case History of a Variable," *American Psychologist* 45 (1990): 489–93; Catherine E. Ross and John Mirowsky, "Social Structure and Psychological Functioning: Distress, Perceived Control, and Trust," in *Handbook of Social Psychology,* ed. John DeLamater (New York: Kluwer Academic/Plenum, 2003), 411–47; C. W. Korn et al., "Depression Is Related to an Absence of Optimistically Biased Belief Updating about Future Life Events," *Psychological Medicine* 44, no. 3 (2014): 579–92.

22 James Austin, *Chase, Chance, and Creativity: The Lucky Art of Novelty* (Cambridge, MA: MIT Press, 2003), 70; Françoys Gagné and Robin M. Schader, "Chance and Talent Development," *Roeper Review* 28, no. 2 (2005): 88–90; Helena Matute, "Learned Helplessness and Superstitious Behavior as Opposite Effects of Uncontrollable Reinforcement in Humans," *Learning and Motivation* 25, no. 2 (1994): 216–32.

CHAPTER 1: BEST IN SHOW

1 Cf. Thomas J. Palmeri and Garrison W. Cottrell, "Modeling Perceptual Expertise," in *Perceptual Expertise: Bridging Brain and Behavior,* ed. Isabel Gauthier, Michael J. Tarr, and Daniel Bub (New York: Oxford University Press, 2010), 197–244; Claudio Babiloni et al., "'Neural Efficiency' of Experts' Brain During Judgment of Actions: A High-Resolution EEG Study in Elite and Amateur Karate Athletes," *Behavioural Brain Research* 207, no. 2 (2010): 466–75; Grit Herzmann and Tim Curran, "Experts' Memory: An ERP Study of Perceptual Expertise Effects on Encoding and Recognition," *Memory and Cognition* 39, no. 3 (2011): 412–32; Claudio Babiloni et al., "Judgment of Actions in Experts: A High-Resolution EEG Study in Elite Athletes," *NeuroImage* 45, no. 2 (2009): 512–21; Nigel Harvey, "Learning Judgment and Decision Making from Feedback," in *Judgment and Decision Making as a Skill,* ed. Mandeep K. Dhami, Anne Schlottmann, and Michael R. Waldman (Cambridge, U.K.: Cambridge University Press, 2012), 200.

2 D. A. Houston, S. J. Sherman, and S. M. Baker, "The Influence of Unique Features and Direction of Comparison on Preferences," *Journal of Experimental Social Psychology* 25 (1989): 121–41; D. A. Houston and S. J. Sherman, "Cancellation and Focus: The Role of Shared and Unique Features in the Choice Process," *Journal of Experimental Social Psychology* 31 (1995): 357–78.

3 For example, Wändi Bruine de Bruin, "Save the Last Dance for Me: Unwanted Serial Position Effects in Jury Evaluations," *Acta Psychologica* 118 (2005): 245–60; Wändi Bruine de Bruin, "Save the Last Dance II: Unwanted Serial Position Effects in Figure Skating Judgments," *Acta Psychologica* 123 (2006): 299–311; J. K. Scheer,

"Effect of Placement in the Order of Competition on Scores of Nebraska High School Students," *Research Quarterly* 44 (1973): 79–85.

4 Mike Penner, "Blithe Lipinski Flies to Gold in Figure Skating: Olympics: Adrenaline Is Great Equalizer as 15-Year-Old Upsets Michelle Kwan of Torrance," *Los Angeles Times,* Feb. 21, 1998, articles.latimes.com/1998/feb/21/news/mn-21416. See video commentary, www.youtube.com/watch?v=Fz3VOFuQ-Ng. First Communion quotation: Jeré Longman, "Birds of a Feather Wear Bad Costumes Together," *New York Times,* Jan. 16, 2010, www.nytimes.com/2010/01/17/sports/olympics/17longman.html?_r=0.

5 Christian Unkelbach et al., "A Calibration Explanation of Serial Position Effects in Evaluative Judgments," *Organizational Behavior and Human Decision Processes* 119, no. 1 (2012): 103–13.

6 Bruine de Bruin, "Save the Last Dance for Me," 245–60; V. E. Wilson, "Objectivity and Effect of Order of Appearance in Judging of Synchronized Swimming Meets," *Perceptual and Motor Skills* 44 (1977): 295–98; R. G. Flôres Jr. and V. A. Ginsburgh, "The Queen Elisabeth Musical Competition: How Fair Is the Final Ranking?," *Statistician* 45 (1996): 97–104; Ye Li and Nicholas Epley, "When the Best Appears to Be Saved for Last: Serial Position Effects on Choice," *Journal of Behavioral Decision Making* 22 (2009): 378–89.

7 The terms "accessibility" and "availability" have been used in differing ways throughout Judgment and Decision Making (JDM) and cognition research. Susan T. Fiske and Shelley E. Taylor make this comment in *Social Cognition: From Brains to Culture,* 2nd ed. (London: Sage, 2013), 74. For the sake of readability, I use the terms "availability" and "accessibility" interchangeably, with a strong preference for the idea "whatever comes to mind," "whatever happens to be floating through your head at the time you have to make a decision," or "whichever marbles are easiest to pick up." Amos Tversky and Daniel Kahneman, "Availability: A Heuristic for Judging Frequency and Probability," *Cognitive Psychology* 5 (1973): 207–32; Amos Tversky, "Features of Similarity," *Psychological Review* 84 (1977): 327–52; Norbert Schwarz et al., "Accessibility Revisited," in *Foundations of Social Cognition: A Festschrift in Honor of Robert S. Wyer Jr.,* ed. Galen V. Bodenhausen and Alan J. Lambert (New York: Psychology Press, 2003), 51–77.

8 Lysann Damisch, Thomas Mussweiler, and Henning Plessner, "Olympic Medals as Fruits of Comparison? Assimilation and Contrast in Sequential Performance Judgments," *Journal of Experimental Psychology: Applied* 12, no. 3 (2006): 166–78; Thomas Mussweiler and Lysann Damisch, "Going Back to Donald: How Comparisons Shape Judgmental Priming Effects," *Journal of Personality and Social Psychology* 95, no. 6 (2008): 1,295–315; Fritz Strack, Štěpán Bahník, and Thomas Mussweiler, "Anchoring: Accessibility as a Cause of Judgmental Assimilation," *Current Opinion in Psychology* 12 (2016): 67–70; Wändi Bruine de Bruin and Gideon Keren, "Order Effects in Sequentially Judged Options Due to the Direction of Comparison," *Organizational Behavior and Human Decision Processes* 92 (2003): 91–101.

9 Shai Danziger, Jonathan Levav, and Liora Avnaim-Pesso, "Extraneous Factors in Judicial Decisions," *Proceedings of the National Academy of Sciences* 108, no. 17 (2011): 6,889–92.

10 Roy F. Baumeister et al., "Ego Depletion: Is the Active Self a Limited Resource?," *Journal of Personality and Social Psychology* 74, no. 5 (1998): 1,252–65.

11 Mark Muraven, Dianne M. Tice, and Roy F. Baumeister, "Self-Control as a Limited Resource: Regulatory Depletion Patterns," *Journal of Personality and Social Psychology* 74, no. 3 (1998): 774–89.

12 Barone, Maddux, and Snyder, *Social Cognitive Psychology,* 42; Alfred H. Fuchs and Katharine S. Milar, "Psychology as a Science," in *Handbook of Psychology,* vol. 1, *History of Psychology,* ed. Donald K. Freedheim (Hoboken, NJ: John Wiley and Sons, 2003), 18–19. Bad case of physics envy: Thomas Hardy Leahey, "Cognition and Learning," in Freedheim, *Handbook of Psychology,* vol. 1, *History of Psychology,* 121–24.

13 Clearly, this is meant in jest and accurately portrays neither the timeline nor the impact of Hull's work. John A. Mills, "The Behaviorist as Research Manager: Clark L. Hull and the Writing of Principles of Behavior," in *Control: A History of Behavioral Psychology* (New York: New York University Press, 1998), 103–22.

14 Clark L. Hull, *Principles of Behavior* (New York: Appleton-Century, 1943), 294.

15 As Daniel Kahneman stated in *Thinking, Fast and Slow,* "If there are several ways of achieving the same goal, people will eventually gravitate to the least demanding course of action. . . . Laziness is built deep into our nature." Daniel Kahneman, *Thinking, Fast and Slow* (New York: Farrar, Straus and Giroux, 2011), 57.

16 Travis Proulx, Michael Inzlicht, and Eddie Harmon-Jones, "Understanding All Inconsistency Compensation as a Palliative Response to Violated Expectations," *Trends in Cognitive Sciences* 16, no. 5 (2012): 285–91.

17 Amitai Shenhav, Matthew M. Botvinick, and Jonathan D. Cohen, "The Expected Value of Control: An Integrative Theory of Anterior Cingulate Cortex Function," *Neuron* 79, no. 2 (2013): 217–40; Markus Ullsperger, Claudia Danielmeier, and Gerhard Jocham, "Neurophysiology of Performance Monitoring and Adaptive Behavior," *Physiological Reviews* 94, no. 1 (2014): 35–79; Clay B. Holroyd and Michael G. H. Coles, "The Neural Basis of Human Error Processing: Reinforcement Learning, Dopamine, and the Error-Related Negativity," *Psychological Review* 109, no. 4 (2002): 679–709.

18 Adele Diamond, "Executive Functions," *Annual Review of Psychology* 64 (2013): 135–68; Todd S. Braver, Michael W. Cole, and Tal Yarkoni, "Vive les Différences! Individual Variation in Neural Mechanisms of Executive Control," *Current Opinion in Neurobiology* 20 (2010): 242–50; Timothy David Noakes, "Fatigue Is a Brain-Derived Emotion That Regulates the Exercise Behavior to Ensure the Protection of Whole Body Homeostasis," *Frontiers in Psychology* 3, no. 82 (2012), doi:10.3389/fphys.2012.00082.

19 Robert Kurzban et al., "An Opportunity Cost Model of Subjective Effort and Task Performance," *Behavioral and Brain Sciences* 36 (2013): 661–726.

20 Robert Schnuerch and Henning Gibbons, "Social Proof in the Human Brain: Elec-trophysiological Signatures of Agreement and Disagreement with the Majority," *Psychophysiology* 52, no. 10 (2015): 1,328–42; Leonie Koban and Gilles Pourtois, "Brain Systems Underlying the Affective and Social Monitoring of Actions: An Integrative Review," *Neuroscience and Biobehavioral Reviews* 46 (2014): 71–84.

21 Bertrand Russell, *Sceptical Essays* (1928; London: Routledge Classics, 2004), 2.

22 Story taken from author interview with Braunohler, Jan. 8, 2016, and "What I Did for Love," *This American Life*, Feb. 10, 2012, www.thisamericanlife.org/radio-archives/episode/457/transcript.

23 James W. Pennebaker et al., "Don't the Girls Get Prettier at Closing Time: A Coun-try and Western Application to Psychology," *Personality and Social Psychology Bulletin* 5, no. 1 (1979): 122–25.

24 Author interview, Jan. 8, 2015.

25 Jerome R. Busemeyer and Peter D. Bruza, "Order Effects on Inference," in *Quan-tum Models of Cognition and Decision* (New York: Cambridge University Press, 2012), 131–42; Seah Chang, Chai-Youn Kim, and Yang Seok Cho, "Sequential Effects in Preference Decision: Prior Preference Assimilates Current Preference," *PLoS ONE* 12, no. 8 (2017): e0182442; Christian Unkelbach and Daniel Mem-mert, "Serial-Position Effects in Evaluative Judgments," *Current Directions in Psy-chological Science* 23, no. 3 (2014): 195–200.

26 Alison P. Lenton et al., "The Heart Has Its Reasons: Social Rationality in Mate Choice," in *Simple Heuristics in a Social World,* ed. Ralph Hertwig, Ulrich Hoffrage, and the ABC Research Group (New York: Oxford University Press, 2013), 445.

27 Stephanie S. Spielmann et al., "Settling for Less out of Fear of Being Single," *Jour-nal of Personality and Social Psychology* 105, no. 6 (2013): 1,049–73.

28 Lionel Page and Katie Page, "Last Shall Be First: A Field Study of Biases in Sequen-tial Performance Evaluation on the Idol Series," *Journal of Economic Behavior and Organization* 73, no. 2 (2010): 186–98. Game shows like *Idol* offer ideal scenarios for examining the evaluation process, especially when we're interested in any inter-national or cultural differences that may arise.

29 Heidi Grant and Laura Gelety, "Goal Content Theories: Why Differences in What We Are Striving for Matter," in *The Psychology of Goals,* ed. Gordon B. Moskowitz and Heidi Grant (New York: Guilford Press, 2009), 83–84; Charles S. Carver and Michael F. Scheier, "Self-Regulation of Action and Affect," in *Handbook of Self-Regulation,* ed. K. D. Vohs and R. F. Baumeister, 2nd ed. (New York: Guilford Press, 2011), 1: 3–21.

CHAPTER 2: THE CHARLIE BREWER PRINCIPLE

 1 Author interview, May 1, 2015; Amitai Shenhav and Randy L. Buckner, "Neural Correlates of Dueling Affective Reactions to Win-Win Choices," *Proceedings of the National Academy of Sciences* 111, no. 30 (2014): 10,978–83.

2 J. O'Doherty et al., "Abstract Reward and Punishment Representations in the Human Orbitofrontal Cortex," *Nature Neuroscience* 4, no. 1 (2001): 95–102; Jay A. Gottfried, John O'Doherty, and Raymond J. Dolan, "Encoding Predictive Reward Value in Human Amygdala and Orbitofrontal Cortex," *Science* 301, no. 5636 (2003): 1,104–7; Morten L. Kringelbach, "The Human Orbitofrontal Cortex: Linking Reward to Hedonic Experience," *Nature Reviews Neuroscience* 6, no. 9 (2005): 691–702; Camillo Padoa-Schioppa and John A. Assad, "Neurons in Orbitofrontal Cortex Encode Economic Value," *Nature* 441, no. 7090 (2006): 223–26; H. Plassmann, John O'Doherty, and Antonio Rangel, "Orbitofrontal Cortex Encodes Willingness to Pay in Everyday Economic Transactions," *Journal of Neuroscience* 27 (2007): 9,984–88; Antonio Rangel, Colin Camerer, and P. Read Montague, "A Framework for Studying the Neurobiology of Value-Based Decision Making," *Nature Reviews Neuroscience* 9, no. 7 (2008): 545–56; Anthony J. Porcelli and Mauricio R. Delgado, "Reward Processing in the Human Brain: Insights from fMRI," in *Handbook of Reward and Decision-Making*, ed. Jean-Claude Dreher and Léon Tremblay (Burlington, MA: Academic Press, 2009), 165–84; Thomas H. B. FitzGerald, Ben Seymour, and Raymond J. Dolan, "The Role of Human Orbitofrontal Cortex in Value Comparison for Incommensurable Objects," *Journal of Neuroscience* 29, no. 26 (2009): 8,388–95.

3 Jacqueline Gottlieb et al., "Information Seeking, Curiosity, and Attention: Computational and Neural Mechanisms," *Trends in Cognitive Science* 17, no. 11 (2013): 585–93.

4 K. Carrie Armel, Aurelie Beaumel, and Antonio Rangel, "Biasing Simple Choices by Manipulating Relative Visual Attention," *Judgment and Decision Making* 3, no. 5 (2008): 396–403; Ian Krajbich and Antonio Rangel, "Multialternative Drift-Diffusion Model Predicts the Relationship Between Visual Fixations and Choice in Value-Based Decisions," *Proceedings of the National Academy of Sciences* 108, no. 33 (2011): 13,852–57.

5 Throughout the book, the process of collecting marbles to be added to one side of the scale or another is used as a metaphor for the drift-diffusion model of decision making, attitude formation, and the process of evaluative conditioning. See also Sudeep Bhatia, "Associations and the Accumulation of Preference," *Psychological Review* 120, no. 3 (2013): 522–43; Milica Milosavljevic et al., "The Drift Diffusion Model Can Account for the Accuracy and Reaction Time of Value-Based Choices under High and Low Time Pressure," *Judgment and Decision Making* 5, no. 6 (2010): 437–49; Gerd Gigerenzer, Anja Dieckmann, and Wolfgang Gaissmaier, "Efficient Cognition Through Limited Search," in *Ecological Rationality: Intelligence in the World,* ed. Peter M. Todd and Gerd Gigerenzer (New York: Oxford University Press, 2012); Peter Fischer et al., "The Cognitive Economy Model of Selective Exposure: Integrating Motivational and Cognitive Accounts of Confirmatory Information Search," in *Social Judgment and Decision Making,* ed. Joachim I. Krueger (New York: Psychology Press, 2012), 21–39. NB: Judgment and decision-making researchers very creatively refer to the point when we "stop search" as the "stopping point."

6 Rolf Reber, Piotr Winkielman, and Norbert Schwarz, "Effects of Perceptual Fluency on Affective Judgments," *Psychological Science* 9, no. 1 (1998): 45–48; cf. Daniel M. Oppenheimer, "The Secret Life of Fluency," *Trends in Cognitive Sciences* 12, no. 6 (2008): 237–41; Christian Unkelbach and Rainer Greifeneder, "A General Model of Fluency Effects in Judgment and Decision Making," in *The Experience of Thinking: How the Fluency of Mental Processes Influences Cognition and Behavior,* ed. Christian Unkelbach and Rainer Greifeneder (New York: Psychology Press, 2013), 11–32; Piotr Winkielman and David E. Huber, "Dynamics and Evaluation: The Warm Glow of Processing Fluency," in *Encyclopedia of Complexity and Systems Science,* ed. Robert A. Meyers (New York: Springer Reference, 2009), 2,242–53; Piotr Winkielman et al., "Fluency of Consistency: When Thoughts Fit Nicely and Flow Smoothly," in *Cognitive Consistency: A Fundamental Principle in Social Cognition,* ed. Bertram Gawronski and Fritz Strack (New York: Guilford Press, 2012), 89–111; P. H. Tannenbaum, "Is Anything Special about Consistency?," in *Theories of Cognitive Consistency: A Sourcebook,* ed. R. P. Abelson et al. (Chicago: Rand McNally, 1968), 343–46.

7 Silvia Galdi, Luciano Arcuri, and Bertram Gawronski, "Automatic Mental Associations Predict Future Choices of Undecided Decision-Makers," *Science* 321 (2008): 1,100–102; Silvia Galdi et al., "Selective Exposure in Decided and Undecided Individuals: Differential Relations to Automatic Associations and Conscious Beliefs," *Personality and Social Psychology Bulletin* 38, no. 5 (2012): 559–69. For a great overview on the Implicit Association Test and other measures of automatic attitudes, see Susan T. Fiske and Michael S. North, "Measures of Stereotyping and Prejudice: Barometers of Bias," in *Measures of Personality and Social Psychological Constructs,* ed. Gregory J. Boyle, Donald H. Saklofske, and Gerald Matthews (New York: Elsevier, 2015), 684–718.

8 Author interview, May 8, 2013.

9 Merryn D. Constable et al., "Self-Generated Cognitive Fluency as an Alternative Route to Preference Formation," *Consciousness and Cognition* 22, no. 1 (2013): 47–52.

10 Leon Festinger, Kurt W. Back, and Stanley Schachter, *Social Pressures in Informal Groups: A Study of Human Factors in Housing,* vol. 3 (Stanford, CA: Stanford University Press, 1950).

11 Robert B. Zajonc, "Attitudinal Effects of Mere Exposure," *Journal of Personality and Social Psychology Monograph Supplement* 9, no. 2 (1968).

12 Author interview, March 30, 2015; Richard L. Moreland and S. R. Beach, "Exposure Effects in the Classroom: The Development of Affinity among Students," *Journal of Experimental Social Psychology* 28, no. 3 (1992): 255–76.

13 Quoted in Lauren Eskreis-Winkler et al., "The Grit Effect: Predicting Retention in the Military, the Workplace, School, and Marriage," *Frontiers in Psychology* 5, no. 36 (2014).

14 Ralph Adolphs, "The Social Brain: Neural Basis of Social Knowledge," *Annual Review of Psychology* 60 (2009): 693–716; Ralph Adolphs, "Cognitive Neuroscience of Human Social Behaviour," *Nature Reviews Neuroscience* 4 (2003): 165–78; Shelly L. Gable and Elliot T. Berkman, "Making Connections and Avoiding Loneliness:

Approach and Avoidance Social Motives and Goals," in *Handbook of Approach and Avoidance Motivation,* ed. Andrew J. Elliot (New York: Taylor & Francis, 2008), 203–16; Jana Nikitin and Simone Schoch, "Social Approach and Avoidance Motivations," in *The Handbook of Solitude: Psychological Perspectives on Social Isolation, Social Withdrawal, and Being Alone,* ed. Robert J. Coplan and Julie C. Bowker, 1st ed. (West Sussex, U.K.: John Wiley & Sons, 2014), 202–23.

15 Thomas F. Pettigrew and Linda R. Tropp, "A Meta-analytic Test of Intergroup Contact Theory," *Journal of Personality and Social Psychology* 90, no. 5 (2006): 751–83; Leslie A. Zebrowitz and Yi Zhang, "Neural Evidence for Reduced Apprehensiveness of Familiarized Stimuli in a Mere Exposure Paradigm," *Social Neuroscience* 7, no. 4 (2012): 347–58.

16 Kristen A. Lindquist et al., "The Brain Basis of Emotion: A Meta-analytic Review," *Behavioral and Brain Sciences* 35 (2012): 121–202; cf. William A. Cunningham, Jay J. Van Bavel, and Ingrid R. Johnsen, "Affective Flexibility: Evaluative Processing Goals Shape Amygdala Activity," *Psychological Science* 19, no. 2 (2008): 152–60; Adolphs, "Social Brain"; Sandra L. Ladd and John D. E. Gabrieli, "Trait and State Anxiety Reduce the Mere Exposure Effect," *Frontiers in Psychology* 6 (2015).

17 Shelley McKeown and John Dixon, "The 'Contact Hypothesis': Critical Reflections and Future Directions," *Social and Personality Psychology Compass* 11, no. 1 (2017); Miles Hewstone and Hermann Swart, "Fifty-Odd Years of Inter-group Contact: From Hypothesis to Integrated Theory," *British Journal of Social Psychology* 50, no. 3 (2011): 374–86.

18 Zajonc, "Attitudinal Effects of Mere Exposure"; Christian Unkelbach et al., "Good Things Come Easy: Subjective Exposure Frequency and the Faster Processing of Positive Information," *Social Cognition* 28, no. 4 (2010): 538–55; Daniel Perlman and Stuart Oskamp, "The Effects of Picture Content and Exposure Frequency on Evaluations of Negroes and Whites," *Journal of Experimental Social Psychology* 7, no. 5 (1971): 503–14.

19 Linda Baker, "Streetless in Seattle," *Metropolis,* May 1, 2006, www.metropolismag .com/uncategorized/streetless-in-seattle/.

20 Daniel Harris, "Age and Occupational Factors in the Residential Propinquity of Marriage Partners," *Journal of Social Psychology* 6 (1935): 257–61; Alvin M. Katz and Reuben Hill, "Residential Propinquity and Marital Selection: A Review of Theory, Method, and Fact," *Marriage and Family Living* 20, no. 1 (1958): 27–35.

21 Beverley Fehr, "Friendship Formation," in *Handbook of Relationship Initiation,* ed. Susan Sprecher, Amy Wenzel, and John Harvey (New York: Psychology Press, 2008), 29–32.

22 Mady Wechsler Segal, "Alphabet and Attraction: An Unobtrusive Measure of the Effect of Propinquity in a Field Setting," *Journal of Personality and Social Psychology* 30, no. 5 (1974): 654–57.

23 Ray Reagans, "Close Encounters: Analyzing How Social Similarity and Propinquity Contribute to Strong Network Connections," *Organization Science* 22, no. 4 (2011): 835–49.

24 Yvonne H. M. van den Berg and Antonius H. N. Cillessen, "Peer Status and Class-room Seating Arrangements: A Social Relations Analysis," *Journal of Experimental Child Psychology* 130 (2015): 19–34.

25 Mitja D. Back, Stefan C. Schmukle, and Boris Egloff, "Becoming Friends by Chance," *Psychological Science* 19, no. 5 (2008): 439–40.

26 Felichism W. Kabo et al., "Proximity Effects on the Dynamics and Outcomes of Scientific Collaborations," *Research Policy* 43, no. 9 (2014): 1,469–85.

27 Pieter A. Gautier, Michael Svarer, and Coen N. Teulings, "Marriage and the City: Search Frictions and Sorting of Singles," *Journal of Urban Economics* 67 (2010): 206–18.

28 Jerker Denrell and Gaël Le Mens, "Social Judgments from Adaptive Samples," in Krueger, *Social Judgment and Decision Making,* 151–69; Harry T. Reis et al., "Familiarity Does Indeed Promote Attraction in Live Interaction," *Journal of Personality and Social Psychology* 101, no. 3 (2011): 557–70.

29 Email exchange with author, Aug. 1, 2014.

30 Formulating attitudes and figuring out what we think of things is a learning process called evaluative conditioning. Richard E. Petty, Duane T. Wegener, and Leandre R. Fabrigar, "Attitudes and Attitude Change," *Annual Review of Psychology* 48, no. 1 (1997): 609–47; Piotr Winkielman et al., "The Hedonic Marking of Processing Fluency: Implications for Evaluative Judgment," in *The Psychology of Evaluation: Affective Processes in Cognition and Emotion,* ed. J. Musch and K. C. Klauer (Mahwah, NJ: Lawrence Erlbaum, 2003), 189–217; Jan De Houwer, Sarah Thomas, and Frank Baeyens, "Association Learning of Likes and Dislikes: A Review of 25 Years of Research on Human Evaluative Conditioning," *Psychological Bulletin* 127, no. 6 (2001): 853–69; Wilhelm Hofmann et al., "Evaluative Conditioning in Humans: A Meta-analysis," *Psychological Bulletin* 136, no. 3 (2010): 390–421.

31 Moshe Bar, "The Proactive Brain: Memory for Predictions," *Philosophical Transactions of the Royal Society of London B: Biological Sciences* 364, no. 1521 (2009): 1,235–43; Moshe Bar, "A Cognitive Neuroscience Hypothesis of Mood and Depression," *Trends in Cognitive Sciences* 13, no. 11 (2009): 456–63; Tad T. Brunyé et al., "Happiness by Association: Breadth of Free Association Influences Affective States," *Cognition* 127, no. 1 (2013): 93–98; Sabrina Trapp et al., "Human Preferences Are Biased Towards Associative Information," *Cognition and Emotion* 29, no. 6 (2015): 1,054–68.

32 Author interview, March 30, 2015.

33 Noola K. Griffiths, "'Posh Music Should Equal Posh Dress': An Investigation into the Concert Dress and Physical Appearance of Female Soloists," *Psychology of Music* 38 (2010): 159–77.

34 Heesu Chung et al., "Doctor's Attire Influences Perceived Empathy in the Patient-Doctor Relationship," *Patient Education and Counseling* 89 (2012): 387–91; cf. Yoann Bazin and Clémence Aubert-Tarby, "Dressing Professional, an Aesthetic Experience of Professions," *Society and Business Review* 8, no. 3 (2013): 251–68;

Y. Kwon and A. Farber, "Attitudes Toward Appropriate Clothing in Perception of Occupational Attributes," *Perceptual and Motor Skills* 74 (1992): 163–68.

35 Author interview, May 21, 2015.

36 Michael I. Norton, Joseph A. Vandello, and John M. Darley, "Casuistry and Social Category Bias," *Journal of Personality and Social Psychology* 87, no. 6 (2004): 817–31.

37 See also Norbert Schwarz, "Feelings-as-Information Theory," in *Handbook of Theories of Social Psychology,* ed. P. Van Lange, A. Kruglanski, and E. Tory Higgins (New York: Sage Knowledge, 2013); Amanda J. Koch, Susan D. D'Mello, and Paul R. Sackett, "A Meta-analysis of Gender Stereotypes and Bias in Experimental Simulations of Employment Decision Making," *Journal of Applied Psychology* 100, no. 1 (2015): 128–61; Lindsay Rice and Joan M. Barth, "A Tale of Two Gender Roles: The Effects of Implicit and Explicit Gender Role Traditionalism and Occupational Stereotype on Hiring Decisions," *Gender Issues* 34, no. 1 (2017): 86–102.

38 Author interview, March 25, 2015.

39 Alex Mesoudi, *Cultural Evolution: How Darwinian Theory Can Explain Human Culture and Synthesize the Social Sciences* (Chicago: University of Chicago Press, 2011); Lewis G. Dean et al., "Human Cumulative Culture: A Comparative Perspective," *Biological Reviews* 89, no. 2 (2014), 284–301; Stefan Voigt and Daniel Kiwit, "The Role and Evolution of Beliefs, Habits, Moral Norms, and Institutions," in *Merits and Limits of Markets,* ed. H Giersch (Heidelberg, Germany: Springer-Verlag Berlin, 1998), 83–110.

40 Eric Sundstrom, *Work Places: The Psychology of the Physical Environment in Offices and Factories* (Cambridge, U.K.: Cambridge University Press, 1986), 33. As quoted in Nikil Saval, *Cubed: A Secret History of the Workplace* (New York: Knopf, 2014) Kindle edition.

41 William H. Leffingwell, *Office Management: Principles and Practice* (New York: A. W. Shaw, 1925), 620–21; quoted in Saval, *Cubed.*

42 Warren Thorngate, Robyn M. Dawes, and Margaret Foddy, *Judging Merit* (New York: Psychology Press, 2008), 32–33.

43 See also Vincent Y. Yzerbyt and Stéphanie Demoulin, "Metacognition in Stereotypes and Prejudice," in *Social Metacognition,* ed. Pablo Briñol and Kenneth G. DeMarree (New York: Taylor & Francis, 2012), 243–62.

44 Eric Luis Uhlmann and Geoffrey L. Cohen, "Constructed Criteria: Redefining Merit to Justify Discrimination," *Psychological Science* 16, no. 6 (2005): 474–80.

45 Author interview, March 24, 2015.

46 Author interview, Sept. 24, 2014.

47 Email correspondence with Kate Y. Hector (media coordinator of University Interscholastic League), April 30, 2015.

48 Author interview, May 13, 2015; Eddie Harmon-Jones, David M. Amodio, and Cindy Harmon-Jones, "Action-Based Model of Dissonance: A Review, Integration, and Expansion of Conceptions of Cognitive Conflict," in *Advances in Experimental Social Psychology,* ed. Mark P. Zanna (Burlington, MA: Academic Press, 2009), 41: 119–66.

49 Lara Mayeux, John J. Houser, and Karmon D. Dyches, "Social Acceptance and Popularity: Two Distinct Forms of Peer Status," in *Popularity in the Peer System,* ed. Antonius H. N. Cillessen, David Schwartz, and Lara Mayeux (New York: Guilford Press, 2011): 87.

CHAPTER 3: BITCHES IN GLASSES

1 Paul Russell, "Actor Breakdowns over Breakdowns: Part 1," *Backstage,* July 9, 2009, www.backstage.com/advice-for-actors/getting-cast/actor-breakdowns-over -breakdowns-part-1/.

2 Ethan S. Bromberg-Martin and Okihide Hikosaka, "Midbrain Dopamine Neurons Signal Preference for Advance Information about Upcoming Rewards," *Neuron* 63 (2009): 119–26.

3 Clark, "Whatever Next?"

4 Robert L. Goldstone and Ji Yun Son, "Similarity," in *The Oxford Handbook of Thinking and Reasoning,* ed. Keith J. Holyoak and Robert G. Morrison (New York: Oxford University Press, 2012), 155–76.

5 W. V. Quine, "Natural Kinds," in *Ontological Relativity, and Other Essays,* ed. W. V. Quine (New York: Columbia University Press, 1969), 116.

6 Brooks King-Casas et al., "Getting to Know You: Reputation and Trust in a Two-Person Economic Exchange," *Science* 308 (2005): 78–83. For an overview of the Trust Game and other similar economic games used in decision making, see Daniel Houser and Kevin McCabe, "Experimental Economics and Experimental Game Theory," in *Neuroeconomics: Decision Making and the Brain,* ed. Paul W. Glimcher and Ernst Fehr, 2nd ed. (London: Elsevier, 2014), 19–34.

7 Lasana T. Harris and Susan T. Fiske, "Neural Regions That Underlie Reinforcement Learning Are Also Active for Social Expectancy Violations," *Social Neuroscience* 5, no. 1 (2010): 76–91; Jasmin Cloutier et al., "An fMRI Study of Violations of Social Expectations: When People Are Not Who We Expect Them to Be," *NeuroImage* 57, no. 2 (2011): 583–88.

8 Michelle de Haan and Margriet Groen, "Neural Bases of Infants' Processing of Social Information in Faces," in *The Development of Social Engagement: Neurobiological Perspectives,* ed. Peter J. Marshall and Nathan A. Fox (New York: Oxford University Press, 2005).

9 Michael J. Tarr and Isabel Gauthier, "FFA: A Flexible Fusiform Area for Subordinate-Level Visual Processing Automatized by Expertise," *Nature Neuroscience* 3 (2000): 764–70; Gauthier, Tarr, and Bub, *Perceptual Expertise;* C. Neil Macrae and Susanne Quadflieg, "Perceiving People," in *Handbook of Social Psychology,* ed. Susan T. Fiske, Daniel T. Gilbert, and Gardner Lindzey, 5th ed. (Hoboken, NJ: John Wiley & Sons, 2010), 428–63; Cindy M. Bukach, Isabel Gauthier, and Michael J. Tarr, "Beyond Faces and Modularity: The Power of an Expertise Framework," *Trends in Cognitive Sciences* 10, no. 4 (2006): 159–66.

10 Zoe Liberman, Amanda L. Woodward, and Katherine D. Kinzler, "Origins of Social Categorization," *Trends in Cognitive Sciences* 21, no. 7 (2017): 556–68; Kristina R. Olson and Yarrow Dunham, "The Development of Implicit Social Cognition," in *Handbook of Implicit Social Cognition: Measurement, Theory, and Applications,* ed. Bertram Gawronski and B. Keith Payne (New York: Guilford Press, 2010), 241–54; Larisa Heiphetz, Elizabeth S. Spelke, and Mahzarin R. Banaji, "The Formation of Belief-Based Social Preferences," *Social Cognition* 32, no. 1 (2014): 22–47; Andrew S. Baron, "Constraints on the Development of Implicit Intergroup Attitudes," *Child Development Perspectives* 9, no. 1 (2015): 50–54; J. Kiley Hamlin, Karen Wynn, and Paul Bloom, "Social Evaluation by Preverbal Infants," *Nature* 450, no. 7169 (2007): 557–59; Katherine D. Kinzler et al., "Accent Trumps Race in Guiding Children's Social Preferences," *Social Cognition* 27, no. 4 (2009): 623–34.

11 Samuel G. Goodrich [Peter Parley], *What to Do, and How to Do It; or, Morals and Manners Taught by Examples* (New York: Lamport, Blakeman and Law, 1844), 28, as quoted in Halttunen, *Confidence Men and Painted Women,* 40–41; Allan Mazur, *Biosociology of Dominance and Deference* (Lanham, MD.: Rowman & Littlefield, 2005), 67.

12 Jamil Zaki, "Cue Integration: A Common Framework for Social Cognition and Physical Perception," *Perspectives on Psychological Science* 8, no. 3 (2013): 296–312; Gordon B. Moskowitz and Michael J. Gill, "Person Perception," in *The Oxford Handbook of Cognitive Psychology,* ed. Daniel Reisberg (New York: Oxford University Press, 2013), 918–42.

13 Author interview, July 17, 2013.

14 Susan M. Andersen and Serena Chen, "The Relational Self: An Interpersonal Social-Cognitive Theory," *Psychological Review* 109, no. 4 (2002): 619–45. Specifically, whether or not someone is wearing a polo shirt, is a certain height, and so on doesn't matter when it comes to the quality of your relationship.

15 Nathaniel Rich, "Silicon Valley's Start-Up Machine," *New York Times Magazine,* May 2, 2013, www.nytimes.com/2013/05/05/magazine/y-combinator-silicon-valleys-start-up-machine.html?pagewanted=all&_r=2.

16 Graham later said repeatedly that he was joking: paulgraham.com/tricked.html. His exact words were "People will probably still repeat that quote, but now if someone does it will be proof that either (a) they didn't do their research or (b) they have an ideological axe to grind."

17 Pawel Lewicki, "Nonconscious Biasing Effects of Single Instances on Subsequent Judgments," *Journal of Personality and Social Psychology* 48, no. 3 (1985): 563–74.

18 Gül Günaydin et al., "I Like You but I Don't Know Why: Objective Facial Resemblance to Significant Others Influences Snap Judgments," *Journal of Experimental Social Psychology* 48 (2012): 350–53.

19 Ashley Mears, *Pricing Beauty: The Making of a Fashion Model* (Berkeley: University of California Press, 2011), 121–69. Quotations about luck on p. 123 and on not finding the words on p. 122. Author interview, Aug. 2, 2013.

20 Goodrich, *What to Do, and How to Do It*, 28, as quoted in Halttunen, *Confidence Men and Painted Women*, 40–41; Mazur, *Biosociology of Dominance and Deference*, 67. [Quote: "If the heart is habitually exercised . . ."] Edward Smedley et al., *The Occult Sciences: Sketches of the Traditions and Superstitions of Past Times, and the Marvels of the Present Day* (London: Richard Griffin, 1855); *The Encyclopedia of Occult Sciences* (New York: Robert M. McBride, 1939); Vicki Bruce and Andy Young, *Face Perception* (New York: Psychology Press, 2012), 135–36; Daniel E. Re and Nicholas O. Rule, "Appearance and Physiognomy," in *APA Handbook of Nonverbal Communication*, ed. David Matsumoto, Hyisung C. Hwang, and Mark G. Frank (Washington, D.C.: American Psychological Association, 2016), 221–56; Alexander Todorov et al., "Social Attributions from Faces: Determinants, Consequences, Accuracy, and Functional Significance," *Annual Review of Psychology* 66 (2015): 519–45.

21 Unkelbach and Greifeneder, "General Model of Fluency Effects in Judgment and Decision Making"; Winkielman et al., "Fluency of Consistency."

22 Michael A. Olson and Russell H. Fazio, "Implicit Attitude Formation Through Classical Conditioning," *Psychological Science* 12, no. 5 (2001): 413–17; De Houwer, Thomas, and Baeyens, "Association Learning of Likes and Dislikes," 853; Gerd Bohner and Nina Dickel, "Attitudes and Attitude Change," *Annual Review of Psychology* 62 (2011): 391–417; Galen V. Bodenhausen and Bertram Gawronski, "Attitude Change," in Reisberg, *Oxford Handbook of Cognitive Psychology*, 957–69; William A. Cunningham and Philip David Zelazo, "Attitudes and Evaluations: A Social Cognitive Neuroscience Perspective," *Trends in Cognitive Sciences* 11, no. 3 (2007): 97–104; Christopher R. Jones, Michael A. Olson, and Russell H. Fazio, "Evaluative Conditioning: The 'How' Question," *Advances in Experimental Social Psychology* 43 (2010): 205–55.

23 Donald G. Dutton and Arthur P. Aron, "Some Evidence for Heightened Sexual Attraction under Conditions of High Anxiety," *Journal of Personality and Social Psychology* 30, no. 4 (1974): 510–17; Lawrence E. Williams and John A. Bargh, "Experiencing Physical Warmth Promotes Interpersonal Warmth," *Science* 322, no. 5901 (2008): 606–7; David R. Kille, Amanda L. Forest, and Joanne V. Wood, "Tall, Dark, and Stable: Embodiment Motivates Mate Selection Preferences," *Psychological Science* 24, no. 1 (2013): 112–14.

24 Mark P. Mattson, "Energy Intake and Exercise as Determinants of Brain Health and Vulnerability to Injury and Disease," *Cell Metabolism* 16, no. 6 (2012): 706–22; Alison P. Lenton and Marco Francesconi, "How Humans Cognitively Manage an Abundance of Mate Options," *Psychological Science* 21, no. 4 (2010): 528–33; cf. Gül Günaydin, Emre Selcuk, and Cindy Hazan, "Finding the One: A Process Model of Human Mate Selection," in *Human Bonding*, ed. Cindy Hazan and M. Campa (New York: Guilford Press, 2013), 103–31.

25 Author interview, Feb. 25, 2015.

26 Christian Rudder, *Dataclysm: Who We Are When We Think No One's Looking* (New York: Crown, 2014), 117–23. See also: life.

27 Ibid., 90.

28 Author interview, April 30, 2015.

29 Nassim Nicholas Taleb, *The Black Swan: The Impact of the Highly Improbable* (New York: Random House, 2007), 102–5.

30 Thorngate, Dawes, and Foddy, *Judging Merit,* 32–33.

31 Author interview, Feb. 23, 2015.

32 Author interview with Toppin, May 22, 2014.

33 Russell, *Sceptical Essays,* 2.

34 Bertram Gawronski, Eva Walther, and Hartmut Blank, "Cognitive Consistency and the Formation of Interpersonal Attitudes: Cognitive Balance Affects the Encoding of Social Information," *Journal of Experimental Social Psychology* 41, no. 6 (2005): 618–26; Eva Walther, "Guilty by Mere Association: Evaluative Conditioning and the Spreading Attitude Effect," *Journal of Personality and Social Psychology* 82, no. 6 (2002): 919–34; Robert B. Zajonc, "Feeling and Thinking: Preferences Need No Inferences," *American Psychologist* 35 (1980): 151–75; Robert B. Zajonc, "Feeling and Thinking: Closing the Debate over the Independence of Affect," in *Feeling and Thinking: The Role of Affect in Social Cognition,* ed. J. P. Forgas (New York: Cambridge University Press, 2000), 31–58; Matthew M. Botvinick, Jonathan D. Cohen, and Cameron S. Carter, "Conflict Monitoring and Anterior Cingulate Cortex: An Update," *Trends in Cognitive Sciences* 8, no. 12 (2004): 539–46; Nick Yeung, Matthew M. Botvinick, and Jonathan D. Cohen, "The Neural Basis of Error Detection: Conflict Monitoring and the Error-Related Negativity," *Psychological Review* 111, no. 4 (2004): 931–59.

35 Robert L. Dipboye, "Self-Fulfilling Prophecies in the Selection-Recruitment Interview," *Academy of Management Review* 7, no. 4 (1982), 579–86; Thomas W. Dougherty, Daniel B. Turban, and John C. Callender, "Confirming First Impressions in the Employment Interview: A Field Study of Interviewer Behavior," *Journal of Applied Psychology* 79, no. 5 (1994), 659–65; Thomas W. Dougherty and Daniel B. Turban, "Behavioral Confirmation of Interviewer Expectations," in *The Employment Interview Handbook,* ed. R. W. Eder and M. M. Harris (Thousand Oaks, CA: Sage: 1999), 217–29; Mark Snyder and Arthur A. Stukas Jr., "Interpersonal Processes: The Interplay of Cognitive, Motivational, and Behavioral Activities in Social Interaction," *Annual Review of Psychology* 50, no. 1 (1999), 273–303; Edgar E. Kausel, Satoris S. Culbertson, and Hector P. Madrid, "Overconfidence in Personnel Selection: When and Why Unstructured Interview Information Can Hurt Hiring Decisions," *Organizational Behavior and Human Decision Processes* 137 (2016), 27–44.

36 Author interview, March 10, 2015.

37 Theodore D. Satterthwaite et al., "Being Right Is Its Own Reward: Load and Performance Related Ventral Striatum Activation to Correct Responses During a Working Memory Task in Youth," *NeuroImage* 61, no. 3 (2012): 723–29; Gilles Pourtois et al., "Errors Recruit Both Cognitive and Emotional Monitoring Systems: Simultaneous Intracranial Recordings in the Dorsal Anterior Cingulate Gyrus and Amygdala Combined with fMRI," *Neuropsychologia* 48, no. 4 (2010): 1,144–59;

Greg Hajcak and Dan Foti, "Errors Are Aversive: Defensive Motivation and the Error-Related Negativity," *Psychological Science* 19, no. 2 (2008): 103–8.

38 Daniel N. Albohn and Reginald B. Adams Jr., "Social Vision: At the Intersection of Vision and Person Perception," in *Neuroimaging Personality, Social Cognition, and Character,* ed. John R. Absher and Jasmin Cloutier (San Diego: Elsevier, 2016), 159–86; Jeffrey A. Brooks and Jonathan B. Freeman, "The Psychology and Neuroscience of Person Perception," in *Stevens' Handbook of Experimental Psychology and Cognitive Neuroscience,* ed. John T. Wixted, 4th ed. (Newark, NJ: Wiley & Sons, 2018), psych.nyu.edu/freemanlab/pubs/Brooks_Freeman_Handbook.pdf; Alex Todorov, "Evaluating Faces on Social Dimensions," in *Social Neuroscience: Toward Understanding the Underpinnings of the Social Mind,* ed. Alexander Todorov, Susan T. Fiske, and D. Prentice (Oxford: Oxford University Press, 2011), 54–76; Reginald B. Adams Jr., Ursula Hess, and Robert E. Kleck, "The Intersection of Gender-Related Facial Appearance and Facial Displays of Emotion," *Emotion Review* 7, no. 1 (2015): 5–13; Ursula Hess et al., "Face Gender and Emotion Expression: Are Angry Women More like Men?," *Journal of Vision* 9, no. 12 (2009): 19.

39 Allan Mazur, "A Biosocial Model of Status in Face-to-Face Groups," in *Evolutionary Perspectives on Social Psychology,* ed. Virgil Zeigler-Hill, Lisa L. M. Welling, and Todd K. Shackelford (New York: Springer, 2015), 303–15; Allan Mazur, Julie Mazur, and Caroline Keating, "Military Rank Attainment of a West Point Class: Effects of Cadets' Physical Features," *American Journal of Sociology* 90, no. 1 (1984): 125–50; Allan Mazur, "A Biosocial Model of Status in Face-to-Face Primate Groups," *Social Forces* 64, no. 2 (1985): 377–402; Alan Booth et al., "Testosterone, and Winning and Losing in Human Competition," *Hormones and Behavior* 23, no. 4 (1989): 556–71; Ulrich Mueller and Allan Mazur, "Facial Dominance of West Point Cadets as a Predictor of Later Military Rank," *Social Forces* 74, (1996): 823–50.

40 Ulrich Mueller and Allan Mazur, "Facial Dominance in Homo Sapiens as Honest Signaling of Male Quality," *Behavioral Ecology* 8, no. 5 (1997): 569–79.

41 Mary Ann Collins and Leslie A. Zebrowitz, "The Contributions of Appearance to Occupational Outcomes in Civilian and Military Settings," *Journal of Applied Social Psychology* 25, no. 2 (1995): 129–63; Leslie A. Zebrowitz and Joann M. Montepare, "Impressions of Babyfaced Individuals Across the Life Span," *Developmental Psychology* 28, no. 6 (1992): 1,143; Carmen E. Lefevre et al., "Telling Facial Metrics: Facial Width Is Associated with Testosterone Levels in Men," *Evolution and Human Behavior* 34, no. 4 (2013): 273–79; Mazur, *Biosociology of Dominance and Deference*; Anthony C. Little and S. Craig Roberts, "Evolution, Appearance, and Occupational Success," *Evolutionary Psychology* 10, no. 5 (2012): 782–801; Mazur, Mazur, and Keating, "Military Rank Attainment of a West Point Class"; Nicholas O. Rule and Nalini Ambady, "Judgments of Power from College Yearbook Photos and Later Career Success," *Social Psychological and Personality Science* 2, no. 2 (2011): 154–58; Christopher D. Watkins and Benedict C. Jones, "Competition-Related Factors Directly Influence Preferences for Facial Cues of Dominance in Allies," *Behavioral*

Ecology and Sociobiology 70, no. 12 (2016): 2,071–79; Margaret E. Ormiston, Elaine M. Wong, and Michael P. Haselhuhn, "Facial-Width-to-Height Ratio Predicts Perceptions of Integrity in Males," *Personality and Individual Differences* 105 (2017): 40–42; Bradley D. Mattan, Jennifer T. Kubota, and Jasmin Cloutier, "How Social Status Shapes Person Perception and Evaluation: A Social Neuroscience Perspective," *Perspectives on Psychological Science* 12, no. 3 (2017): 468–507; Re and Rule, "Appearance and Physiognomy."

42 Claire O'Callaghan et al., "Predictions Penetrate Perception: Converging Insights from Brain, Behaviour, and Disorder," *Consciousness and Cognition* 47 (2017): 63–74; Moshe Bar, "The Proactive Brain: Using Analogies and Associations to Generate Predictions," *Trends in Cognitive Sciences* 11, no. 7 (2007): 280–89; Christopher Y. Olivola, Friederike Funk, and Alexander Todorov, "Social Attributions from Faces Bias Human Choices," *Trends in Cognitive Sciences* 18, no. 11 (2014): 566–70; Alexander Todorov et al., "Social Attributions from Faces: Determinants, Consequences, Accuracy, and Functional Significance," *Annual Review of Psychology* 66 (2015): 519–45.

43 Leslie A. Zebrowitz, P. Matthew Bronstad, and Joann M. Montepare, "An Ecological Theory of Face Perception," in *The Science of Social Vision,* ed. Reginald B. Adams et al. (New York: Oxford University Press, 2011), 3–30; Joann M. Montepare, "'Cue, View, Action': An Ecological Approach to Person Perception," in *Social Psychology of Visual Perception,* ed. Emily Balcetis and G. Daniel Lassiter (New York: Psychology Press, 2010), 299–323.

CHAPTER 4: HOW SARAH PALIN HAPPENED

1 Michael Joseph Gross, "Sarah Palin: The Sound and the Fury," *Vanity Fair,* Sept. 1, 2010, www.vanityfair.com/news/2010/10/sarah-palin-201010/; Nick Allen, "Beauty Queen Who Beat Sarah Palin in Miss Alaska Aims for Political Career," *Telegraph,* May 1, 2010, www.telegraph.co.uk/news/worldnews/sarah-palin/7661230/Beauty -queen-who-beat-Sarah-Palin-in-Miss-Alaska-aims-for-political-career.html. When questioned about Heath, Blackburn later told reporters, "Everybody liked her, but I could tell she was very calculating. She was always asking questions, figuring out what she needed to do to get ahead." Sarah Palin's biography taken from www.biography .com/people/sarah-palin-360398#early-life. Jonathan Martin, "The Story Behind the Palin Surprise," *Politico,* Aug. 29, 2008, www.politico.com/story/2008/08/the-story -behind-the-palin-surprise-012988; Jane Mayer, "The Insiders: How John McCain Came to Pick Sarah Palin," *New Yorker,* Oct. 27, 2008, www.newyorker.com/maga zine/2008/10/27/the-insiders; Leonard Doyle, "In Alaska, Reputation of Palin Is Still Whiter than White," *Independent,* Sept. 3, 2008, www.independent.co.uk/voices /commentators/leonard-doyle-in-alaska-reputation-of-palin-is-still-whiter-than -white-918066.html; Tom Kizzia, "Rising Star," *Anchorage Daily News,* Oct. 23,

2006, www.webcitation.org/60oWlVgHw?url=http://www.adn.com/2006/10/23
/510447/part-1–fresh-face-launched-carries.html.

2   www.youtube.com/watch?v=UioYqnnBf3Y.

3   Gross, "Sarah Palin."

4   Todd Purdum, "It Came from Wasilla," *Vanity Fair,* June 30, 2009, www.vanity
fair.com/news/2009/08/sarah-palin200908. See also Andrew Edward White and
Douglas T. Kenrick, "Why Attractive Candidates Win," *New York Times,* Nov. 1,
2013, www.nytimes.com/2013/11/03/opinion/sunday/health-beauty-and-the
-ballot.html?hp&rref=opinion&_r=1&.

5   Madeline E. Heilman and Lois R. Saruwatari, "When Beauty Is Beastly: The Ef-
fects of Appearance and Sex on Evaluations of Job Applicants for Managerial and
Nonmanagerial Jobs," *Organizational Behavior and Human Performance* 23, no. 3
(1979): 360–72; Madeline E. Heilman and Melanie H. Stopeck, "Being Attractive,
Advantage or Disadvantage? Performance-Based Evaluations and Recommended
Personnel Actions as a Function of Appearance, Sex, and Job Type," *Organizational
Behavior and Human Decision Processes* 35, no. 2 (1985): 202–15; Alice H. Eagly
and Steven J. Karau, "Role Congruity Theory of Prejudice Toward Female Lead-
ers," *Psychological Review* 109, no. 3 (2002): 573–98.

6   Most research in this chapter is from Alice H. Eagly et al., "What Is Beautiful Is
Good, But: A Meta-analytic Review of Research on the Physical Attractiveness
Stereotype," *Psychological Bulletin* 110, no. 1 (1991): 109–28; Alan Feingold, "Good
Looking People Are Not What We Think," *Psychological Bulletin* 111, no. 2 (1992):
304–41; Judith H. Langlois et al., "Maxims or Myths of Beauty? A Meta-analytic
and Theoretical Review," *Psychological Bulletin* 126, no. 3 (2000): 390–423; An-
thony C. Little and David I. Perrett, "Facial Attractiveness," in Adams et al., *Science
of Social Vision*; Macrae and Quadflieg, "Perceiving People"; Ray Bull and Nichola
Rumsey, *The Social Psychology of Facial Appearance* (New York: Springer, 1988);
Gordon L. Patzer, *The Physical Attractiveness Phenomena* (New York: Plenum Press,
1985); Nancy Etcoff, *Survival of the Prettiest: The Science of Beauty* (New York:
Doubleday, 1999); Anthony C. Little and Benedict C. Jones, "The Evolutionary
Cognitive Neuropsychology of Face Preferences," in *Foundations in Evolutionary
Cognitive Neuroscience,* ed. Steven M. Platek and Todd K. Shackelford (Cambridge,
U.K.: Cambridge University Press, 2009), 175–204; Deborah L. Rhode, *The Beauty
Bias: The Injustice of Appearance in Life and Law* (New York: Oxford University
Press, 2010); Daniel S. Hamermesh, *Beauty Pays: Why Attractive People Are More
Successful* (Princeton, NJ: Princeton University Press, 2011); Bruce and Young, *Face
Perception*; Nichola Rumsey and Diana Harcourt, *The Psychology of Appearance*
(New York: Open University Press, 2005); J. L. Rennels, "Physical Attractiveness
Stereotyping," in *Encyclopedia of Body Image and Human Appearance* (Boston: Else-
vier, 2012), 2: 636–43; Dario Maestripieri, Andrea Henry, and Nora Nickels, "Ex-
plaining Financial and Prosocial Biases in Favor of Attractive People:
Interdisciplinary Perspectives from Economics, Social Psychology, and

Evolutionary Psychology," *Behavioral and Brain Sciences* (2017), doi:10.1017/S0140525X16000340, e19.

7   D. R. Osborn, "Measurement and Stability of Physical Attractiveness Judgments," in *Encyclopedia of Body Image and Human Appearance,* vol. 2, doi:10.1016/B978–0–12–384925–0.00080–8.

8   For more on Galton, see Nicholas W. Gillham, *A Life of Sir Francis Galton: From African Exploration to the Birth of Eugenics* (New York: Oxford University Press, 2001); Wade E. Pickren and Alexandra Rutherford, *A History of Modern Psychology in Context* (Hoboken, NJ: John Wiley & Sons, 2010); Gregory J. Feist, *The Psychology of Science and the Origins of the Scientific Mind* (New Haven, CT: Yale University Press, 2006), 23, 72, 115.

9   Francis Galton, "Composite Portraits, Made by Combining Those of Many Different Persons into a Single Resultant Figure," *Journal of the Anthropological Institute of Great Britain and Ireland* 8 (1879): 132–44.

10 Thomas Gilovich et al., *Social Psychology* (New York: W. W. Norton, 2013), 374. See also Rolf Reber, Norbert Schwarz, and Piotr Winkielman, "Processing Fluency and Aesthetic Pleasure: Is Beauty in the Perceiver's Processing Experience?," *Personality and Social Psychology Review* 8, no. 4 (2004): 364–82; Judith H. Langlois and L. A. Roggman, "Attractive Faces Are Only Average," *Psychological Science* 1 (1990): 115–21.

11 Logan T. Trujillo, Jessica M. Jankowitsch, and Judith H. Langlois, "Beauty Is in the Ease of the Beholding: A Neurophysiological Test of the Averageness Theory of Facial Attractiveness," *Cognitive, Affective, and Behavioral Neuroscience* 14, no. 3 (2014): 1,061–76; Winkielman et al., "Fluency of Consistency."

12 Doug Jones and Kim Hill, "Criteria of Facial Attractiveness in Five Populations," *Human Nature* 4 (1993): 271–96; Jamin Halberstadt and Gillian Rhodes, "The Attractiveness of Nonface Averages: Implications for an Evolutionary Explanation of the Attractiveness of Average Faces," *Psychological Science* 11, no. 4 (2000): 285–89.

13 Alan Slater et al., "Newborn Infants Prefer Attractive Faces," *Infant Behavior and Development* 21 (1998): 345–54; Alan Slater et al., "Newborn Infants' Preference for Attractive Faces: The Role of Internal and External Facial Features," *Infancy* 1, no. 2 (2000): 265–74; Jennifer L. Ramsey et al., "Origins of a Stereotype: Categorization of Facial Attractiveness by 6-Month-Old Infants," *Developmental Science* 7, no. 2 (2004): 201–11; T. M. Field et al., "Mother-Stranger Face Discrimination by the Newborn," *Infant Behavior and Development* 7 (1984): 19–25.

14 Rebecca A. Hoss and Judith H. Langlois, "Infants Prefer Attractive Faces," in *The Development of Face Processing in Infancy and Early Childhood,* ed. Olivier Pascalis and Alan Slater (Hauppauge, NY: Nova Science, 2003), 27–38; Judith H. Langlois et al., "Infant Preferences for Attractive Faces: Rudiments of a Stereotype?," *Developmental Psychology* 23, no. 3 (1987): 363–69.

15 Anthony C. Little, "Attraction and Human Mating," in Zeigler-Hill, Welling, and Shackelford, *Evolutionary Perspectives on Social Psychology,* 319–32.

16 David A. Puts, "Beauty and the Beast: Mechanisms of Sexual Selection in Humans," *Evolution and Human Behavior* 31 (2010): 157–75; David A. Puts, Benedict C. Jones, and Lisa M. DeBruine, "Sexual Selection on Human Faces and Voices," *Journal of Sex Research* 49 (2012): 227–43; R. Thornhill and S. W. Gangestad, "Human Facial Beauty: Averageness, Symmetry, and Parasite Resistance," *Human Nature* 4 (1993): 237–69; R. Thornhill and S. W. Gangestad, "Facial Attractiveness," *Trends in Cognitive Sciences* 3 (1999): 452–60.

17 Gillian Rhodes, "The Evolutionary Psychology of Facial Beauty," *Annual Review of Psychology* 57 (2006): 199–226; Joanna E. Scheib, Steven W. Gangestad, and Randy Thornhill, "Facial Attractiveness, Symmetry, and Cues of Good Genes," *Proceedings of the Royal Society of London B: Biological Sciences* 266, no. 1431 (1999): 1,913–17; cf. Little and Perrett, "Facial Attractiveness."

18 Michael L. Platt and Hilke Plassmann, "Multistage Valuation Signals and Common Neural Currencies," in *Neuroeconomics: Decision Making and the Brain,* ed. Paul W. Glimcher and Ernst Fehr, 2nd ed. (London: Elsevier, 2014), 237–58; Christian C. Ruff and Ernst Fehr, "The Neurobiology of Rewards and Values in Social Decision Making," *Nature Reviews Neuroscience* 15, no. 8 (2014): 549–62; Benedetto De Martino et al., "The Neurobiology of Reference-Dependent Value Computation," *Journal of Neuroscience* 29, no. 12 (2009): 3,833–42. FWIW, you should always go to the birthday party. Porcelli and Delgado, "Reward Processing in the Human Brain"; Kringelbach, "Human Orbitofrontal Cortex"; Rangel, Camerer, and Montague, "Framework for Studying the Neurobiology of Value-Based Decision Making."

19 Jasmin Cloutier et al., "Are Attractive People Rewarding? Sex Differences in the Neural Substrates of Facial Attractiveness," *Journal of Cognitive Neuroscience* 20, no. 6 (2008): 941–51.

20 Guillaume Sescousse, Jérôme Redouté, and Jean-Claude Dreher, "The Architecture of Reward Value Coding in the Human Orbitofrontal Cortex," *Journal of Neuroscience* 30, no. 39 (2010): 13,095–104.

21 E. T. Rolls, Z. J. Sienkiewicz, and S. Yaxley, "Hunger Modulates the Responses to Gustatory Stimuli of Single Neurons in the Caudolateral Orbitofrontal Cortex of the Macaque Monkey," *European Journal of Neuroscience* 1 (1989): 53–60; M. L. Kringelbach et al., "Activation of the Human Orbitofrontal Cortex to a Liquid Food Stimulus Is Correlated with Its Subjective Pleasantness," *Cerebral Cortex* 13 (2003): 1,064–71.

22 Owen Hargie, *Skilled Interpersonal Communication: Research, Theory, and Practice,* 5th ed. (New York: Routledge, 2010), 84–85; cf. Ingrid R. Olson and Christy Marshuetz, "Facial Attractiveness Is Appraised at a Glance," *Emotion* 5 (2005): 186–201; M. L. Van Leeuwen and C. N. Macrae, "Is Beautiful Always Good? Implicit Benefits of Facial Attractiveness," *Social Cognition* 22 (2004): 637–49. See also social exchange theory, J. Thibaut and H. H. Kelley, *The Social Psychology of Groups* (New York: Wiley, 1959); G. Homans, *Social Behavior: Its Elementary Forms* (New York: Harcourt, Brace & World, 1961).

23 Paul W. Eastwick et al., "Implicit and Explicit Preferences for Physical Attractiveness in a Romantic Partner: A Double Dissociation in Predictive Validity," *Journal of Personality and Social Psychology* 101, no. 5 (2011): 993; Sascha Krause et al., "Implicit Interpersonal Attraction in Small Groups: Automatically Activated Evaluations Predict Actual Behavior Toward Social Partners," *Social Psychological and Personality Science* 5, no. 6 (2014): 671–79. More cognitive resources: Laura K. Morgan and Michael A. Kisley, "The Effects of Facial Attractiveness and Perceiver's Mate Value on Adaptive Allocation of Central Processing Resources," *Evolution and Human Behavior* 35 (2014): 96–102.

24 Ladd Wheeler and Youngmee Kim, "What Is Beautiful Is Culturally Good: The Physical Attractiveness Stereotype Has Different Content in Collectivist Cultures," *Personality and Social Psychology Bulletin* 23 (1997): 795–800.

25 Judith H. Langlois et al., "Infant Attractiveness Predicts Maternal Behaviors and Attitudes," *Developmental Psychology* 31, no. 3 (1995): 464–72. We instinctively do not like ugly babies, as evidenced by one of the most depressing journal article titles of all time: Stevie S. Schein and Judith H. Langlois, "Unattractive Infant Faces Elicit Negative Affect from Adults," *Infant Behavior and Development* 38 (2015): 130–34.

26 Rick K. Wilson and Catherine C. Eckel, "Judging a Book by Its Cover: Beauty and Expectations in the Trust Game," *Political Research Quarterly* 59, no. 2 (2006): 189–202.

27 S. Michael Kalick, "Physical Attractiveness as a Status Cue," *Journal of Experimental Social Psychology* 24, no. 6 (1988): 469–89.

28 Peter L. Benson, Stuart A. Karabenick, and Richard M. Lerner, "Pretty Pleases: The Effects of Physical Attractiveness, Race, and Sex on Receiving Help," *Journal of Experimental Social Psychology* 12, no. 5 (1976): 409–15.

29 Debra Umberson and Michael Hughes, "The Impact of Physical Attractiveness on Achievement and Psychological Well-Being," *Social Psychology Quarterly* 50, no. 3 (1987): 227–36.

30 G. P. Elovitz and J. Salvia, "Attractiveness as a Biasing Factor in the Judgments of School Psychologists," *Journal of School Psychology* 20 (1982): 339–45.

31 Pamela Kenealy, Neil Frude, and William Shaw, "Influence of Children's Physical Attractiveness on Teacher Expectations," *Journal of Social Psychology* 128, no. 3 (1988): 373–83; Pamela Kenealy, Neil Frude, and William Shaw, "Teacher Expectations as Predictors of Academic Success," *Journal of Social Psychology* 131, no. 2 (1991): 305–6; M. T. French et al., "Effects of Physical Attractiveness, Personality, and Grooming on High School GPA," *Labour Economics* 16, no. 4 (2009): 373–82; David Landy and Harold Sigall, "Beauty Is Talent: Task Evaluation as a Function of the Performer's Physical Attractiveness," *Journal of Personality and Social Psychology* 29, no. 3 (1974): 299–304.

32 Shawn Bauldry et al., "Attractiveness Compensates for Low Status Background in the Prediction of Educational Attainment," *PLoS ONE* 11, no. 6 (2016): e0155313, doi:10.1371/journal.pone.0155313.

33 Daniel S. Hamermesh and Jeff E. Biddle, "Beauty and the Labor Market," *American Economic Review* 84, no. 5 (1994): 1,174–94; Markus M. Mobius and Tanya S. Rosenblat, "Why Beauty Matters," *American Economic Review* 96 (2006): 222–35; J. M. Fletcher, "Beauty vs. Brains: Early Labor Market Outcomes of High School Graduates," *Economics Letters* 105 (2009): 321–25.

34 Michael Ahearne, Thomas W. Gruen, and Cheryl Burke Jarvis, "If Looks Could Sell: Moderation and Mediation of the Attractiveness Effect on Salesperson Performance," *International Journal of Research in Marketing* 16, no. 4 (1999): 269–84; Elaine Hatfield, "Physical Attractiveness in Social Interaction," in *The Psychology of Cosmetic Treatments* (New York: Praeger, 1985), 77–92; Cameron Anderson et al., "Who Attains Social Status? Effects of Personality and Physical Attractiveness in Social Groups," *Journal of Personality and Social Psychology* 81, no. 1 (2001): 116–32; Michael G. Efran, "The Effect of Physical Appearance on the Judgment of Guilt, Interpersonal Attraction, and Severity of Recommended Punishment in a Simulated Jury Task," *Journal of Research in Personality* 8, no. 1 (1974): 45–54; Harold Sigall and Nancy Ostrove, "Beautiful but Dangerous: Effects of Offender Attractiveness and Nature of the Crime on Juridic Judgment," *Journal of Personality and Social Psychology* 31, no. 3 (1975): 410–14; Tammy L. Anderson et al., "Aesthetic Capital: A Research Review on Beauty Perks and Penalties," *Sociology Compass* 4, no. 8 (2010): 564–75; C. Green, "Effects of Counselor and Subject Race and Counselor Physical Attractiveness on Impressions and Expectations of a Female Counselor," *Journal of Counseling Psychology* 33 (1986): 349–52; S. Romano and J. Bordiere, "Physical Attractiveness Stereotypes and Students' Perceptions of College Professors," *Psychological Reports* 64 (1989): 1,099–102; Daniel S. Hamermesh and Amy Parker, "Beauty in the Classroom: Instructors' Pulchritude and Putative Pedagogical Productivity," *Economics of Education Review* 24, no. 4 (2005): 369–76; Todd C. Riniolo et al., "Hot or Not: Do Professors Perceived as Physically Attractive Receive Higher Student Evaluations?," *Journal of General Psychology* 133, no. 1 (2006): 19–35.

35 Mark Snyder, Elizabeth Decker Tanke, and Ellen Berscheid, "Social Perception and Interpersonal Behavior: On the Self-Fulfilling Nature of Social Stereotypes," *Journal of Personality and Social Psychology* 35, no. 9 (1977): 656–66; Mark Snyder, "When Belief Creates Reality," *Advances in Experimental Social Psychology* 18 (1984): 247–305; Olivier Klein and Mark Snyder, "Stereotypes and Behavioral Confirmation: From Interpersonal to Intergroup Perspectives," *Advances in Experimental Social Psychology* 35 (2003): 153–234.

36 Author interview, Feb. 20, 2015; cf. Tor D. Wager and Lauren Y. Atlas, "The Neuroscience of Placebo Effects: Connecting Context, Learning, and Health," *Nature Reviews Neuroscience* 16 (2015): 403–18.

37 Katharina A. Schwarz, Roland Pfister, and Christian Büchel, "Rethinking Explicit Expectations: Connecting Placebos, Social Cognition, and Contextual Perception," *Trends in Cognitive Sciences* 20, no. 6 (2016): 469–80.

38 James J. Gibson, *The Ecological Approach to Visual Perception* (New York: Psychology Press, 1986).

39 Thanks to James A. Coan for his insights. Lane Beckes and James A. Coan, "Social Baseline Theory: The Role of Social Proximity in Emotion and Economy of Action," *Social and Personality Psychology Compass* 5, no. 12 (2011): 976–88; Lane Beckes and James A. Coan, "Toward an Integrative Neuroscience of Relationships," in *The Oxford Handbook of Close Relationships,* ed. Jeffry Simpson and Lorne Campbell (New York: Oxford University Press, 2013), 684–710; James A. Coan and David A. Sbarra, "Social Baseline Theory: The Social Regulation of Risk and Effort," *Current Opinion in Psychology* 1 (2015): 87–91; James A. Coan, Casey L. Brown, and Lane Beckes, "Our Social Baseline: The Role of Social Proximity in Economy of Action," in *Mechanisms of Social Connection: From Brain to Group,* ed. Mario Mikulincer and Phillip R. Shaver (Washington, D.C.: American Psychological Association, 2014), 89–104.

40 Rodolfo Mendoza-Denton and Özlem Ayduk, "Personality and Social Interaction: Interpenetrating Processes," in *The Oxford Handbook of Personality and Social Psychology,* ed. Kay Deaux and Mark Snyder (New York: Oxford University Press, 2012), doi:10.1093/oxfordhb/9780195398991.001.0001.

41 Roy F. Baumeister and Mark R. Leary, "The Need to Belong: Desire for Interpersonal Attachments as a Fundamental Human Motivation," *Psychological Bulletin* 117 (1995): 497–529; cf. Leslie A. Zebrowitz and Joann M. Montepare, "Social Psychological Face Perception: Why Appearance Matters," *Social and Personality Psychology Compass* 2 (2008): 1,497–517; White and Kenrick, "Why Attractive Candidates Win."

42 Zebrowitz and Montepare, "Social Psychological Face Perception"; White and Kenrick, "Why Attractive Candidates Win."

43 Cecilia L. Ridgeway and Sandra Nakagawa, "Status," in *Handbook of the Social Psychology of Inequality,* ed. Jane D. McLeod, Edward J. Lawler, and Michael Schwalbe (New York: Springer, 2014), 3–26.

44 Sigall and Ostrove, "Beautiful but Dangerous."

45 James Andreoni and Ragan Petrie, "Beauty, Gender, and Stereotypes: Evidence from Laboratory Experiments," *Journal of Economic Psychology* 29 (2008): 73–93; Sunyoung Lee et al., "When Beauty Helps and When It Hurts: An Organizational Context Model of Attractiveness Discrimination in Selection Decisions," *Organizational Behavior and Human Decision Processes* 128 (2015): 15–28; Anderson et al., "Aesthetic Capital."

46 Rotem Kowner, "Susceptibility to Physical Attractiveness Comparison on the Role of Attributions in Protecting Self-Esteem," *Psychologia* 39 (1996): 150–62; Maria Agthe, Matthias Spörrle, and Jon K. Maner, "Does Being Attractive Always Help? Positive and Negative Effects of Attractiveness on Social Decision Making," *Personality and Social Psychology Bulletin* 37, no. 8 (2011): 1,042–54; Maria Agthe et al., "Looking up versus Looking down: Attractiveness-Based Organizational Biases Are Moderated by Social Comparison Direction," *Journal of Applied Social Psychology* 44, no. 1 (2014): 40–45.

47 Author interview, Oct. 18, 2013.

48 Anderson et al., "Who Attains Social Status?"; Kalick, "Physical Attractiveness as a Status Cue"; Anne Haas and Stanford W. Gregory, "The Impact of Physical Attractiveness on Women's Social Status and Interactional Power," *Sociological Forum* 20, no. 3 (2005): 449–71; Tonya K. Frevert and Lisa Slattery Walker, "Physical Attractiveness and Social Status," *Sociology Compass* 8, no. 3 (2014): 313–23.

49 Author interview, Aug. 9, 2015.

50 Ridgeway and Nakagawa, "Status."

51 Jacob L. Moreno, *Who Shall Survive?* (Washington, D.C.: Nervous and Mental Disease Publishing Company, 1934). For an introduction to Moreno, see Willard W. Hartup, "Critical Issues and Theoretical Viewpoints," in *Handbook of Peer Interactions, Relationships, and Groups,* ed. Kenneth H. Rubin, William M. Bukowski, and Brett Laursen (New York: Guilford Press, 2009), 3–19. Shelley Hymel et al., "Social Status among Peers: From Sociometric Attraction to Peer Acceptance to Perceived Popularity," in *The Wiley-Blackwell Handbook of Childhood Social Development,* ed. Peter K. Smith and Craig H. Hart, 2nd ed. (Malden, MA.: Blackwell, 2011), 375–92; Janice R. Kelly, Megan K. McCarty, and Nicole E. Iannone, "Interaction in Small Groups," in *Handbook of Social Psychology,* ed. John DeLamater and Amanda Ward, 2nd ed. (New York: Springer, 2013), 413–38.

52 Timothy A. Judge, Charlice Hurst, and Lauren S. Simon, "Does It Pay to Be Smart, Attractive, or Confident (or All Three)? Relationships among General Mental Ability, Physical Attractiveness, Core Self-Evaluations, and Income," *Journal of Applied Psychology* 94, no. 3 (2009): 742–55; Mary E. Gifford-Smith and Celia A. Brownell, "Childhood Peer Relationships: Social Acceptance, Friendships, and Peer Networks," *Journal of School Psychology* 41 (2003): 235–84.

53 Hymel et al., "Social Status among Peers." Self-esteem shows stability over time: Abraham Tesser, "Self-Esteem," in *Blackwell Handbook of Social Psychology: Intraindividual Processes,* ed. Abraham Tesser and Norbert Schwarz (Hoboken, NJ: Blackwell, 2001), 479–98.

54 For a discussion of how the social comparison process influences our self-concept, see Ulrich Trautwein and Jens Möller, "Self-Concept: Determinants and Consequences of Academic Self-Concept in School Contexts," in *Psychosocial Skills and School Systems in the 21st Century: Theory, Research, and Applications,* ed. A. Lipnevich, F. Preckel, and R. Roberts (Berlin: Springer, 2016), 187–214.

55 Mark R. Leary et al., "Self-Esteem as an Interpersonal Monitor: The Sociometer Hypothesis," *Journal of Personality and Social Psychology* 68, no. 3 (1995): 518–30; Mark R. Leary and Jennifer Guadagno, "The Sociometer, Self-Esteem, and the Regulation of Interpersonal Behavior," in *Handbook of Self-Regulation: Research, Theory, and Applications,* ed. Kathleen D. Vohs and Roy F. Baumeister, 2nd ed. (New York: Guilford Press, 2011), 339–54.

56 Author interview, March 30, 2015.

57 Genevieve L. Lorenzo, Jeremy C. Biesanz, and Lauren J. Human, "What Is Beautiful Is Good and More Accurately Understood: Physical Attractiveness and Accuracy in First Impressions of Personality," *Psychological Science* 21, no. 12 (2010): 1,777–82; Edward P. Lemay, Margaret S. Clark, and Aaron Greenberg, "What Is Beautiful Is Good Because What Is Beautiful Is Desired: Physical Attractiveness Stereotyping as Projection of Interpersonal Goals," *Personality and Social Psychology Bulletin* 36, no. 3 (2010): 339–53.

58 Ryan T. McKay and Daniel C. Dennett, "The Evolution of Misbelief," *Behavioral and Brain Sciences* 32 (2009): 493–561. See also Constantine Sedikides and Mark D. Alicke, "Self-Enhancement and Self-Protection Motives," in *The Oxford Handbook of Human Motivation*, ed. Richard M. Ryan (New York: Oxford University Press, 2013); Peter Sheridan Dodds et al., "Human Language Reveals a Universal Positivity Bias," *Proceedings of the National Academy of Sciences* 112, no. 8 (2015): 2,389–94; Tali Sharot, *The Optimism Bias: A Tour of the Irrationally Positive Brain* (New York: Vintage, 2011).

59 Raffael Kalisch, Marianne B. Müller, and Oliver Tüscher, "A Conceptual Framework for the Neurobiological Study of Resilience," *Behavioral and Brain Sciences* 38 (2015): e92; William Von Hippel and Robert Trivers, "The Evolution and Psychology of Self-Deception," *Behavioral and Brain Sciences* 34, no. 1 (2011): 1–16; Shelley E. Taylor and Jonathon D. Brown, "Illusion and Well-Being: A Social Psychological Perspective on Mental Health," *Psychological Bulletin* 103, no. 2 (1988): 193–210; Michael F. Scheier and Charles S. Carver, "Effects of Optimism on Psychological and Physical Well-Being: Theoretical Overview and Empirical Update," *Cognitive Therapy and Research* 16, no. 2 (1992): 201–28; Shelley E. Taylor et al., "Psychological Resources, Positive Illusions, and Health," *American Psychologist* 55, no. 1 (2000): 99–109.

60 Lars Penke et al., "How Self-Assessments Can Guide Human Mating Decisions," in *Mating Intelligence: New Insights into Intimate Relationships, Human Sexuality, and the Mind's Reproductive System*, ed. G. Geher and G. F. Miller (Mahwah, NJ: Lawrence Erlbaum, 2007), 37–75; Peter M. Todd and Geoffrey F. Miller, "From Pride and Prejudice to Persuasion: Satisficing in Mate Search," in *Simple Heuristics That Make Us Smart*, ed. Gerd Gigerenzer, Peter M. Todd, and the ABC Research Group (New York: Oxford University Press, 1999), 287–308; Peter M. Todd, "Co-evolved Cognitive Mechanisms in Mate Search: Making Decisions in a Decision-Shaped World," in *Evolution and the Social Mind: Evolutionary Psychology and Social Cognition*, ed. J. P. Forgas, M. G. Haselton, and W. von Hippel (New York: Psychology Press, 2007), 145–59; A. Feingold, "Matching for Attractiveness in Romantic Partners and Same-Sex Friends: A Meta-analysis and Theoretical Critique," *Psychological Bulletin* 104 (1988): 226–35; Peter M. Todd, Skyler S. Place, and Robert I. Bowers, "Simple Heuristics for Mate Choice Decisions," in Krueger, *Social Judgment and Decision Making*, 193–207; Lenton et al., "Heart Has Its Reasons," 433–57; Matthew S. Sullivan, "Mate Choice as an Information Gathering

Process under Time Constraint: Implications for Behaviour and Signal Design," *Animal Behaviour* 47, no. 1 (1994): 141–51.

61 Gable and Berkman, "Making Connections and Avoiding Loneliness"; Nikitin and Schoch, "Social Approach and Avoidance Motivations"; Taishi Kawamoto, Mitsuhiro Ura, and Hiroshi Nittono, "Intrapersonal and Interpersonal Processes of Social Exclusion," *Frontiers in Neuroscience* 9 (2015): 62; Christopher G. Davey et al., "Being Liked Activates Primary Reward and Midline Self-Related Brain Regions," *Human Brain Mapping* 31, no. 4 (2010): 660–68.

62 Peter Belmi and Margaret Neale, "Mirror, Mirror on the Wall, Who's the Fairest of Them All? Thinking That One Is Attractive Increases the Tendency to Support Inequality," *Organizational Behavior and Human Decision Processes* 124, no. 2 (2014): 133–49.

63 Peter M. Todd et al., "Different Cognitive Processes Underlie Human Mate Choices and Mate Preferences," *Proceedings of the National Academy of Sciences* 104, no. 38 (2007): 15,011–16; David M. Buss and Todd K. Shackelford, "Attractive Women Want It All: Good Genes, Economic Investment, Parenting Proclivities, and Emotional Commitment," *Evolutionary Psychology* 6, no. 1 (2008): 134–46.

64 Joyce Carol Oates, *Faithless: Tales of Transgression* (New York: Ecco Press, 2009), 17.

65 Judge, Hurst, and Simon, "Does It Pay to Be Smart, Attractive, or Confident (Or All Three)?"; Kali H. Trzesniewski, M. Brent Donnellan, and Richard W. Robins, "Development of Self-Esteem," in *Self-Esteem,* ed. Virgil Zeigler-Hill (New York: Psychology Press, 2013), 60–79; Jennifer Crocker and Connie T. Wolfe, "Contingencies of Self-Worth," *Psychological Review* 108, no. 3 (2001): 593–623; Jennifer Crocker and Lora E. Park, "Contingencies of Self-Worth," in *Handbook of Self and Identity,* ed. Mark Leary and June Price Tangney, 2nd ed. (New York: Guilford Press, 2012), 309–26; Lora E. Park and Jennifer Crocker, "Contingencies of Self-Worth and Responses to Negative Interpersonal Feedback," *Self and Identity* 7, no. 2 (2008): 184–203; Jennifer Crocker and Katherine M. Knight, "Contingencies of Self-Worth," *Current Directions in Psychological Science* 14, no. 4 (2005): 200–3; Tom Pyszczynski et al., "Why Do People Need Self-Esteem? A Theoretical and Empirical Review," *Psychological Bulletin* 130, no. 3 (2004): 435–68; Jennifer Crocker and Lora E. Park, "The Costly Pursuit of Self-Esteem," *Psychological Bulletin* 130 (2004): 392–414; John P. Hewitt, "The Social Construction of Self-Esteem," in Snyder and Lopez, *Handbook of Positive Psychology,* 135–47.

66 Paul W. Eastwick and Lucy L. Hunt, "Relational Mate Value: Consensus and Uniqueness in Romantic Evaluations," *Journal of Personality and Social Psychology* 106, no. 5 (2014): 728–51; Gary W. Lewandowski Jr., Arthur Aron, and Julie Gee, "Personality Goes a Long Way: The Malleability of Opposite-Sex Physical Attractiveness," *Personal Relationships* 14 (2007): 571–85; Lucy L. Hunt, Paul W. Eastwick, and Eli J. Finkel, "Leveling the Playing Field: Longer Acquaintance Predicts Reduced Assortative Mating on Attractiveness," *Psychological Science* 26, no. 7 (2015): 1,046–53.

67 Author interview, July 17, 2013.

68 Samantha Kwan and Mary Nell Trautner, "Beauty Work: Individual and Institutional Rewards, the Reproduction of Gender, and Questions of Agency," *Sociology Compass* 3, no. 1 (2009): 49–71; Mark D. Alicke, Richard H. Smith, and M. L. Klotz, "Judgments of Physical Attractiveness: The Role of Faces and Bodies," *Personality and Social Psychology Bulletin* 12, no. 4 (1986): 381–89; Jaclyn S. Wong and Andrew M. Penner, "Gender and the Returns to Attractiveness," *Research in Social Stratification and Mobility* 44 (2016): 113–23.

69 Olga Khazan, "The Makeup Tax: Women Who Wear Makeup Earn More and Are Treated Better. This Has Steep Costs, in Both Money and Time," *Atlantic,* Aug. 5, 2015, www.theatlantic.com/business/archive/2015/08/the-makeup-tax/400478/; Wong and Penner, "Gender and the Returns to Attractiveness."

70 Brian P. Meier et al., "Are Sociable People More Beautiful? A Zero-Acquaintance Analysis of Agreeableness, Extraversion, and Attractiveness," *Journal of Research in Personality* 44, no. 2 (2010): 293–96.

71 Anderson et al., "Aesthetic Capital."

72 Ben Child, "Carrie Fisher Blasts Star Wars Body Shamers on Twitter," *The Guardian,* Dec. 30, 2015, www.theguardian.com/film/2015/dec/30/carrie-fisher-blasts-star-wars-body-shamers-twitter-social-media.

CHAPTER 5: I GOT THIS

1 While reporting this book, I joined the Parents League of New York and attended several admissions sessions, fairs, and panels over the years. With one obvious exception, fragments of anecdotes have been compiled and some details have been modified in order to protect the identities of people who just wanted to go there to help their kids. History: "The Parents League: Its Place in Time," Parent's League of New York, www.parentsleague.org/about_us/history/index.aspx.

2 "Nursery School Scandal," *ABC News,* Jan. 5, 2006, abcnews.go.com/2020/story?id=123782&page=1; Jane Gross, "No Talking out of Preschool; Favoritism in Nursery School Entrance? No Comment," *New York Times,* Nov. 15, 2002, www.nytimes.com/2002/11/15/nyregion/no-talking-out-of-preschool-favoritism-in-nursery-school-entrance-no-comment.html; Rebecca Mead, "Tales out of Preschool," *New Yorker,* Dec. 2, 2002, www.newyorker.com/magazine/2002/12/02/tales-out-of-preschool; Chloe Malle, "Stock-Goosing Grubman to Sell Townhouse for $19.6 M," *New York Observer,* March 16, 2010, observer.com/2010/03/stockgoosing-grubman-to-sell-townhouse-for-196-m/. See also www.pbs.org/wgbh/pages/frontline/shows/wallstreet/wcom/92memo.html. The email: "You know everyone thinks I upgraded [AT&T] to get lead for [AT&T Wireless]. Nope. I used Sandy to get my kids in 92nd ST Y pre-school (which is harder than Harvard) and Sandy needed Armstrong's vote on our board to nuke Reed in showdown. Once coast was clear for both of us (ie Sandy clear victor and my kids confirmed) I went back to my normal

negative self on [AT&T]. Armstrong never knew that we both (Sandy and I) played him like a fiddle."

3 Winnie Hu and Kyle Spencer, "Your 4-Year-Old Scored a 95? Better Luck Next Time: Abandoning E.R.B. Test May Also Put End to a Status Symbol," *New York Times,* Sept. 25, 2013, www.nytimes.com/2013/09/26/education/on-entrance-test-whose -days-appear-numbered-a-95–just-wasnt-good-enough.html?_r=2&#_jmp0_.

4 Recorded at panel discussion on Oct. 1, 2014.

5 Author interview, Dec. 5, 2017.

6 Jenny Anderson and Rachel Ohmjan, "Bracing for $40,000 at New York City Private Schools," *New York Times,* Jan. 27, 2012, www.nytimes.com/2012/01/29 /nyregion/scraping-the-40000–ceiling-at-new-york-city-private-schools.html.

7 To be honest, I still do not understand quite what happened, leaving me to conclude that Krakowski simply materialized in the front of the line.

8 McKay and Dennett, "Evolution of Misbelief"; Corey L. M. Keyes and Shane J. Lopez, "Toward a Science of Mental Health: Positive Directions in Diagnosis and Interventions," in Snyder and Lopez, *Handbook of Positive Psychology,* 49; Daniel Campbell-Meiklejohn and Chris D. Frith, "Social Factors and Preference Change," in *Neuroscience of Preference and Choice,* ed. Raymond J. Dolan and Tali Sharot (New York: Academic Press, 2012), 181–82; Dominic D. P. Johnson and James H. Fowler, "The Evolution of Overconfidence," *Nature* 477, no. 7364 (2011): 317–20; Cameron Anderson et al., "A Status-Enhancement Account of Overconfidence," *Journal of Personality and Social Psychology* 103, no. 4 (2012): 718–35.

9 McKay and Dennett, "Evolution of Misbelief"; Keyes and Lopez, "Toward a Science of Mental Health," 49; Campbell-Meiklejohn and Frith, "Social Factors and Preference Change," 181–82; Johnson and Fowler, "Evolution of Overconfidence"; Anderson et al., "Status-Enhancement Account of Overconfidence"; Stephen M. Fleming and Nathaniel D. Daw, "Self-Evaluation of Decision-Making: A General Bayesian Framework for Metacognitive Computation," *Psychological Review* 124, no. 1 (2017): 91–114; cf. Holroyd and Coles, "Neural Basis of Human Error Processing"; Melle J. W. Vander Molen, "Fear of Negative Evaluation Modulates Electrocortical and Behavioral Responses When Anticipating Social Evaluative Feedback," *Frontiers in Human Neuroscience* 7, no. 936 (2014), doi:10.3389/ fnhum.2013.00936; Koban and Pourtois, "Brain Systems Underlying the Affective and Social Monitoring of Actions"; Rongjun Yu, "Choking under Pressure: The Neuropsychological Mechanisms of Incentive-Induced Performance Decrements," *Frontiers in Behavioral Neuroscience* 9, no. 19 (2014), doi:10.3389/fnbeh.2015.00019.

10 John D. Salamone, Michael S. Cousins, and Sherri Bucher, "Anhedonia or Anergia? Effects of Haloperidol and Nucleus Accumbens Dopamine Depletion on Instrumental Response Selection in a T-Maze Cost/Benefit Procedure," *Behavioural Brain Research* 65 (1994): 221–29; John D. Salamone, "The Involvement of Nucleus Accumbens Dopamine in Aversive Motivation," *Behavioural Brain Research* 61 (1994): 117–33; J. E. Aberman and John D. Salamone, "Nucleus Accumbens Dopamine

Depletions Make Rats More Sensitive to High Ratio Requirements but Do Not Impair Primary Food Reinforcement," *Neuroscience* 92 (1999) 545–52; John D. Salamone and Merce Correa, "Motivational Views of Reinforcement: Implications for Understanding the Behavioral Functions of Nucleus Accumbens Dopamine," *Behavioural Brain Research* 137 (2002): 3–25; John D. Salamone et al., "Nucleus Accumbens Dopamine and the Regulation of Effort in Food-Seeking Behavior: Implications for Studies of Natural Motivation, Psychiatry, and Drug Abuse," *Journal of Pharmacology and Experimental Therapeutics* 305, no. 1 (2003): 1–8; Michael T. Treadway et al., "Dopaminergic Mechanisms of Individual Differences in Human Effort-Based Decision-Making," *Journal of Neuroscience* 32, no. 18 (2012): 6,170–76; John D. Salamone et al., "The Pharmacology of Effort-Related Choice Behavior: Dopamine, Depression, and Individual Differences," *Behavioural Processes* 127 (2016) 3–17.

11 McKay and Dennett, "Evolution of Misbelief"; Keyes and Lopez, "Toward a Science of Mental Health," 49; Campbell-Meiklejohn and Frith, "Social Factors and Preference Change," 181–82; Johnson and Fowler, "Evolution of Overconfidence"; Anderson et al., "Status-Enhancement Account of Overconfidence."

12 Rodica Ioana Damian et al., "Can Personality Traits and Intelligence Compensate for Background Disadvantage? Predicting Status Attainment in Adulthood," *Journal of Personality and Social Psychology* 109, no. 3 (2015): 473–89; Michael J. Shanahan et al., "Personality and the Reproduction of Social Class," *Social Forces* 93, no. 1 (2014): 209–40; Andrew J. Elliot and Martin V. Covington, "Approach and Avoidance Motivation," *Educational Psychology Review* 13, no. 2 (2001): 73–92; Colin G. DeYoung, "Cybernetic Big Five Theory," *Journal of Research in Personality* 56 (2015): 33–58. General discussion of cybernetics and personality: Gordon B. Moskowitz, "The Representation and Regulation of Goals," in *Goal-Directed Behavior,* ed. Henk Aarts and Andrew J. Elliot (New York: Psychology Press, 2012), 1–47.

13 Luke D. Smillie, Natalie J. Loxton, and Rachel E. Avery, "Reinforcement Sensitivity Theory, Research, Applications, and Future," in *The Wiley-Blackwell Handbook of Individual Differences,* ed. Tomas Chamorro-Premuzic, Sophie von Stumm, and Adrian Furnham (Malden, MA: Wiley-Blackwell, 2011), 101–31; O. C. Schultheiss and M. M. Wirth, "Biopsychological Aspects of Motivation," in *Motivation and Action,* ed. Jutta Heckhausen and Heinz Heckhausen (Cambridge, U.K.: Cambridge University Press, 2012), 256–58; P. J. Corr, "Reinforcement Sensitivity Theory (RST): Introduction," in *The Reinforcement Sensitivity Theory of Personality,* ed. P. L. Corr (Cambridge, U.K.: Cambridge University Press, 2008), 1–43; Andrew J. Elliot and Todd M. Thrash, "Approach-Avoidance Motivation in Personality: Approach and Avoidance Temperaments and Goals," *Journal of Personality and Social Psychology* 82, no. 5 (2002): 804–18; Elliot, *Handbook of Approach and Avoidance Motivation.* Jeffrey Gray and his co-conspirator McNaughton revised the BAS/BIS model in 2000, upon publication of the second edition of *The Neuropsychology of Anxiety: An Enquiry into the Functions of the Septo-Hippocampal System,* to include

FFFS, the fight/flight/freeze system. FFFS responds to fear. In his old model, all behavior could be explained through differences in the behavioral activation system and the behavioral inhibition system. In the new model, the BAS responds to good things, the FFFS responds to bad things, and the BIS puts the brakes on your behavior until you figure out what the heck you're going to do.

14 Cameron Anderson, John Angus D. Hildreth, and Laura Howland, "Is the Desire for Status a Fundamental Human Motive? A Review of the Empirical Literature," *Psychological Bulletin* 141, no. 3 (2015): 574–601.

15 Ann Marie T. Russell and Susan T. Fiske, "Power and Social Perception," in *The Social Psychology of Power,* ed. Ana Guinote and Theresa K. Vescio (New York: Guilford Press, 2010), 231; Keely A. Muscatell et al., "Social Status Modulates Neural Activity in the Mentalizing Network," *NeuroImage* 60, no. 3 (2012): 1,771–77; Cameron Anderson, Oliver P. John, and Dacher Keltner, "The Personal Sense of Power," *Journal of Personality* 80, no. 2 (2012): 313–44; Pamela K. Smith et al., "Lacking Power Impairs Executive Functions," *Psychological Science* 19, no. 5 (2008): 441–47; Pamela K. Smith and Yaacov Trope, "You Focus on the Forest When You're in Charge of the Trees: Power Priming and Abstract Information Processing," *Journal of Personality and Social Psychology* 90, no. 4 (2006): 578–96; Yaacov Trope and N. Liberman, "Temporal Construal," *Psychological Review* 110 (2003): 403–21; Joe C. Magee and Adam D. Galinsky, "Social Hierarchy: The Self-Reinforcing Nature of Power and Status," *Academy of Management Annals* 2, no. 1 (2008): 351–98; Joe C. Magee and Pamela K. Smith, "The Social Distance Theory of Power," *Personality and Social Psychology Review* 17, no. 2 (2013): 158–86; Michael W. Kraus et al., "Social Class, Solipsism, and Contextualism: How the Rich Are Different from the Poor," *Psychological Review* 119, no. 3 (2012): 546; Martin Reimann et al., "Embodiment in Judgment and Choice," *Journal of Neuroscience, Psychology, and Economics* 5, no. 2 (2012): 104–23; Aaron W. Lukaszewski et al., "The Role of Physical Formidability in Human Social Status Allocation," *Journal of Personality and Social Psychology* 110, no. 3 (2016): 385–406; Hugo Toscano et al., "Physical Strength as a Cue to Dominance: A Data-Driven Approach," *Personality and Social Psychology Bulletin* 42, no. 12 (2016): 1,603–16.

16 Laura Van Berkel et al., "Hierarchy, Dominance, and Deliberation: Egalitarian Values Require Mental Effort," *Personality and Social Psychology Bulletin* 41, no. 9 (2015): 1,207–22; Nir Halevy, Eileen Y. Chou, and Adam D. Galinsky, "A Functional Model of Hierarchy: Why, How, and When Vertical Differentiation Enhances Group Performance," *Organizational Psychology Review* 1, no. 1 (2011): 32–52; Larissa Z. Tiedens and Alison R. Fragale, "Power Moves: Complementarity in Dominant and Submissive Nonverbal Behavior," *Journal of Personality and Social Psychology* 84, no. 3 (2003): 558–68; Emily M. Zitek and Larissa Z. Tiedens, "The Fluency of Social Hierarchy: The Ease with Which Hierarchical Relationships Are Seen, Remembered, Learned, and Liked," *Journal of Personality and Social Psychology* 102, no. 1 (2012): 98–115; Daniel A. McFarland, Dan Jurafsky, and Craig Rawlings, "Making the Connection: Social Bonding in Courtship Situations,"

American Journal of Sociology 118, no. 6 (2013): 1,596–649; Roy F. Baumeister and Kathleen D. Vohs, "Sexual Economics: Sex as Female Resource for Social Exchange in Heterosexual Interactions," *Personality and Social Psychology Review* 8, no. 4 (2004): 339–63.

17 Author interview, Nov. 10, 2015.

18 Van Berkel et al., "Hierarchy, Dominance, and Deliberation"; Halevy, Chou, and Galinsky, "Functional Model of Hierarchy"; Tiedens and Fragale, "Power Moves"; Zitek and Tiedens, "Fluency of Social Hierarchy"; McFarland, Jurafsky, and Rawlings, "Making the Connection"; Baumeister and Vohs, "Sexual Economics."

19 Pierre Bourdieu, *Distinction: A Social Critique of the Judgement of Taste* (Cambridge, Mass.: Harvard University Press, 1984).

20 Bourdieu, *Distinction*; Adam Howard, *Learning Privilege: Lessons of Power and Identity in Affluent Schooling* (New York: Taylor & Francis, 2008); William H. Sewell and Vimal P. Shah, "Social Class, Parental Encouragement, and Educational Aspirations," *American Journal of Sociology* 73, no. 5 (1968): 559–72; Susan T. Fiske and Hazel Rose Markus, eds., *Facing Social Class: How Societal Rank Influences Interaction* (New York: Russell Sage Foundation, 2012); Jessi Streib, "Class Reproduction by Four Year Olds," *Qualitative Sociology* 34, no. 2 (2011): 337–52; Bernice Lott, "The Social Psychology of Class and Classism," *American Psychologist* 67, no. 8 (2012): 650–58; Daniel Potter and Josipa Roksa, "Accumulating Advantages over Time: Family Experiences and Social Class Inequality in Academic Achievement," *Social Science Research* 42, no. 4 (2013): 1,018–32; S. Michael Gaddis, "The Influence of Habitus in the Relationship Between Cultural Capital and Academic Achievement," *Social Science Research* 42, no. 1 (2013): 1–13; Nicole M. Stephens, Hazel Rose Markus, and L. Taylor Phillips, "Social Class Culture Cycles: How Three Gateway Contexts Shape Selves and Fuel Inequality," *Annual Review of Psychology* 65 (2014): 611–34; Annette Lareau, "Cultural Knowledge and Social Inequality," *American Sociological Review* 80, no. 1 (2015): 1–27; Anthony Abraham Jack, "(No) Harm in Asking: Class, Acquired Cultural Capital, and Academic Engagement at an Elite University," *Sociology of Education* 89, no. 1 (2016): 1–19; Mads Meier Jæger and Richard Breen, "A Dynamic Model of Cultural Reproduction," *American Journal of Sociology* 121, no. 4 (2016): 1,079–115; Sue Ellen Henry, "Bodies at Home and at School: Toward a Theory of Embodied Social Class Status," *Educational Theory* 63, no. 1 (2013): 1–16; Omar Lizardo, "The Cognitive Origins of Bourdieu's Habitus," *Journal for the Theory of Social Behaviour* 34, no. 4 (2004): 375–401.

21 John M. Darley and Paget H. Gross, "A Hypothesis-Confirming Bias in Labeling Effects," *Journal of Personality and Social Psychology* 44, no. 1 (1983): 20–33; Gloria B. Solomon, "Improving Performance by Means of Action-Cognition Coupling in Athletes and Coaches," in *Performance Psychology: Perception, Action, Cognition, and Emotion,* ed. Markus Raab et al. (San Diego: Academic Press, 2016), 87–101.

22 Lisa Dawn Hamilton et al., "Social Neuroendocrinology of Status: A Review and Future Directions," *Adaptive Human Behavior and Physiology* 1 (2015): 202–30; Kathleen V. Casto and David A. Edwards, "Testosterone, Cortisol, and Human Competition," *Hormones and Behavior* 82 (2016): 21–37; Peter B. Gray, Timothy S. McHale, and Justin M. Carré, "A Review of Human Male Field Studies of Hormones and Behavioral Reproductive Effort," *Hormones and Behavior* (2016); Matthew J. Fuxjager et al., "Winning Territorial Disputes Selectively Enhances Androgen Sensitivity in Neural Pathways Related to Motivation and Social Aggression," *Proceedings of the National Academy of Sciences* 107, no. 27 (2010): 12,393–98; Justin M. Carré et al., "Changes in Testosterone Mediate the Effect of Winning on Subsequent Aggressive Behaviour," *Psychoneuroendocrinology* 38, no. 10 (2013): 2,034–41; Neha A. John-Henderson et al., "The Role of Interpersonal Processes in Shaping Inflammatory Responses to Social-Evaluative Threat," *Biological Psychology* 110 (2015): 134–37; A. B. Losecaat Vermeer, I. Riečanský, and C. Eisenegger, "Competition, Testosterone, and Adult Neurobehavioral Plasticity," *Progress in Brain Research* 229 (2016): 213–38; Julie L. Hall, Steven J. Stanton, and Oliver C. Schultheiss, "Biopsychological and Neural Processes of Implicit Motivation," in *Implicit Motives,* ed. Oliver Schultheiss and Joachim Brunstein (New York: Oxford University Press, 2010); Erik L. Knight and Pranjal H. Mehta, "Hormones and Hierarchies," in *The Psychology of Social Status,* ed. Joey T. Cheng, Jessica L. Tracy, and Cameron Anderson (New York: Springer, 2014), 269–301.

23 Cameron Anderson et al., "The Local-Ladder Effect: Social Status and Subjective Well-Being," *Psychological Science* 23, no. 7 (2012): 764–71; Fred Luthans, Carolyn M. Youssef-Morgan, and Bruce J. Avolio, *Psychological Capital and Beyond* (New York: Oxford University Press, 2015), 45–78.

24 Eva Ranehill et al., "Assessing the Robustness of Power Posing: No Effect on Hormones and Risk Tolerance in a Large Sample of Men and Women," *Psychological Science* 26, no. 5 (2015): 653–56; Andrew Gelman and Kaiser Fung, "The Power of the 'Power Pose': Amy Cuddy's Famous Finding Is the Latest Example of Scientific Overreach," *Slate,* Jan. 19, 2016, www.slate.com/articles/health_and_science/sci ence/2016/01/amy_cuddy_s_power_pose_research_is_the_latest_example_of_sci entific_overreach.html. Dana Carney's paper refuting power poses is available at faculty.haas.berkeley.edu/dana_carney/pdf_My%20position%20on%20power %20poses.pdf. Booth et al., "Testosterone, and Winning and Losing in Human Competition."

25 Robert M. Sapolsky, "The Influence of Social Hierarchy on Primate Health," *Science* 308, no. 5722 (2005): 648–52. See also Erik L. Knight and Pranjal H. Mehta, "Hierarchy Stability Moderates the Effect of Status on Stress and Performance in Humans," *Proceedings of the National Academy of Sciences* 114, no. 1 (2017): 78–83.

26 K. Dedovic, C. D'Aguiar, and J. C. Pruessner, "What Stress Does to Your Brain: A Review of Neuroimaging Studies," *Canadian Journal of Psychiatry* 54 (2009): 6–15;

J. Amat et al., "Previous Experience with Behavioral Control over Stress Blocks the Behavioral and Dorsal Raphe Nucleus Activating Effects of Later Uncontrollable Stress: Role of the Ventral Medial Prefrontal Cortex," *Journal of Neuroscience* 26 (2006): 13,264–72; Sally S. Dickerson and Margaret E. Kemeny, "Acute Stressors and Cortisol Responses: A Theoretical Integration and Synthesis of Laboratory Research," *Psychological Bulletin* 130, no. 3 (2004): 355–91; Robert M. Sapolsky, "Stress and the Brain: Individual Variability and the Inverted-U," *Nature Neuroscience* 18, no. 10 (2015): 1,344–46; J. John Mann et al., "Neurobiology of Severe Mood and Anxiety Disorders," in *Basic Neurochemistry: Principles of Molecular, Cellular, and Medical Neurobiology,* ed. Scott T. Brady et al., 8th ed. (Waltham, MA: Academic Press, 2012), 1,021–36.

27 Arthur M. Glenberg, "Embodiment as a Unifying Perspective for Psychology," *Wiley Interdisciplinary Reviews: Cognitive Science* 1, no. 4 (2010): 586–96.

28 Andrei Cimpian, Yan Mu, and Lucy C. Erickson, "Who Is Good at This Game? Linking an Activity to a Social Category Undermines Children's Achievement," *Psychological Science* 23, no. 5 (2012): 533–41.

29 Jaap J. A. Denissen, Marcel A. G. van Aken, and Brent W. Roberts, "Personality Development Across the Life Span," in Chamorro-Premuzic, von Stumm, and Furnham, *Wiley-Blackwell Handbook of Individual Differences,* 86; A. Cimpian and E. M. Markman, "The Generic/Nongeneric Distinction Influences How Children Interpret New Information about Social Others," *Child Development* 82, no. 2 (2011): 471–92; Michael S. North and Susan T. Fiske, "Social Categories Create and Reflect Inequality: Psychological and Sociological Insights," in Cheng, Tracy, and Anderson, *Psychology of Social Status,* 243–65; Mark R. Leary, Katrina P. Jongman-Sereno, and Kate J. Diebels, "The Pursuit of Status: A Self-Presentational Perspective on the Quest for Social Value," in Cheng, Tracy, and Anderson, *Psychology of Social Status*; Dana H. Lindsley, Daniel J. Brass, and James B. Thomas, "Efficacy-Performing Spirals: A Multilevel Perspective," *Academy of Management Review* 20, no. 3 (1995): 645–78.

30 Daeun Park et al., "How Do Generic Statements Impact Performance? Evidence for Entity Beliefs," *Developmental Science* (2016): 1–8.

31 Carol Dweck, *Mindset: The New Psychology of Success* (New York: Random House, 2006); Lisa S. Blackwell, Kali H. Trzesniewski, and Carol Dweck, "Implicit Theories of Intelligence Predict Achievement across an Adolescent Transition: A Longitudinal Study and an Intervention," *Child Development* 78, no. 1 (2007): 246–63; Claudia M. Mueller and Carol S. Dweck, "Praise for Intelligence Can Undermine Children's Motivation and Performance," *Journal of Personality and Social Psychology* 75, no. 1 (1998): 33–52; Andrei Cimpian, "The Impact of Generic Language about Ability on Children's Achievement Motivation," *Developmental Psychology* 46, no. 5 (2010): 1,333–40.

32 Andrei Cimpian and Erika Salomon, "The Inherence Heuristic: An Intuitive Means of Making Sense of the World, and a Potential Precursor to Psychological Essentialism," *Behavioral and Brain Sciences* 37, no. 5 (2014): 461–80.

33 See also Carol Lynn Martin, "Children's Use of Gender-Related Information in Making Social Judgments," *Developmental Psychology* 25, no. 1 (1989): 80–88.

34 Cecilia Ridgeway, "The Social Construction of Status Value: Gender and Other Nominal Characteristics," *Social Forces* 70, no. 2 (1991): 367–86; Susan T. Fiske, "Interpersonal Stratification: Status, Power, and Subordination," in Fiske, Gilbert, and Lindzey, *Handbook of Social Psychology*, 941–82; Noah P. Mark, Lynn Smith-Lovin, and Cecilia L. Ridgeway, "Why Do Nominal Characteristics Acquire Status Value? A Minimal Explanation for Status Construction," *American Journal of Sociology* 115, no. 3 (2009): 832–62.

35 Matthias Sutter and Daniela Glätzle-Rützler, "Gender Differences in the Willingness to Compete Emerge Early in Life and Persist," *Management Science* 61, no. 10 (2014): 2,339–54; Anna Dreber, Emma von Essen, and Eva Ranehill, "Gender and Competition in Adolescence: Task Matters," *Experimental Economics* 17, no. 1 (2014): 154–72.

36 Karen P. Maruska, "Social Transitions Cause Rapid Behavioral and Neuroendocrine Changes," *Integrative and Comparative Biology* 55, no. 2 (2015): 294–306; Wendy Wood and Alice H. Eagly, "Biosocial Construction of Sex Differences and Similarities in Behavior," *Advances in Experimental Social Psychology* 46, no. 1 (2012): 55–123; Aïna Chalabaev et al., "The Influence of Sex Stereotypes and Gender Roles on Participation and Performance in Sport and Exercise: Review and Future Directions," *Psychology of Sport and Exercise* 14, no. 2 (2013): 136–44; Wendy Wood and Alice H. Eagly, "Biology or Culture Alone Cannot Account for Human Sex Differences and Similarities," *Psychological Inquiry* 24, no. 3 (2013): 241–47; Janet Shibley Hyde, "Gender Similarities and Differences," *Annual Review of Psychology* 65 (2014): 373–98; Sari M. van Anders, Jeffrey Steiger, and Katherine L. Goldey, "Effects of Gendered Behavior on Testosterone in Women and Men," *Proceedings of the National Academy of Sciences* 112, no. 45 (2015): 13,805–10.

37 Ridgeway and Nakagawa, "Status."

38 Author interview, Aug. 9, 2015.

39 Pranjal H. Mehta and Robert A. Josephs, "Testosterone and Cortisol Jointly Regulate Dominance: Evidence for a Dual-Hormone Hypothesis," *Hormones and Behavior* 58, no. 5 (2010): 898–906; Pranjal H. Mehta, Amanda C. Jones, and Robert A. Josephs, "The Social Endocrinology of Dominance: Basal Testosterone Predicts Cortisol Changes and Behavior Following Victory and Defeat," *Journal of Personality and Social Psychology* 94, no. 6 (2008): 1,078–93; Justin M. Carré and Pranjal H. Mehta, "Importance of Considering Testosterone-Cortisol Interactions in Predicting Human Aggression and Dominance," *Aggressive Behavior* 37, no. 6 (2011): 489–91.

40 Arline T. Geronimus et al., "'Weathering' and Age Patterns of Allostatic Load Scores among Blacks and Whites in the United States," *American Journal of Public Health* 96, no. 5 (2006): 826–33; George A. Bonanno et al., "Psychological Resilience after Disaster: New York City in the Aftermath of the September 11th Terrorist Attack," *Psychological Science* 17, no. 3 (2006): 181–86; George A. Bonanno et al., "What Predicts Psychological Resilience after Disaster? The Role of

Demographics, Resources, and Life Stress," *Journal of Consulting and Clinical Psychology* 75, no. 5 (2007): 671–82; Robert-Paul Juster, Bruce S. McEwen, and Sonia J. Lupien, "Allostatic Load Biomarkers of Chronic Stress and Impact on Health and Cognition," *Neuroscience and Biobehavioral Reviews* 35, no. 1 (2010): 2–16; Clyde Hertzman and Tom Boyce, "How Experience Gets under the Skin to Create Gradients in Developmental Health," *Annual Review of Public Health* 31 (2010): 329–47; Bruce S. McEwen, "Brain on Stress: How the Social Environment Gets under the Skin," *Proceedings of the National Academy of Sciences* 109, no. S2 (2012): 17,180–85; S. Jay Olshansky et al., "Differences in Life Expectancy Due to Race and Educational Differences Are Widening, and Many May Not Catch Up," *Health Affairs* 31, no. 8 (2012): 1,803–13; Pilyoung Kim et al., "Effects of Childhood Poverty and Chronic Stress on Emotion Regulatory Brain Function in Adulthood," *Proceedings of the National Academy of Sciences* 110, no. 46 (2013): 18,442–47; Bruce S. McEwen et al., "Mechanisms of Stress in the Brain," *Nature Neuroscience* 18, no. 10 (2015): 1,353–63; Rachel E. Norman et al., "Trait Anxiety Moderates the Relationship between Testosterone Responses to Competition and Aggressive Behavior," *Adaptive Human Behavior and Physiology* 1, no. 3 (2015): 312–24; Jon K. Maner et al., "Dispositional Anxiety Blocks the Psychological Effects of Power," *Personality and Social Psychology Bulletin* 38, no. 11 (2012): 1,383–95; Lorenz Goette et al., "Stress Pulls Us Apart: Anxiety Leads to Differences in Competitive Confidence under Stress," *Psychoneuroendocrinology* 54 (2015): 115–23; Vander Molen, "Fear of Negative Evaluation Modulates Electrocortical and Behavioral Responses When Anticipating Social Evaluative Feedback"; E. R. Montoya et al., "Cortisol Administration Induces Global Down-Regulation of the Brain's Reward Circuitry," *Psychoneuroendocrinology* 47 (2014): 31–42.

41 Roland G. Fryer and Steven D. Levitt, "An Empirical Analysis of the Gender Gap in Mathematics," *American Economic Journal: Applied Economics* 2, no. 2 (2010): 210–40.

42 Angelica Moè and Francesca Pazzaglia, "Following the Instructions! Effects of Gender Beliefs in Mental Rotation," *Learning and Individual Differences* 16 (2006): 369–77; Tuulia M. Ortner and Monika Sieverding, "Where Are the Gender Differences? Male Priming Boosts Spatial Skills in Women," *Sex Roles* 59, no. 3 (2008): 274–81; Angelica Moè, "Are Males Always Better than Females in Mental Rotation? Exploring a Gender Belief Explanation," *Learning and Individual Differences* 19, no. 1 (2009): 21–27; Zachary Estes and Sydney Felker, "Confidence Mediates the Sex Difference in Mental Rotation Performance," *Archives of Sexual Behavior* 41 (2012): 557–70; Sarah Neuburger et al., "A Threat in the Classroom: Gender Stereotype Activation and Mental-Rotation Performance in Elementary-School Children," *Zeitschrift für Psychologie* (2015). See also Michelle G., "Picture Yourself as a Stereotypical Male," MIT Admissions Blog, mitadmissions.org/blogs/entry/picture-yourself-as-a-stereotypical-male.

43 Emily R. Kaskan and Ivy K. Ho, "Microaggressions and Female Athletes," *Sex Roles* 74, no. 7–8 (2016): 275–87; Aïna Chalabaev et al., "Can Stereotype Threat Affect

Motor Performance in the Absence of Explicit Monitoring Processes? Evidence Using a Strength Task," *Journal of Sport and Exercise Psychology* 35, no. 2 (2013): 211–15; Caroline Heidrich and Suzete Chiviacowsky, "Stereotype Threat Affects the Learning of Sport Motor Skills," *Psychology of Sport and Exercise* 18 (2015): 42–46; Johanna M. Hermann and Regina Vollmeyer, "'Girls Should Cook, Rather than Kick!'—Female Soccer Players under Stereotype Threat," *Psychology of Sport and Exercise* 26 (2016): 94–101.

44 Steven J. Spencer, Christine Logel, and Paul G. Davies, "Stereotype Threat," *Annual Review of Psychology* 67 (2016): 415–37; Michael Inzlicht et al., "Lingering Effects: Stereotype Threat Hurts More than You Think," *Social Issues and Policy Review* 5, no. 1 (2011): 227–56; Wendy Berry Mendes and Jeremy Jamieson, "Embodied Stereotype Threat: Exploring Brain and Body Mechanisms Underlying Performance Impairments," *Stereotype Threat: Theory, Process, and Application* (2011): 51–68; Colleen M. Ganley et al., "An Examination of Stereotype Threat Effects on Girls' Mathematics Performance," *Developmental Psychology* 49, no. 10 (2013): 1,886–97; Anne M. Koenig and Alice H. Eagly, "Stereotype Threat in Men on a Test of Social Sensitivity," *Sex Roles* 52, no. 7–8 (2005): 489–96; Neil A. Lewis and Denise Sekaquaptewa, "Beyond Test Performance: A Broader View of Stereotype Threat," *Current Opinion in Psychology* 11 (2016): 40–43; Lana J. Ozen and Myra A. Fernandes, "Effects of 'Diagnosis Threat' on Cognitive and Affective Functioning Long after Mild Head Injury," *Journal of the International Neuropsychological Society* 17, no. 2 (2011): 219–29.

45 Vincent Pillaud, David Rigaud, and Alain Clémence, "The Influence of Chronic and Situational Social Status on Stereotype Susceptibility," *PLoS ONE* 10, no. 12 (2015): e0144582; Sandra Ludwig, Gerlinde Fellner-Röhling, and Carmen Thoma, "Do Women Have More Shame than Men? An Experiment on Self-Assessment and the Shame of Overestimating Oneself," *European Economic Review* 92 (2017): 31–46.

46 Formal clothing: Hajo Adam and Adam Galinsky, "Enclothed Cognition," *Journal of Experimental Social Psychology* 48 (2012): 918–25; Sandra Blakeslee, "Mind Games: Sometimes a White Coat Isn't Just a White Coat," *New York Times,* April 2, 2012, www.nytimes.com/2012/04/03/science/clothes-and-self-perception.html; Michael L. Slepian et al., "The Cognitive Consequences of Formal Clothing," *Social Psychological and Personality Science* 6, no. 6 (2015): 661–68.

47 Judee K. Burgoon and Norah E. Dunbar, "Nonverbal Expressions of Dominance and Power in Human Relationships," *The Sage Handbook of Nonverbal Communication,* ed. Valerie Manusov and Miles L. Patterson (New York: Sage, 2006), 279–99.

48 Cameron Anderson and Gavin J. Kilduff, "Why Do Dominant Personalities Attain Influence in Face-to-Face Groups? The Competence-Signaling Effects of Trait Dominance," *Journal of Personality and Social Psychology* 96, no. 2 (2009): 491–503.

49 Alison Wood Brooks, "Get Excited: Reappraising Pre-performance Anxiety as Excitement," *Journal of Experimental Psychology: General* 143, no. 3 (2014): 1,144–58;

Jeremy P. Jamieson, Wendy Berry Mendes, and Matthew K. Nock, "Improving Acute Stress Responses: The Power of Reappraisal," *Current Directions in Psychological Science* 22, no. 1 (2013): 51–56; Neha A. John-Henderson, Michelle L. Rheinschmidt, and Rodolfo Mendoza-Denton, "Cytokine Responses and Math Performance: The Role of Stereotype Threat and Anxiety Reappraisals," *Journal of Experimental Social Psychology* 56 (2015): 203–6; Adam L. Alter et al., "Rising to the Threat: Reducing Stereotype Threat by Reframing the Threat as a Challenge," *Journal of Experimental Social Psychology* 46, no. 1 (2010): 166–71.

50 Caroline F. Keating, "Why and How the Silent Self Speaks Volumes: Functional Approaches to Nonverbal Impression Management," in Manusov and Patterson, *Sage Handbook of Nonverbal Communication,* 321–40; Caroline F. Keating, "Charismatic Faces: Social Status Cues Put Face Appeal in Context," in *Facial Attractiveness: Evolutionary, Cognitive, and Social Perspectives,* ed. G. Rhodes and L. A. Zebrowitz (Westport, CT: Ablex, 2002), 153–92.

51 Author interview, Aug. 9, 2015.

52 Derald Wing Sue, *Microaggressions in Everyday Life: Race, Gender, and Sexual Orientation* (Hoboken, NJ: John Wiley & Sons, 2010); Derald Wing Sue et al., "Racial Microaggressions in Everyday Life: Implications for Clinical Practice," *American Psychologist* 62, no. 4 (2007): 271–86; Mesmin Destin and Régine Debrosse, "Upward Social Mobility and Identity," *Current Opinion in Psychology* 18 (2017): 99–104.

53 C. D. Hardin and E. Tory Higgins, "Shared Reality: How Social Verification Makes the Subjective Objective," in *Handbook of Motivation and Cognition,* ed. R. M. Sorrentino and E. Tory Higgins (New York: Guilford Press, 1996), 28–84; Ivy Yee-Man Lau, Chi-Yue Chiu, and Sau-Lai Lee, "Communication and Shared Reality: Implications for the Psychological Foundations of Culture," *Social Cognition* 19, no. 3 (2001): 350–71; William Samuelson and Richard Zeckhauser, "Status Quo Bias in Decision Making," *Journal of Risk and Uncertainty* 1, no. 1 (1988): 7–59; Young Eun Huh, Joachim Vosgerau, and Carey K. Morewedge, "Social Defaults: Observed Choices Become Choice Defaults," *Journal of Consumer Research* 41, no. 3 (2014): 746–60. See discussion in Mkael Symmonds and Raymond J. Dolan, "The Neurobiology of Preferences," in Dolan and Sharot, *Neuroscience of Preference and Choice,* 3–31; Cimpian and Salomon, "The Inherence Heuristic"; Scott Eidelman and Christian S. Crandall, "Bias in Favor of the Status Quo," *Social and Personality Psychology Compass* 6, no. 3 (2012): 270–81; Daniel Kahneman, Jack L. Knetsch, and Richard H. Thaler, "Anomalies: The Endowment Effect, Loss Aversion, and Status Quo Bias," *Journal of Economic Perspectives* 5, no. 1 (1991): 193–206; Scott Eidelman and Christian S. Crandall, "A Psychological Advantage for the Status Quo," in *Social and Psychological Bases of Ideology and System Justification,* ed. John T. Jost, Aaron C. Kay, and Hulda Thorisdottir (New York: Oxford University Press, 2009), 85–106; Carolyn L. Hafer and Becky L. Choma, "Belief in a Just World, Perceived Fairness, and Justification of the Status Quo," in Jost, Kay,

and Thorisdottir, *Social and Psychological Bases of Ideology and System Justification,* 107–25.

54 Emily Pronin, Daniel Y. Lin, and Lee Ross, "The Bias Blind Spot: Perceptions of Bias in Self versus Others," *Personality and Social Psychology Bulletin* 28, no. 3 (2002): 369–81; Emily Pronin, "Perception and Misperception of Bias in Human Judgment," *Trends in Cognitive Sciences* 11, no. 1 (2007): 37–43; cf. Emily Pronin, "Perception and Misperception of Bias in Human Judgment," *Trends in Cognitive Science* 11, no. 1 (2006); Glenn D. Reeder, "Attribution as a Gateway to Social Cognition," in *The Oxford Handbook of Social Cognition,* ed. Donal E. Carlston (New York: Oxford University Press, 2013), 95–117.

55 Monica Biernat and Diane Kobrynowicz, "Gender- and Race-Based Standards of Competence: Lower Minimum Standards but Higher Ability Standards for Devalued Groups," *Journal of Personality and Social Psychology* 72, no. 3 (1997): 544–57; Christian S. Crandall and Amy Eshleman, "A Justification-Suppression Model of the Expression and Experience of Prejudice," *Psychological Bulletin* 129, no. 3 (2003): 414–46; Uhlmann and Cohen, "Constructed Criteria"; Emilio J. Castilla, "Gender, Race, and Meritocracy in Organizational Careers," *American Journal of Sociology* 113, no. 6 (2008): 1,479–526; Monica Biernat, *Standards and Expectancies: Contrast and Assimilation in Judgments of Self and Others* (New York: Psychology Press, 2005); Ridgeway and Nakagawa, "Status"; Steven Foy et al., "Emotions and Affect as Source, Outcome, and Resistance to Inequality," in McLeod, Lawler, and Schwalbe, *Handbook of the Social Psychology of Inequality,* 295–324; Monica Biernat, "Stereotypes and Shifting Standards," in *Handbook of Prejudice, Stereotyping, and Discrimination,* ed. Todd D. Nelson (New York: Psychology Press, 2009), 137–52; Gregory M. Walton and Geoffrey L. Cohen, "A Question of Belonging: Race, Social Fit, and Achievement," *Journal of Personality and Social Psychology* 92, no. 1 (2007): 82–96; Magee and Galinsky, "Social Hierarchy"; Devah Pager, Bruce Western, and Bart Bonikowski, "Discrimination in a Low-Wage Labor Market: A Field Experiment," *American Sociological Review* 74, no. 5 (2009): 777–99; Martha Foschi, "Double Standards for Competence: Theory and Research," *Annual Review of Sociology* 26 (2000): 21–42; Monica Biernat and Kathleen Fuegen, "Shifting Standards and the Evaluation of Competence: Complexity in Gender-Based Judgment and Decision Making," *Journal of Social Issues* 57, no. 4 (2001): 707–24; Emilio J. Castilla and Stephen Benard, "The Paradox of Meritocracy in Organizations," *Administrative Science Quarterly* 55, no. 4 (2010): 543–676.

56 Shannon K. McCoy and Brenda Major, "Priming Meritocracy and the Psychological Justification of Inequality," *Journal of Experimental Social Psychology* 43 (2007): 341–51; Miguel M. Unzueta, Brian S. Lowery, and Eric D. Knowles, "How Believing in Affirmative Action Quotas Protects White Men's Self-Esteem," *Organizational Behavior and Human Decision Processes* 105, no. 1 (2008): 1–13; Michael I. Norton and Samuel R. Sommers, "Whites See Racism as a Zero-Sum Game That They Are Now Losing," *Perspectives on Psychological Science* 6, no. 3 (2011): 215–18; Eric D. Knowles

and Brian S. Lowery, "Meritocracy, Self-Concerns, and Whites' Denial of Racial Inequity," *Self and Identity* 11, no. 2 (2012): 202–12; Jennifer Katherine Bosson et al., "American Men's and Women's Beliefs about Gender Discrimination: For Men, It's Not Quite a Zero-Sum Game," *Masculinities and Social Change* 1, no. 3 (2012): 210–39; Clara L. Wilkins, Joseph D. Wellman, and Cheryl R. Kaiser, "Status Legitimizing Beliefs Predict Positivity Toward Whites Who Claim Anti-white Bias," *Journal of Experimental Social Psychology* 49, no. 6 (2013): 1,114–19; Shannon K. McCoy et al., "Is the Belief in Meritocracy Palliative for Members of Low Status Groups? Evidence for a Benefit for Self-Esteem and Physical Health via Perceived Control," *European Journal of Social Psychology* 43 (2013): 307–18; Clara L. Wilkins and Cheryl R. Kaiser, "Racial Progress as Threat to the Status Hierarchy: Implications for Perceptions of Anti-white Bias," *Psychological Science* 25, no. 2 (2014): 439–46; Miguel M. Unzueta, Benjamin A. Everly, and Angélica S. Gutiérrez, "Social Dominance Orientation Moderates Reactions to Black and White Discrimination Claimants," *Journal of Experimental Social Psychology* 54 (2014): 81–88; Christopher W. Bauman, Sophie Trawalter, and Miguel M. Unzueta, "Diverse According to Whom? Racial Group Membership and Concerns about Discrimination Shape Diversity Judgments," *Personality and Social Psychology Bulletin* 40, no. 10 (2014): 1,354–72; Evelyn R. Carter and Mary C. Murphy, "Group-Based Differences in Perceptions of Racism: What Counts, to Whom, and Why?," *Social and Personality Psychology Compass* 9, no. 6 (2015): 269–80.

57 Shai Davidai and Thomas Gilovich, "The Headwinds/Tailwinds Asymmetry: An Availability Bias in Assessments of Barriers and Blessings," *Journal of Personality and Social Psychology* 111, no. 6 (2016): 835–51; Peggy McIntosh, "White Privilege: Unpacking the Invisible Knapsack," in *Re-visioning Family Therapy: Race, Culture, and Gender in Clinical Practice,* ed. Monica McGoldrick (New York: Guilford Press, 1998), 147–52; L. Taylor Phillips and Brian S. Lowery; "The Hard-Knock Life? Whites Claim Hardships in Response to Racial Inequity," *Journal of Experimental Social Psychology* 61 (2015): 12–18; Isaac F. Young and Daniel Sullivan, "Competitive Victimhood: A Review of the Theoretical and Empirical Literature," *Current Opinion in Psychology* 11 (2016): 30–34.

58 Roy F. Baumeister et al., "Bad Is Stronger than Good," *Review of General Psychology* 5, no. 4 (2001): 323–70; Clara L. Wilkins et al., "You Can Win but I Can't Lose: Bias against High-Status Groups Increases Their Zero-Sum Beliefs about Discrimination," *Journal of Experimental Social Psychology* 57 (2015): 1–14; Tessa L. Dover, Brenda Major, and Cheryl R. Kaiser, "Members of High-Status Groups Are Threatened by Pro-diversity Organizational Messages," *Journal of Experimental Social Psychology* 62 (2016): 58–67.

59 Jessica E. Koski, Hongling Xie, and Ingrid R. Olson, "Understanding Social Hierarchies: The Neural and Psychological Foundations of Status Perception," *Social Neuroscience* 10, no. 5 (2015): 527–50; Maarten A. S. Boksem et al., "Social Status Determines How We Monitor and Evaluate Our Performance," *Social Cognitive*

and Affective Neuroscience 7, no. 3 (2012): 304–13; Michael W. Kraus and Jun W. Park, "The Undervalued Self: Social Class and Self-Evaluation," *Frontiers in Psychology* 5, no. 1404 (2014); Jie Hu et al., "Low Social Status Decreases the Neural Salience of Unfairness," *Frontiers in Behavioral Neuroscience* 8, no. 402 (2014); Jie Hu et al., "Social Status Modulates the Neural Response to Unfairness," *Social Cognitive and Affective Neuroscience* 11, no. 1 (2016): 1–10.

60 Laurie T. O'Brien and Christian S. Crandall, "Perceiving Self-Interest: Power, Ideology, and Maintenance of the Status Quo," *Social Justice Research* 18, no. 1 (2005): 1–24.

61 Michael E. McCullough et al., "Rumination, Fear, and Cortisol: An In Vivo Study of Interpersonal Transgressions," *Health Psychology* 26, no. 1 (2007): 126–32; Louisa C. Michl et al., "Rumination as a Mechanism Linking Stressful Life Events to Symptoms of Depression and Anxiety: Longitudinal Evidence in Early Adolescents and Adults," *Journal of Abnormal Psychology* 122, no. 2 (2013): 339–52; Hannes Rakoczy, Felix Warneken, and Michael Tomasello, "The Sources of Normativity: Young Children's Awareness of the Normative Structure of Games," *Developmental Psychology* 44, no. 3 (2008): 875–81; Joshua W. Buckholtz, "Social Norms, Self-Control, and the Value of Antisocial Behavior," *Current Opinion in Behavioral Sciences* 3 (2015): 122–29; Rick O'Gorman, David Sloan Wilson, and Ralph R. Miller, "An Evolved Cognitive Bias for Social Norms," *Evolution and Human Behavior* 29, no. 2 (2008): 71–78; Julie C. Coultas and Edwin J. C. van Leeuwen, "Conformity: Definitions, Types, and Evolutionary Grounding," in Zeigler-Hill, Welling, and Shackelford, *Evolutionary Perspectives on Social Psychology,* 189–202; Michael Tomasello and Amrisha Vaish, "Origins of Human Cooperation and Morality," *Annual Review of Psychology* 64 (2013): 231–55.

62 Gardner Lindzey, Martin Manosevitz, and Harvey Winston, "Social Dominance in the Mouse," *Psychonomic Science* 5, no. 11 (1966): 451–52; G. J. Syme, "Competitive Orders as Measures of Social Dominance," *Animal Behaviour* 22, no. 4 (1974): 931–40; Serge Guimond et al., "Social Comparison, Self-Stereotyping, and Gender Differences in Self-Construals," *Journal of Personality and Social Psychology* 90, no. 2 (2006): 221–42; Wendy Wood and Alice H. Eagly, "Biosocial Construction of Sex Differences and Similarities in Behavior;" Katherine E. Powers, Robert S. Chavez, and Todd F. Heatherton, "Individual Differences in Response of Dorsomedial Prefrontal Cortex," *Social Cognitive and Affective Neuroscience* (2015); Anderson, John, and Keltner, "Personal Sense of Power"; Christopher von Rueden, "The Roots and Fruits of Social Status in Small-Scale Human Societies," in Cheng, Tracy, and Anderson, *Psychology of Social Status,* 180–81.

63 Guimond et al., "Social Comparison, Self-Stereotyping, and Gender Differences in Self-Construals"; Wood and Eagly, "Biosocial Construction of Sex Differences and Similarities in Behavior"; Koski, Xie, and Olson, "Understanding Social Hierarchies"; Peter Mende-Siedlecki, Yang Cai, and Alexander Todorov, "The Neural Dynamics of Updating Person Impressions," *Social Cognitive and Affective Neuroscience*

8, no. 6 (2013): 623–31; Powers, Chavez, and Heatherton, "Individual Differences in Response of Dorsomedial Prefrontal Cortex"; Anderson, John, and Keltner, "Personal Sense of Power"; von Rueden, "Roots and Fruits of Social Status in Small-Scale Human Societies," 180–81.

64 Amber R. Massey-Abernathy, Jennifer Byrd-Craven, and CaSandra L. Swearingen, "The Biological Diary of a Woman: Physiological Consequences of Status and Social Evaluative Threat," *Evolutionary Psychological Science* 1, no. 1 (2015): 37–43.

65 Email exchange with author, Sept. 18, 2015.

66 Patrick M. Egan and Edward R. Hirt, "Flipping the Switch: Power, Social Dominance, and Expectancies of Mental Energy Change," *Personality and Social Psychology Bulletin* 41, no. 3 (2015): 336–50; Barbara L. Fredrickson and Tomi-Ann Roberts, "Objectification Theory: Toward Understanding Women's Lived Experiences and Mental Health Risks," *Psychology of Women Quarterly* 21, no. 2 (1997): 173–206; Bonnie Moradi and Yu-Ping Huang, "Objectification Theory and Psychology of Women: A Decade of Advances and Future Directions," *Psychology of Women Quarterly* 32, no. 4 (2008): 377–98; Keely A. Muscatell et al., "Social Status Modulates Neural Activity in the Mentalizing Network," *NeuroImage* 60, no. 3 (2012): 1,771–77.

67 Toscano et al., "Physical Strength as a Cue to Dominance"; William B. Strean and Joseph P. Mills, "The Body and Performance," in *The Oxford Handbook of Sport and Performance Psychology,* ed. Shane M. Murphy (New York: Oxford University Press, 2012); Michael M. Kasumovic and Jeffrey H. Kuznekoff, "Insights into Sexism: Male Status and Performance Moderates Female-Directed Hostile and Amicable Behaviour," *PLoS ONE* 10, no. 7 (2015): e0131613; Eftychia Stamkou et al., "How Norm Violations Shape Social Hierarchies: Those on Top Block Norm Violators from Rising Up," *Group Processes and Intergroup Relations* 19, no. 5 (2016): 608–29; Park and Crocker, "Contingencies of Self-Worth and Responses to Negative Interpersonal Feedback."

68 Joseph A. Vandello and Jennifer K. Bosson, "Hard Won and Easily Lost: A Review and Synthesis of Theory and Research on Precarious Manhood," *Psychology of Men and Masculinity* 14, no. 2 (2013): 101–13; Kevin S. Weaver and Theresa K. Vescio, "The Justification of Social Inequality in Response to Masculinity Threats," *Sex Roles* 72 (2015): 521–35; Ekaterina Netchaeva, Maryam Kouchaki, and Leah D. Sheppard, "A Man's (Precarious) Place: Men's Experienced Threat and Self-Assertive Reactions to Female Superiors," *Personality and Social Psychology Bulletin* 41, no. 9 (2015): 1,247–59.

69 Mary C. Murphy and Valerie Jones Taylor, "The Role of Situational Cues in Signaling and Maintaining Stereotype Threat," in *Stereotype Threat: Theory, Process, and Application,* ed. Michael Inzlicht and Toni Schmader (New York: Oxford University Press, 2012), 17–33; Paul G. Davies, Steven J. Spencer, and Claude M. Steele, "Clearing the Air: Identity Safety Moderates the Effects of Stereotype Threat on

Women's Leadership Aspirations," *Journal of Personality and Social Psychology* 88, no. 2 (2005): 276–87.

70 Geoffrey L. Cohen et al., "Reducing the Racial Achievement Gap: A Social-Psychological Intervention," *Science* 313, no. 5791 (2006): 1,307–10. List of values available at science.sciencemag.org/content/suppl/2006/08/29/313.5791.1307.DC1.

71 Karen O'Leary, Siobhan O'Neill, and Samantha Dockray, "A Systematic Review of the Effects of Mindfulness Interventions on Cortisol," *Journal of Health Psychology* 21, no. 9 (2016): 2,108–21.

CHAPTER 6: FIND YOUR THING

1 David Epstein, *The Sports Gene: Inside the Science of Extraordinary Athletic Performance* (New York: Current/Penguin, 2013), 27–33.

2 K. Anders Ericsson and Robert Pool, *Peak: Secrets from the New Science of Expertise* (New York: Houghton Mifflin Harcourt, 2016).

3 Joseph Durso, "Fearless Fosbury Flops to Glory," *New York Times,* Oct. 20, 1968, www.nytimes.com/packages/html/sports/year_in_sports/10.20.html; Simon Burnton, "50 Stunning Olympic Moments No. 28: Dick Fosbury Introduces 'the Flop,'" *Guardian,* May 8, 2012, www.theguardian.com/sport/blog/2012/may/08/50–stunning-olympic-moments-dick-fosbury.

4 Peter M. McGinnis, *Biomechanics of Sport and Exercise,* 3rd ed. (Champaign, IL: Human Kinetics, 2013), 149–50.

5 Ruud J. R. Den Hartigh et al., "A Dynamic Network Model to Explain the Development of Excellent Human Performance," *Frontiers in Psychology* 7, no. 532 (2016). See also Robert Gaschler et al., "Playing Off the Curve: Testing Quantitative Predictions of Skill Acquisition Theories in Development of Chess Performance," *Frontiers in Psychology* 5, no. 923 (2014); Fernand Gobet and Morgan H. Ereku, "Checkmate to Deliberate Practice: The Case of Magnus Carlsen," *Frontiers in Psychology* 5, no. 878 (2014): 148.

6 Author interview, Aug. 8, 2016.

7 Michael D. Roberts and Chad M. Kerksick, "Vitamins/Minerals: Invaluable Cellular Components for Optimal Physiological Function," in *Nutrient Timing: Metabolic Optimization for Health, Performance, and Recovery,* ed. Chad M. Kerksick (Boca Raton, FL: CRC Press, 2012), 81; D. G. MacArthur and K. N. North, "Genes and Human Elite Athletic Performance," *Human Genetics* 116, no. 5 (2005): 331–39; Claude Bouchard and Robert M. Malina, "Genetics of Physiological Fitness and Motor Performance," *Exercise and Sport Sciences Reviews* 11, no. 1 (1983): 306; Nir Eynon et al., "Genes and Elite Athletes: A Roadmap for Future Research," *Journal of Physiology* 589, no. 13 (2011): 3,063–70; S. Voisin et al., "Exercise Training and DNA Methylation in Humans," *Acta Physiologica* 213, no. 1 (2015): 39–59; Ildus I. Ahmetov et al., "Genes and Athletic Performance: An Update," in *Genetics and Sports,* ed. M. Posthumus and M. Collins, 2nd ed. (Basel:

Karger, 2016), 41–54; Marleen H. M. De Moor et al., "Genome-Wide Linkage Scan for Athlete Status in 700 British Female DZ Twin Pairs," *Twin Research and Human Genetics* 10, no. 6 (2007): 812–20.

8 Tim Rees et al., "The Great British Medalists Project: A Review of Current Knowledge on the Development of the World's Best Sporting Talent," *Sports Medicine* 46, no. 8 (2016): 1,041–58; Ildus I. Ahmetov and Olga N. Fedotovskaya, "Current Progress in Sports Genomics," *Advances in Clinical Chemistry* 70 (2015): 247–314.

9 Ahmetov et al., "Genes and Athletic Performance."

10 Sharon A. Plowman and Denise L. Smith, *Exercise Physiology for Health, Fitness, and Performance*, 4th ed. (Baltimore: Lippincott Williams & Wilkins, 2014), 528–36.

11 Naotaka Sakai and Satoshi Shimawaki, "Measurement of a Number of Indices of Hand and Movement Angles in Pianists with Overuse Disorders," *Journal of Hand Surgery, European Volume* 35, no. 6 (2010): 494–98; C. H. Wagner, "The Pianist's Hand: Anthropometry and Biomechanics," *Ergonomics* 31, no. 1 (1988): 97–131.

12 Shinichi Furuya et al., "Secrets of Virtuoso: Neuromuscular Attributes of Motor Virtuosity in Expert Musicians," *Scientific Reports* 5, no. 15750 (2015): 1–8, doi:10.1038/srep15750.

13 Daniel F. Chambliss, "The Mundanity of Excellence: An Ethnographic Report on Stratification and Olympic Swimmers," *Sociological Theory* 7, no. 1 (1989): 70–86.

14 Author interview, Sept. 15, 2016.

15 Davidai and Gilovich, "Headwinds/Tailwinds Asymmetry"; Robert H. Frank, "Why Luck Matters More Than You Might Think," *The Atlantic,* May 2016, http://www.theatlantic.com/magazine/archive/2016/05/why-luck-matters-more-than-you-might-think/476394/; Jesse Singal, "Why Americans Ignore the Role of Luck in Everything," *New York,* May 12, 2016, http://nymag.com/scienceofus/2016/05/why-americans-ignore-the-role-of-luck-in-everything.html.

16 Author interview, Aug. 12, 2016.

17 Halttunen, *Confidence Men and Painted Women,* 206.

18 Neil Charness et al., "The Role of Deliberate Practice in Chess Expertise," *Applied Cognitive Psychology* 19, no. 2 (2005): 151–65.

19 Miriam A. Mosing et al., "Practice Does Not Make Perfect: No Causal Effect of Music Practice on Music Ability," *Psychological Science* 25, no. 9 (2014): 1,795–803.

20 Karl Anders Ericsson, Ralf T. Krampe, and Clemens Tesch-Römer, "The Role of Deliberate Practice in the Acquisition of Expert Performance," *Psychological Review* 100, no. 3 (1993): 363–406. Stops at the age of six: Plowman and Smith, *Exercise Physiology for Health, Fitness, and Performance,* 83, 528–36.

21 Author interview, Sept. 15, 2016.

22 Tilmann A. Klein et al., "Genetically Determined Differences in Learning from Errors," *Science* 318, no. 5856 (2007): 1,642–45; Sylvia M. L. Cox et al., "Striatal D1 and D2 Signaling Differentially Predict Learning from Positive and Negative Outcomes," *NeuroImage* 109 (2015): 95–101; Jean-Claude Dreher et al., "Variation in Dopamine Genes Influences Responsivity of the Human Reward System," *Proceedings of the National Academy of Sciences* 106, no. 2 (2009): 617–22; Dara G.

Ghahremani et al., "Striatal Dopamine D2/D3 Receptors Mediate Response Inhibition and Related Activity in Frontostriatal Neural Circuitry in Humans," *Journal of Neuroscience* 32, no. 21 (2012): 7,316–24.

23 Donny M. Camera, William J. Smiles, and John A. Hawley, "Exercise-Induced Skeletal Muscle Signaling Pathways and Human Athletic Performance," *Free Radical Biology and Medicine* 98 (2016): 131–43; N. Jones et al., "A Genetic-Based Algorithm for Personalized Resistance Training," *Biology of Sport* 33, no. 2 (2016): 117–26.

24 Paul Farhi, "Where the Rich and Elite Meet to Compete," *Washington Post,* Feb. 5, 2006, www.washingtonpost.com/wp-dyn/content/article/2006/02/03/AR2006020302280.html.

25 Chambliss, "Mundanity of Excellence."

26 Adele Diamond and Daphne S. Ling, "Conclusions about Interventions, Programs, and Approaches for Improving Executive Functions That Appear Justified and Those That, Despite Much Hype, Do Not," *Developmental Cognitive Neuroscience* 18 (2016): 34–48; Duarte Araújo et al., "The Role of Ecological Constraints on Expertise Development," *Talent Development and Excellence* 2, no. 2 (2010): 165–79.

27 Gregory D. Myer et al., "Sport Specialization, Part I: Does Early Sports Specialization Increase Negative Outcomes and Reduce the Opportunity for Success in Young Athletes?," *Sports Health* 7, no. 5 (2015): 437–42; Gregory D. Myer et al., "Sports Specialization, Part II: Alternative Solutions to Early Sport Specialization in Youth Athletes," *Sports Health* 8, no. 1 (2016): 65–73; Robert F. LaPrade et al., "AOSSM Early Sport Specialization Consensus Statement," *Orthopaedic Journal of Sports Medicine* 4, no. 4 (2016).

28 Rhodri S. Lloyd et al., "National Strength and Conditioning Association Position Statement on Long-Term Athletic Development," *Journal of Strength and Conditioning Research* 30, no. 6 (2016): 1,491–509.

29 Thomas Lin, "How Badminton Helped Federer's Game," *New York Times,* May 29, 2009, straightsets.blogs.nytimes.com/2009/05/29/not-just-tennis/?_r=1.

30 Ericsson, Krampe, and Tesch-Romer, "Role of Deliberate Practice in the Acquisition of Expert Performance." Additional data on percentage of winning: Joanne Ruthsatz et al., "Becoming an Expert in the Musical Domain: It Takes More than Just Practice," *Intelligence* 36, no. 4 (2008): 330–38.

31 Ethan Zell, Mark D. Alicke, and Jason E. Strickhouser, "Referent Status Neglect: Winners Evaluate Themselves Favorably Even When the Competitor Is Incompetent," *Journal of Experimental Social Psychology* 56 (2015): 18–23; cf. Hamilton et al., "Social Neuroendocrinology of Status": Casto and Edwards, "Testosterone, Cortisol, and Human Competition"; Gray, McHale, and Carré, "Review of Human Male Field Studies of Hormones and Behavioral Reproductive Effort"; Fuxjager et al., "Winning Territorial Disputes Selectively Enhances Androgen Sensitivity in Neural Pathways Related to Motivation and Social Aggression"; Carré et al., "Changes in Testosterone Mediate the Effect of Winning on Subsequent Aggressive

Behaviour"; John-Henderson et al., "Role of Interpersonal Processes in Shaping Inflammatory Responses to Social-Evaluative Threat"; Losecaat Vermeer, Riečanský, and Eisenegger, "Competition, Testosterone, and Adult Neurobehavioral Plasticity"; Hewitt, "Social Construction of Self-Esteem."

32 Clay B. Holroyd et al., "When Is an Error Not a Prediction Error? An Electrophysiological Investigation," *Cognitive, Affective, and Behavioral Neuroscience* 9, no. 1 (2009): 59–70. Interested in outcomes: Nick Yeung, Clay B. Holroyd, and Jonathan D. Cohen, "ERP Correlates of Feedback and Reward Processing in the Presence and Absence of Response Choice," *Cerebral Cortex* 15, no. 5 (2005): 535–44; Matthew M. Walsh and John R. Anderson, "Learning from Experience: Event-Related Potential Correlates of Reward Processing, Neural Adaptation, and Behavioral Choice," *Neuroscience and Biobehavioral Reviews* 36, no. 8 (2012): 1,870–84; Ullsperger, Danielmeier, and Jocham, "Neurophysiology of Performance Monitoring and Adaptive Behavior."

33 L. Verburgh et al., "The Key to Success in Elite Athletes? Explicit and Implicit Motor Learning in Youth Elite and Non-elite Soccer Players," *Journal of Sports Sciences* 34, no. 18 (2016): 1,782–90; Patrícia Coutinho, Isabel Mesquita, and António M. Fonseca, "Talent Development in Sport: A Critical Review of Pathways to Expert Performance," *International Journal of Sports Science and Coaching* 11, no. 2 (2016): 279–93; Pablo Greco, Daniel Memmert, and Juan C. P. Morales, "The Effect of Deliberate Play on Tactical Performance in Basketball," *Perceptual and Motor Skills* 110, no. 3 (2010): 849–56; Paul R. Ford et al., "The Role of Deliberate Practice and Play in Career Progression in Sport: The Early Engagement Hypothesis," *High Ability Studies* 20, no. 1 (2009): 65–75.

34 Matt Richtel, "How Big Data Is Playing Recruiter for Specialized Workers," *New York Times,* April 27, 2013, www.nytimes.com/2013/04/28/technology/how-big-data-is-playing-recruiter-for-specialized-workers.html?pagewanted=all&_r=1&#_jmp0_; Adam Sandel, "Vivienne Ming: The Transformative Power of Being Yourself," *Advocate,* Nov. 26, 2013, www.advocate.com/business/2013/11/26/vivienne-ming-transformative-power-being-yourself/; Zach Church, "Facing Down Employment Discrimination with an Algorithm: Vivienne Ming on Where Meritocracy Fails, and How Big Data Might Help," *MIT,* Oct. 13, 2016, mitsloan.mit.edu/newsroom/articles/facing-down-employment-discrimination-with-an-algorithm/; Becky Catherine Harris, "This Man Changed His Name from José to Joe and Immediately Got More Job Interviews," *BuzzFeed,* Aug. 30, 2014, www.buzzfeed.com/beckycatherineharris/jose-vs-joe; Jenny Anderson, "A Scientist Calculated the Cost of Not Being a Straight Man, and She Wants a Tax Cut," *Quartz,* March 7, 2016, qz.com/631455/a-scientist-cacluated-the-cost-of-not-being-a-straight-man-and-she-wants-a-tax-cut/.

35 Author interview, March 24, 2015.

36 Zell, Alicke, and Strickhouser, "Referent Status Neglect"; cf. Hamilton et al., "Social Neuroendocrinology of Status"; Casto and Edwards, "Testosterone, Cortisol,

and Human Competition"; Gray, McHale, and Carré, "Review of Human Male Field Studies of Hormones and Behavioral Reproductive Effort"; Fuxjager et al., "Winning Territorial Disputes Selectively Enhances Androgen Sensitivity in Neural Pathways Related to Motivation and Social Aggression"; Carré et al., "Changes in Testosterone Mediate the Effect of Winning on Subsequent Aggressive Behaviour"; John-Henderson et al., "Role of Interpersonal Processes in Shaping Inflammatory Responses to Social-Evaluative Threat"; Losecaat Vermeer, Riečanský, and Eisenegger, "Competition, Testosterone, and Adult Neurobehavioral Plasticity"; Hewitt, "Social Construction of Self-Esteem."

37 Coutinho, Mesquita, and Fonseca, "Talent Development in Sport"; Araújo et al., "Role of Ecological Constraints on Expertise Development"; Megan A. Rendell et al., "Implicit Practice for Technique Adaptation in Expert Performers," *International Journal of Sports Science and Coaching* 6, no. 4 (2011): 553–66.

38 Author interview, Aug. 8, 2016.

39 Mathieu Roy, Daphna Shohamy, and Tor D. Wager, "Ventromedial Prefrontal Subcortical Systems and the Generation of Affective Meaning," *Trends in Cognitive Sciences* 16, no. 3 (2012): 147–56.

40 Amy Winecoff et al., "Ventromedial Prefrontal Cortex Encodes Emotional Value," *Journal of Neuroscience* 33, no. 27 (2013): 11,032–39; Andreja Bubic and Anna Abraham, "Neurocognitive Bases of Future Oriented Cognition," *Review of Psychology* 21, no. 1 (2014): 3–15; Yaacov Trope and N. Liberman, "Temporal Construal"; Roland G. Benoit, Karl K. Szpunar, and Daniel L. Schacter, "Ventromedial Prefrontal Cortex Supports Affective Future Simulation by Integrating Distributed Knowledge," *Proceedings of the National Academy of Sciences* 111, no. 46 (2014): 16,550–55. See also Schultheiss and Wirth, "Biopsychological Aspects of Motivation."

41 Author interview, Feb. 23, 2015.

42 Brent L. Hughes and Jamil Zaki, "The Neuroscience of Motivated Cognition," *Trends in Cognitive Sciences* 19, no. 2 (2015): 62–64; Clayton R. Critcher and Melissa J. Ferguson, "'Whether I Like It or Not, It's Important': Implicit Importance of Means Predicts Self-Regulatory Persistence and Success," *Journal of Personality and Social Psychology* 110, no. 6 (2016): 818–39.

43 James E. Maddux, "Self-Efficacy: The Power of Believing You Can," in Snyder and Lopez, *Oxford Handbook of Positive Psychology*, 335–43; Albert Bandura, "Self-Efficacy: Toward a Unifying Theory of Behavioral Change," *Psychological Review* 84, no. 2 (1977): 191–215; Albert Bandura, "Self-Efficacy Mechanism in Human Agency," *American Psychologist* 37, no. 2 (1982): 122–47; Alexander D. Stajkovic and Fred Luthans, "Self-Efficacy and Work-Related Performance: A Meta-analysis," *Psychological Bulletin* 124, no. 2 (1998): 240–61; Barry J. Zimmerman, "Self-Efficacy: An Essential Motive to Learn," *Contemporary Educational Psychology* 25, no. 1 (2000): 82–91; Mark R. Beauchamp, Ben Jackson, and Katie L. Morton, "Efficacy Beliefs and Human Performance: From Independent Action to Interpersonal Functioning," in Murphy, *Oxford Handbook of Sport and Performance Psychology*, 273–93.

44 Andrei Cimpian et al., "Subtle Linguistic Cues Affect Children's Motivation," *Psychological Science* 18, no. 4 (2007): 314–16; Gabriele Wulf and Rebecca Lewthwaite, "Optimizing Performance through Intrinsic Motivation and Attention for Learning: The Optimal Theory of Motor Learning," *Psychonomic Bulletin and Review* 23, no. 5 (2016): 1–33.

45 Kristin L. Sommer and Roy F. Baumeister, "Self-Evaluation, Persistence, and Performance Following Implicit Rejection: The Role of Trait Self-Esteem," *Personality and Social Psychology Bulletin* 28, no. 7 (2002): 926–38; Roy F. Baumeister et al., "Does High Self-Esteem Cause Better Performance, Interpersonal Success, Happiness, or Healthier Lifestyles?," *Psychological Science in the Public Interest* 4, no. 1 (2003): 1–44; Tiffiny Bernichon, Kathleen E. Cook, and Jonathon D. Brown, "Seeking Self-Evaluative Feedback: The Interactive Role of Global Self-Esteem and Specific Self-Views," *Journal of Personality and Social Psychology* 84, no. 1 (2003): 194–204; Jennifer Crocker and Amy Canevello, "Self and Identity: Dynamics of Persons and Their Situations," in Deaux and Snyder, *Oxford Handbook of Personality and Social Psychology,* 263–86.

46 David Shenk, "The 32-Million Word Gap," *Atlantic,* March 9, 2010, www.theatlantic.com/technology/archive/2010/03/the-32-million-word-gap/36856/.

47 Jason Weaver, Jennifer Filson Moses, and Mark Snyder, "Self-Fulfilling Prophecies in Ability Settings," *Journal of Social Psychology* 156, no. 2 (2016): 179–89; Gloria B. Solomon, "The Influence of Coach Expectations on Athlete Development," *Journal of Sport Psychology in Action* 1, no. 2 (2010): 76–85; Marcia A. Wilson and Dawn E. Stephens, "Great Expectations: An Examination of the Differences between High and Low Expectancy Athletes' Perception of Coach Treatment," *Journal of Sport Behavior* 30, no. 3 (2007): 358–73; Athanasios Mouratidis et al., "The Motivating Role of Positive Feedback in Sport and Physical Education: Evidence for a Motivational Model," *Journal of Sport and Exercise Psychology* 30, no. 2 (2008): 240–68.

48 Gabriele Wulf, Charles Shea, and Rebecca Lewthwaite, "Motor Skill Learning and Performance: A Review of Influential Factors," *Medical Education* 44 (2010): 75–84.

49 Kaitlin Woolley and Ayelet Fishbach, "Immediate Rewards Predict Adherence to Long-Term Goals," *Personality and Social Psychology Bulletin* 43, no. 2 (2017): 151–62; Kaitlin Woolley and Ayelet Fishbach, "Harnessing Immediate Rewards to Increase Intrinsic Motivation," in *The Motivation-Cognition Interface: From the Lab to the Real World,* ed. C. Kopetz and Ayelet Fishbach (New York: Routledge, 2017), home.uchicago.edu/~kwoolley/IntrinsicMotivationChapter.pdf; Julius Kuhl, Markus Quirin, and Sander L. Koole, "Being Someone: The Integrated Self as a Neuropsychological System," *Social and Personality Psychology Compass* 9, no. 3 (2015): 115–32; Nora H. Hope et al., "The Humble Path to Progress: Goal-Specific Aspirational Content Predicts Goal Progress and Goal Vitality," *Personality and Individual Differences* 90 (2016): 99–107.

50 Charles S. Carver and Michael F. Scheier, "Goals and Emotion," in *Handbook of Cognition and Emotion,* ed. Michael D. Robinson, Edward R. Watkins, and Eddie Harmon-Jones (New York: Guilford Press, 2013), 176–95; A. Fishbach, J. Steinmetz, and Y. Tu, "Motivation in a Social Context: Coordinating Personal and Shared Goal Pursuits with Others," in *Advances in Motivation Science* (New York: Elsevier, 2016), 3: 35–79.

51 J. Richard Eiser and Russell H. Fazio, "How Approach and Avoidance Decisions Influence Attitude Formation and Change," in Elliot, *Handbook of Approach and Avoidance Motivation.*

CHAPTER 7: CHECK YOURSELF PRIOR TO WRECKING YOURSELF

1 Interviews with Sivers at CD Baby in Portland, Oregon, Sept. 2007; Eliot Van Buskirk, "Derek Sivers Sold CD Baby for $22 Million, Giving Most of It Away," *Wired,* Oct. 24, 2008, www.wired.com/2008/10/derek-sivers-so/.

2 Everett M. Rogers, *Diffusion of Innovations,* 5th ed. (New York: Free Press, 2003).

3 Angela Lee Duckworth and Eli Tsukayama, "Domain-Specificity in Self-Control," in *Character: New Directions from Philosophy, Psychology, and Theology,* ed. Christian B. Miller et al. (New York: Oxford University Press, 2015), 393–411.

4 Kira O. McCabe and William Fleeson, "Are Traits Useful? Explaining Trait Manifestations as Tools in the Pursuit of Goals," *Journal of Personality and Social Psychology* 110, no. 2 (2016): 287–301. For an excellent look at the full impact of time scarcity, see Sendhil Mullainathan and Eldar Shafir, *The New Science of Having Less and How It Defines Our Lives* (New York: Picador, 2014).

5 DeYoung, "Cybernetic Big Five Theory." General discussion of cybernetics and personality: Moskowitz, "Representation and Regulation of Goals."

6 Elliot T. Berkman, "Self-Regulation Training," in *Handbook of Self-Regulation: Research, Theory, and Applications,* ed. K. D. Vohs and R. F. Baumeister, 3rd ed. (New York: Guilford Press, 2016): 440–57; Carver and Scheier, "Self-Regulation of Action and Affect." See also Giulio Costantini and Marco Perugini, "The Network of Conscientiousness," *Journal of Research in Personality* 65 (2016): 68–88.

7 Eva Krapohl et al., "The High Heritability of Educational Achievement Reflects Many Genetically Influenced Traits, Not Just Intelligence," *Proceedings of the National Academy of Sciences* 111, no. 42 (2014): 15,273–78.

8 First referred to as noncognitive traits in Samuel Bowles and Herbert Gintis, *Schooling in Capitalist America* (New York: Basic Books, 1976), 57: 135. Point made in George Farkas, "Cognitive Skills and Noncognitive Traits and Behaviors in Stratification Processes," *Annual Review of Sociology* 29 (2003): 541–62. See also Arthur E. Poropat, "A Meta-analysis of the Five-Factor Model of Personality and Academic Performance," *Psychological Bulletin* 135, no. 2 (2009): 322–38; Daniel A. Briley, Matthew Domiteaux, and Elliot M. Tucker-Drob, "Achievement-Relevant Personality: Relations with the Big Five and Validation of an Efficient Instrument,"

Learning and Individual Differences 32 (2014) 26–39; Erik E. Noftle and Richard W. Robins, "Personality Predictors of Academic Outcomes: Big Five Correlates of GPA and SAT Scores," *Journal of Personality and Social Psychology* 93, no. 1 (2007): 116–30; Marcus Credé and Nathan R. Kuncel, "Study Habits, Skills, and Attitudes: The Third Pillar Supporting Collegiate Academic Performance," *Perspectives on Psychological Science* 3, no. 6 (2008): 425–53; Terrie E. Moffitt et al., "A Gradient of Childhood Self-Control Predicts Health, Wealth, and Public Safety," *Proceedings of the National Academy of Sciences* 108, no. 7 (2011): 2,693–98. Grit doesn't add anything beyond conscientiousness: Kaili Rimfeld et al., "True Grit and Genetics: Predicting Academic Achievement from Personality," *Journal of Personality and Social Psychology* 111, no. 5 (2016): 780–89; Barbara Dumfart and Aljoscha C. Neubauer, "Conscientiousness Is the Most Powerful Noncognitive Predictor of School Achievement in Adolescents," *Journal of Individual Differences* 37, no. 1 (2016): 8–15.

9 Marcus Credé, Michael C. Tynan, and Peter D. Harms, "Much Ado About Grit: A Meta-analytic Synthesis of the Grit Literature," *Journal of Personality and Social Psychology* 113, no. 3 (2017): 492–511; Angela L. Duckworth and Martin E. P. Seligman, "The Science and Practice of Self-Control," *Perspectives on Psychological Science* 12, no. 5 (2017): 715–18.

10 Chambliss, "Mundanity of Excellence."

11 Daniel J. Ozer and Veronica Benet-Martinez, "Personality and the Prediction of Consequential Outcomes," *Annual Review of Psychology* 57 (2006): 401–21; Carver and Scheier, "Self-Regulation of Action and Affect." See also Costantini and Perugini, "Network of Conscientiousness"; David J. Bridgett et al., "Intergenerational Transmission of Self-Regulation: A Multidisciplinary Review and Integrative Conceptual Framework," *Psychological Bulletin* 141, no. 3 (2015): 602–54.

12 Francesca Righetti and Catrin Finkenauer, "If You Are Able to Control Yourself, I Will Trust You: The Role of Perceived Self-Control in Interpersonal Trust," *Journal of Personality and Social Psychology* 100, no. 5 (2011): 874–86.

13 Christopher F. Chabris et al., "The Fourth Law of Behavior Genetics," *Current Directions in Psychological Science* 24, no. 4 (2015): 304–12.

14 Walter Mischel, Yuichi Shoda, and Monica I. Rodriguez, "Delay of Gratification in Children," *Science* 244, no. 4907 (1989): 933–38.

15 Jean-Claude Dreher et al., "Variation in Dopamine Genes Influences Responsivity of the Human Reward System," *Proceedings of the National Academy of Sciences* 106, no. 2 (2009): 617–22; Konstantin A. Pavlov, Dimitry A. Chistiakov, and Vladimir P. Chekhonin, "Genetic Determinants of Aggression and Impulsivity in Humans," *Journal of Applied Genetics* 53, no. 1 (2012): 61–82; Catharine A. Winstanley et al., "Double Dissociation Between Serotonergic and Dopaminergic Modulation of Medial Prefrontal and Orbitofrontal Cortex During a Test of Impulsive Choice," *Cerebral Cortex* 16, no. 1 (2006): 106–14; David Goldman, *Our Genes, Our Choices: How Genotype and Gene Interactions Affect Behavior* (New York: Academic Press, 2012), 21–23; Aaron A. Duke et al., "Revisiting the Serotonin-Aggression

Relation in Humans: A Meta-analysis," *Psychological Bulletin* 139, no. 5 (2013): 1,148–72; Benjamin T. Saunders and Terry E. Robinson, "Individual Variation in Resisting Temptation: Implications for Addiction," *Neuroscience and Biobehavioral Reviews* 37, no. 9 (2013): 1,955–75; Pierre Trifilieff and Diana Martinez, "Imaging Addiction: D2 Receptors and Dopamine Signaling in the Striatum as Biomarkers for Impulsivity," *Neuropharmacology* 76 (2014): 498–509; Marci R. Mitchell and Marc N. Potenza, "Recent Insights into the Neurobiology of Impulsivity," *Current Addiction Reports* 1, no. 4 (2014): 309–19; Bridgett et al., "Intergenerational Transmission of Self-Regulation."

16 B. J. Casey et al., "Behavioral and Neural Correlates of Delay of Gratification 40 Years Later," *Proceedings of the National Academy of Sciences* 108, no. 36 (2011): 14,998–15,003.

17 E. Tory Higgins et al., "Achievement Orientations from Subjective Histories of Success: Promotion Pride versus Prevention Pride," *European Journal of Social Psychology* 31, no. 1 (2001): 3–23; Jason P. Mitchell et al., "Medial Prefrontal Cortex Predicts Intertemporal Choice," *Journal of Cognitive Neuroscience* 23, no. 4 (2011): 857–66.

18 Author interview, Aug. 29, 2016; Daniel W. Belsky et al., "The Genetics of Success: How Single-Nucleotide Polymorphisms Associated with Educational Attainment Relate to Life-Course Development," *Psychological Science* 27, no. 7 (2016): 957–72; Mitchell et al., "Medial Prefrontal Cortex Predicts Intertemporal Choice."

19 Author interview, Aug. 29, 2016.

20 Walter Mischel and Ervin Staub, "Effects of Expectancy on Working and Waiting for Larger Reward," *Journal of Personality and Social Psychology* 2, no. 5 (1965): 625–33.

21 Richard T. Walls and Tennie S. Smith, "Development of Preference for Delayed Reinforcement in Disadvantaged Children," *Journal of Educational Psychology* 61, no. 2 (1970): 118–23.

22 Laura Michaelson et al., "Delaying Gratification Depends on Social Trust," *Frontiers in Psychology* 4, no. 355 (2013), doi:10.3389/fpsyg.2013.00355.

23 Author interview, Oct. 18, 2013.

24 Jutta Beckmann and Heinz Heckhausen, "Motivation as a Function of Expectancy and Incentive," in Heckhausen and Heckhausen, *Motivation and Action,* 101.

25 Paola Giuliano and Antonio Spilimbergo, "Growing up in a Recession," *Review of Economic Studies* 81, no. 2 (2014): 787–817.

26 John J. Ray, "Locus of Control as a Moderator of the Relationship between Level of Aspiration and Achievement Motivation," *Journal of Social Psychology* 124, no. 1 (1984): 131–32; David L. Palenzuela, "Refining the Theory and Measurement of Expectancy of Internal vs External Control of Reinforcement," *Personality and Individual Differences* 9, no. 3 (1988): 607–29; Hielke Buddelmeyer and Nattavudh Powdthavee, "Can Having Internal Locus of Control Insure against Negative Shocks? Psychological Evidence from Panel Data," *Journal of Economic Behavior*

and Organization 122 (2016): 88–109; Korn et al., "Depression Is Related to an Absence of Optimistically Biased Belief Updating about Future Life Events."

27 Cendri A. Hutcherson et al., "Cognitive Regulation during Decision Making Shifts Behavioral Control between Ventromedial and Dorsolateral Prefrontal Value Systems," *Journal of Neuroscience* 32, no. 39 (2012): 13,543–54; Ian C. Ballard et al., "Dorsolateral Prefrontal Cortex Drives Mesolimbic Dopaminergic Regions to Initiate Motivated Behavior," *Journal of Neuroscience* 31, no. 28 (2011): 10,340–46; Todd A. Hare, Shabnam Hakimi, and Antonio Rangel, "Activity in dlPFC and Its Effective Connectivity to vmPFC Are Associated with Temporal Discounting," *Frontiers in Neuroscience* 8 (2014): 50.

28 Todd A. Hare, Colin F. Camerer, and Antonio Rangel, "Self-Control in Decision-Making Involves Modulation of the vmPFC Valuation System," *Science* 324, no. 5927 (2009): 646–48; Todd A. Hare, Jonathan Malmaud, and Antonio Rangel, "Focusing Attention on the Health Aspects of Foods Changes Value Signals in vmPFC and Improves Dietary Choice," *Journal of Neuroscience* 31, no. 30 (2011): 11,077–87; Antonio Rangel, "Regulation of Dietary Choice by the Decision-Making Circuitry," *Nature Neuroscience* 16, no. 12 (2013): 1,717–24; Nicolette Sullivan et al., "Dietary Self-Control Is Related to the Speed with Which Attributes of Healthfulness and Tastiness Are Processed," *Psychological Science* 26, no. 2 (2015): 122–34; Martin Weygandt et al., "Impulse Control in the Dorsolateral Prefrontal Cortex Counteracts Post-diet Weight Regain in Obesity," *NeuroImage* 109 (2015): 318–27.

29 Author interview, Aug. 5, 2016.

30 Note: Physiological mechanisms prevent us from using our brain 24/7. Niels Birbaumer, Sergio Ruiz, and Ranganatha Sitaram, "Learned Regulation of Brain Metabolism," *Trends in Cognitive Sciences* 17, no. 6 (2013): 295–302; Giulio Tononi and Chiara Cirelli, "Sleep and the Price of Plasticity: From Synaptic and Cellular Homeostasis to Memory Consolidation and Integration," *Neuron* 81, no. 1 (2014): 12–34; David Attwell and Alasdair Gibb, "Neuroenergetics and the Kinetic Design of Excitatory Synapses," *Nature Reviews Neuroscience* 6, no. 11 (2005): 841–49. See section on "transient hypofrontality" in Arne Dietrich and Oliver Stoll, "Effortless Attention, Hypofrontality, and Perfectionism," in *Effortless Attention: A New Perspective in the Cognitive Science of Attention and Action,* ed. Brian Bruya (Cambridge, MA: MIT Press, 2010), 159–78; Tom Verguts, Eliana Vassena, and Massimo Silvetti, "Adaptive Effort Investment in Cognitive and Physical Tasks: A Neurocomputational Model," *Frontiers in Behavioral Neuroscience* 9, no. 57 (2015); Adele Diamond, "Executive Functions," *Annual Review of Psychology* 64 (2013): 135–68; Akira Miyake and Naomi P. Friedman, "The Nature and Organization of Individual Differences in Executive Functions: Four General Conclusions," *Current Directions in Psychological Science* 21, no. 1 (2012): 8–14.

31 Lulu Xie et al., "Sleep Drives Metabolite Clearance from the Adult Brain," *Science* 342, no. 6156 (2013): 373–77; Akira Ishii, Masaaki Tanaka, and Yasuyoshi Watanabe, "Neural Mechanisms of Mental Fatigue," *Reviews in the Neurosciences* 25, no.

4 (2014): 469–79; Romain Meeusen and Bart Roelands, "Fatigue: Is It All Neuro-chemistry?," *European Journal of Sport Science* 18, no. 1 (2018): 1–10; Timothy David Noakes, "Fatigue Is a Brain-Derived Emotion That Regulates the Exercise Behavior to Ensure the Protection of Whole Body Homeostasis," *Frontiers in Psychology* 3, no. 82 (2012), doi:10.3389/fphys.2012.00082.

32 Koban and Pourtois, "Brain Systems Underlying the Affective and Social Monitoring of Actions"; Wouter Kool et al., "Neural and Behavioral Evidence for an Intrinsic Cost of Self-Control," *PLoS ONE* 8, no. 8 (2013): e72626; Andrew Westbrook and Todd S. Braver, "Cognitive Effort: A Neuroeconomic Approach," *Cognitive, Affective, and Behavioral Neuroscience* 15, no. 2 (2015): 395–415; Hiroki P. Kotabe and Wilhelm Hofmann, "On Integrating the Components of Self-Control," *Perspectives on Psychological Science* 10, no. 5 (2015): 618–38; S. Thomas Christie and Paul Schrater, "Cognitive Cost as Dynamic Allocation of Energetic Resources," *Frontiers in Neuroscience* 9 (2015); William M. Kelley, Dylan D. Wagner, and Todd F. Heatherton, "In Search of a Human Self-Regulation System," *Annual Review of Neuroscience* 38 (2015): 389–411.

33 Kristien Aarts, Jan De Houwer, and Gilles Pourtois, "Evidence for the Automatic Evaluation of Self-Generated Actions," *Cognition* 124, no. 2 (2012): 117–27; Ullsperger, Danielmeier, and Jocham, "Neurophysiology of Performance Monitoring and Adaptive Behavior"; Koban and Pourtois, "Brain Systems Underlying the Affective and Social Monitoring of Actions"; cf. Amy F. T. Arnsten, "Stress Weakens Prefrontal Networks: Molecular Insults to Higher Cognition," *Nature Neuroscience* 18, no. 10 (2015): 1,376–85; Amy F. T. Arnsten, "Stress Signalling Pathways That Impair Prefrontal Cortex Structure and Function," *Nature Reviews Neuroscience* 10, no. 6 (2009): 410–22; Jamil P. Bhanji, Eunbin S. Kim, and Mauricio R. Delgado, "Perceived Control Alters the Effect of Acute Stress on Persistence," *Journal of Experimental Psychology: General* 145, no. 3 (2016): 356–65.

34 Author interviews with von Sperling, July 24, 2013, and Aug. 2, 2013.

35 Irmgard Tischner and Helen Malson, "Understanding the 'Too Fat' Body and the 'Too Thin' Body: A Critical Psychological Perspective," in *Oxford Handbook of the Psychology of Appearance,* ed. Nichola Rumsey and Diana Harcourt (New York: Oxford University Press, 2012); Henry, "Bodies at Home and at School"; Lizardo, "Cognitive Origins of Bourdieu's Habitus"; Kate Cregan, *The Sociology of the Body: Mapping the Abstraction of Embodiment* (London: SAGE, 2006); Eve Shapiro, "Social Psychology and the Body," in *Handbook of Social Psychology,* ed. John DeLamater and Amanda Ward, 2nd ed. (New York: Springer, 2013), 191–224.

36 Catherine F. Moore et al., "Neuroscience of Compulsive Eating Behavior," *Frontiers in Neuroscience* 11 (2017): 469; David Mathar et al., "Failing to Learn from Negative Prediction Errors: Obesity Is Associated with Alterations in a Fundamental Neural Learning Mechanism," *Cortex* 95 (2017): 222–37; Rea Lehner et al., "Food-Predicting Stimuli Differentially Influence Eye Movements and Goal-Directed Behavior in Normal-Weight, Overweight, and Obese Individuals," *Frontiers in Psychiatry* 8 (2017); Lieneke K. Janssen et al., "Loss of Lateral Prefrontal Cortex

Control in Food-Directed Attention and Goal-Directed Food Choice in Obesity," *NeuroImage* 146 (2017): 148–56.

37 Katrin E. Giel et al., "Stigmatization of Obese Individuals by Human Resource Professionals: An Experimental Study," *BMC Public Health* 12 (2012): 525, www.biomedcentral.com/1471-2458/12/525. Discussion of the relationship between BMI and college: Rebecca Puhl and Kelly D. Brownell, "Bias, Discrimination, and Obesity," *Obesity Research* 9, no. 12 (2001): 788–805; Regina Pingitore et al., "Bias against Overweight Job Applicants in a Simulated Employment Interview," *Journal of Applied Psychology* 79, no. 6 (1994): 909–17; Jens Agerström and Dan-Olof Rooth, "The Role of Automatic Obesity Stereotypes in Real Hiring Discrimination," *Journal of Applied Psychology* 96, no. 4 (2011): 790–805; M. R. Hebl and L. M. Mannix, "The Weight of Obesity in Evaluating Others: A Mere Proximity Effect," *Personality and Social Psychology Bulletin* 29, no. 1 (2003): 28–38.

38 Timothy A. Judge and Daniel M. Cable, "When It Comes to Pay, Do the Thin Win? The Effect of Weight on Pay for Men and Women," *Journal of Applied Psychology* 96, no. 1 (2011): 95–112.

39 Lenny R. Vartanian and Keri M. Silverstein, "Obesity as a Status Cue: Perceived Social Status and the Stereotypes of Obese Individuals," *Journal of Applied Social Psychology* 43 (2013): E319–E328; Lindsay McLaren, "Socioeconomic Status and Obesity," *Epidemiologic Reviews* 29, no. 1 (2007): 29–48; Fred C. Pampel, Patrick M. Krueger, and Justin T. Denney, "Socioeconomic Disparities in Health Behaviors," *Annual Review of Sociology* 36 (2010): 349–70; Karen A. Matthews and Linda C. Gallo, "Psychological Perspectives on Pathways Linking Socioeconomic Status and Physical Health," *Annual Review of Psychology* 62 (2011): 501–30; Jacqueline J. Rivers and Robert A. Josephs, "Dominance and Health: The Role of Social Rank in Physiology and Illness," in Guinote and Vescio, *Social Psychology of Power*, 87–112; N. E. Adler et al., "Relationship of Subjective and Objective Social Status with Psychological and Physiological Functioning: Preliminary Data in Healthy White Women," *Health Psychology: Official Journal of the Division of Health Psychology, American Psychological Association* 19, no. 6 (2000): 586–92.

40 Marina Milyavskaya and Michael Inzlicht, "What's So Great about Self-Control? Examining the Importance of Effortful Self-Control and Temptation in Predicting Real-Life Depletion and Goal Attainment," *Social Psychological and Personality Science* (2017); Michelle R. VanDellen et al., "In Good Company: Managing Interpersonal Resources That Support Self-Regulation," *Personality and Social Psychology Bulletin* 41, no. 6 (2015): 869–82; Michael R. Ent, Roy F. Baumeister, and Dianne M. Tice, "Trait Self-Control and the Avoidance of Temptation," *Personality and Individual Differences* 74 (2015): 12–15; Angela L. Duckworth, Tamar Szabó Gendler, and James J. Gross, "Situational Strategies for Self-Control," *Perspectives on Psychological Science* 11, no. 1 (2016): 35–55; Michelle R. vanDellen, Matthew K. Meisel, and Bridget P. Lynch, "Dynamics of Self-Control in Egocentric Social Networks," *Personality and Individual Differences* 106 (2017): 196–202; Gráinne M. Fitzsimons, Eli J. Finkel, and Michelle R. vanDellen, "Transactive Goal

Dynamics," *Psychological Review* 122, no. 4 (2015): 648–73; Tila M. Pronk and Francesca Righetti, "How Executive Control Promotes Happy Relationships and a Well-Balanced Life," *Current Opinion in Psychology* 1 (2015): 14–17; Denise de Ridder et al., "Taking Stock of Self-Control: A Meta-analysis of How Trait Self-Control Relates to a Wide Range of Behaviors," *Personality and Social Psychology Review* 16, no. 1 (2012): 76–99; Traci Mann, Denise de Ridder, and Kentaro Fujita, "Self-Regulation of Health Behavior: Social Psychological Approaches to Goal Setting and Goal Striving," *Health Psychology* 32, no. 5 (2013): 487–98.

41 Righetti and Finkenauer, "If You Are Able to Control Yourself, I Will Trust You."

42 Milyavskaya and Inzlicht, "What's So Great about Self-Control?"; vanDellen et al., "In Good Company"; Ent, Baumeister, and Tice, "Trait Self-Control and the Avoidance of Temptation"; vanDellen, Meisel, and Lynch, "Dynamics of Self-Control in Egocentric Social Networks"; Fitzsimons, Finkel, and vanDellen, "Transactive Goal Dynamics"; Christy Zhou Koval et al., "The Burden of Responsibility: Interpersonal Costs of High Self-Control," *Journal of Personality and Social Psychology* 108, no. 5 (2015): 750; Jeni L. Burnette et al., "Mind-Sets Matter: A Meta-analytic Review of Implicit Theories and Self-Regulation," *Psychological Bulletin* 139, no. 3 (2013): 655–701.

43 Duckworth, Gendler, and Gross, "Situational Strategies for Self-Control"; Bhatia, "Associations and the Accumulation of Preference"; Todd F. Heatherton and Dylan D. Wagner, "Cognitive Neuroscience of Self-Regulation Failure," *Trends in Cognitive Sciences* 15, no. 3 (2011): 132–39.

44 Elliot T. Berkman et al., "Self-Control as Value-Based Choice," *Current Directions in Psychological Science* 26, no. 5 (2017): 422–28; Hare, Camerer, and Rangel, "Self-Control in Decision-Making Involves Modulation of the vmPFC Valuation System"; Hare, Malmaud, and Rangel, "Focusing Attention on the Health Aspects of Foods Changes Value Signals in vmPFC and Improves Dietary Choice"; Rangel, "Regulation of Dietary Choice by the Decision-Making Circuitry"; Hutcherson et al., "Cognitive Regulation during Decision Making Shifts Behavioral Control Between Ventromedial and Dorsolateral Prefrontal Value Systems"; Sullivan et al., "Dietary Self-Control Is Related to the Speed with Which Attributes of Healthfulness and Tastiness Are Processed"; Weygandt et al., "Impulse Control in the Dorsolateral Prefrontal Cortex Counteracts Post-diet Weight Regain in Obesity"; Walid Briki, "Trait Self-Control: Why People with a Higher Approach (Avoidance) Temperament Can Experience Higher (Lower) Subjective Wellbeing," *Personality and Individual Differences* 120 (2018): 112–17.

45 Woolley and Fishbach, "Immediate Rewards Predict Adherence to Long-Term Goals"; Patty Van Cappellen et al., "Positive Affective Processes Underlie Positive Health Behaviour Change," *Psychology and Health* 33, no. 1 (2018): 77–97; Dominika Kwasnicka et al., "Theoretical Explanations for Maintenance of Behaviour Change: A Systematic Review of Behaviour Theories," *Health Psychology Review* 10, no. 3 (2016): 277–96; Denise de Ridder and Marleen Gillebaart, "Lessons Learned from Trait Self-Control in Well-Being: Making the Case for Routines and

Initiation as Important Components of Trait Self-Control," *Health Psychology Review* 11, no. 1 (2017): 89–99.

46 Christine Haughney, "Every Penny Counts," *New York Times,* July 29, 2007, www
.nytimes.com/2007/07/29/realestate/29cov.html.

47 Crystal L. Park et al., "Daily Stress and Self-Control," *Journal of Social and Clinical Psychology* 35, no. 9 (2016): 738–53; Patrick L. Hill and Joshua J. Jackson, "The Invest-and-Accrue Model of Conscientiousness," *Review of General Psychology* 20, no. 2 (2016): 141–54.

48 vanDellen et al., "In Good Company"; Ent, Baumeister, and Tice, "Trait Self-Control and the Avoidance of Temptation"; vanDellen, Meisel, and Lynch, "Dynamics of Self-Control in Egocentric Social Networks"; Fitzsimons, Finkel, and vanDellen, "Transactive Goal Dynamics"; Zhou Koval et al., "Burden of Responsibility"; Hanna Suh, Philip B. Gnilka, and Kenneth G. Rice, "Perfectionism and Well-Being: A Positive Psychology Framework," *Personality and Individual Differences* 111 (2017): 25–30. Marriage: Brent W. Roberts and Timothy Bogg, "A Longitudinal Study of the Relationships between Conscientiousness and the Social-Environmental Factors and Substance-Use Behaviors That Influence Health," *Journal of Personality* 72, no. 2 (2004): 325–54.

49 Author interview, Sept. 15, 2016.

50 June P. Tangney, Roy F. Baumeister, and Angie Luzio Boone, "High Self-Control Predicts Good Adjustment, Less Pathology, Better Grades, and Interpersonal Success," *Journal of Personality* 72, no. 2 (2004): 271–324.

51 Hester R. Trompetter, Elian de Kleine, and Ernst T. Bohlmeijer, "Why Does Positive Mental Health Buffer against Psychopathology? An Exploratory Study on Self-Compassion as a Resilience Mechanism and Adaptive Emotion Regulation Strategy," *Cognitive Therapy and Research* 41, no. 3 (2017): 459–68; Suh, Gnilka, and Rice, "Perfectionism and Well-Being."

52 Author interview, Aug. 29, 2016; Belsky et al., "Genetics of Success."

53 Hargie, *Skilled Interpersonal Communication,* 100; Barone, Maddux, and Snyder, *Social Cognitive Psychology,* 52–54; Rotter, "Generalized Expectancies for Internal versus External Control of Reinforcement"; Rotter, "Some Problems and Misconceptions Related to the Construct of Internal versus External Control of Reinforcement"; Rotter, "Internal versus External Control of Reinforcement"; Korn et al., "Depression Is Related to an Absence of Optimistically Biased Belief Updating about Future Life Events."

54 Adam B. Cohen and Michael E. W. Varnum, "Beyond East vs. West: Social Class, Region, and Religion as Forms of Culture," *Current Opinion in Psychology* 8 (2016): 5–9; Adam B. Cohen, "Many Forms of Culture," *American Psychologist* 64, no. 3 (2009): 194–204; Heejung S. Kim and Joni Y. Sasaki, "Cultural Neuroscience: Biology of the Mind in Cultural Contexts," *Annual Review of Psychology* 65 (2014): 487–514; Michèle Lamont, Stefan Beljean, and Matthew Clair, "What Is Missing? Cultural Processes and Causal Pathways to Inequality," *Socio-economic Review* 12, no. 3 (2014): 573–608.

55 Tomasello, *Natural History of Human Thinking*, 7.

56 Brent W. Roberts, Patrick L. Hill, and Jordan P. Davis, "How to Change Conscientiousness: The Sociogenomic Trait Intervention Model," *Personality Disorders:
Theory, Research, and Treatment* 8, no. 3 (2017): 199–205; Marleen Gillebaart and
Denise de Ridder, "Effortless Self-Control: A Novel Perspective on Response Conflict Strategies in Trait Self-Control," *Social and Personality Psychology Compass* 9,
no. 2 (2015): 88–99.

CHAPTER 8: YOU HAD ME AT HELLO

1 Elements of Steinberg's story are taken from an interview with him on June 26,
2014, and his book *Super Agent* (New York: St. Martin's Press, 2014). Kathleen E.
Mitchell, Al S. Levin, and John D. Krumboltz, "Planned Happenstance: Constructing Unexpected Career Opportunities," *Journal of Counseling and Development* 77, no. 2 (1999): 115–24; Tom Pelissero, "Leigh Steinberg: Can He Return to
Superagent Status?," *USA Today*, Oct. 4, 2013, www.usatoday.com/story/sports/nfl
/2013/10/04/leigh-steinberg-agent-comeback/2919259/; Jessica Iavazzi, "Bartkowski: 'Guys Are Crying for Help,'" *Columbia Sports Journalism,* columbiasports
journalism.com/2014/03/12/steve-bartkowski-guys-are-crying-for-help/.

2 Author originally interviewed Steinberg for chapter 10.

3 Morten L. Kringelbach and Kent C. Berridge, "Brain Mechanisms of Pleasure: The
Core Affect Component of Emotion," in *The Psychological Construction of Emotion,*
ed. Lisa Feldman Barrett and James A. Russell (New York: Guilford Press, 2015),
230; cf. A. Bartels and S. Zeki, "The Neural Correlates of Maternal and Romantic
Love," *NeuroImage* 21, no. 3 (2004): 1,155–66.

4 Ruth Feldman, "The Neurobiology of Human Attachments," *Trends in Cognitive
Sciences* 21, no. 2 (2017): 80–99; Coan and Sbarra, "Social Baseline Theory"; Inga
D. Neumann and David A. Slattery, "Oxytocin in General Anxiety and Social
Fear: A Translational Approach," *Biological Psychiatry* 79, no. 3 (2016): 213–21;
Markus Heinrichs et al., "Social Support and Oxytocin Interact to Suppress Corti-
sol and Subjective Responses to Psychosocial Stress," *Biological Psychiatry* 54, no. 12
(2003): 1,389–98; Sidney Cobb, "Social Support as a Moderator of Life Stress,"
Psychosomatic Medicine 38, no. 5 (1976): 300–314; Bert N. Uchino, "Social Support
and Health: A Review of Physiological Processes Potentially Underlying Links to
Disease Outcomes," *Journal of Behavioral Medicine* 29, no. 4 (2006): 377–87; John
T. Caciopppo et al., "The Neuroendocrinology of Social Isolation," *Annual Review of
Psychology* 66 (2015): 733–67.

5 Thanks to James A. Coan for his insights. Lane Beckes and James A. Coan, "Social
Baseline Theory: The Role of Social Proximity in Emotion and Economy of Action," *Social and Personality Psychology Compass* 5, no. 12 (2011): 976–88; Lane
Beckes and James A. Coan, "Toward an Integrative Neuroscience of Relationships,"
in *The Oxford Handbook of Close Relationships*, ed. Jeffry Simpson and Lorne Campbell (New York: Oxford University Press, 2013), 684–710; James A. Coan and

David A. Sbarra, "Social Baseline Theory: The Social Regulation of Risk and Effort," *Current Opinion in Psychology* 1 (2015): 87–91; James A. Coan, Casey L. Brown, and Lane Beckes, "Our Social Baseline: The Role of Social Proximity in Economy of Action," in *Mechanisms of Social Connection: From Brain to Group,* ed. Mario Mikulincer and Phillip R. Shaver (Washington, D.C.: American Psychological Association, 2014), 89–104.

6 Kyle Nash et al., "Muted Neural Response to Distress among Securely Attached People," *Social Cognitive and Affective Neuroscience* 9, no. 8 (2013): 1,239–45.

7 Valentina Colonnello et al., "Positive Social Interactions in a Lifespan Perspective with a Focus on Opioidergic and Oxytocinergic Systems: Implications for Neuroprotection," *Current Neuropharmacology* 15, no. 4 (2017): 543–61; A. J. Machin and R. I. M. Dunbar, "The Brain Opioid Theory of Social Attachment: A Review of the Evidence," *Behaviour* 148, no. 9 (2011): 985–1,025; Lauri Nummenmaa et al., "Adult Attachment Style Is Associated with Cerebral μ-Opioid Receptor Availability in Humans," *Human Brain Mapping* 36, no. 9 (2015): 3,621–28; Adrienne Santiago, Chiye Aoki, and Regina M. Sullivan, "From Attachment to Independence: Stress Hormone Control of Ecologically Relevant Emergence of Infants' Responses to Threat," *Current Opinion in Behavioral Sciences* 14 (2017): 78–85.

8 Jennifer A. Bartz et al., "Social Effects of Oxytocin in Humans: Context and Person Matter," *Trends in Cognitive Sciences* 15, no. 7 (2011): 301–9; Ruth Feldman et al., "Evidence for a Neuroendocrinological Foundation of Human Affiliation: Plasma Oxytocin Levels across Pregnancy and the Postpartum Period Predict Mother-Infant Bonding," *Psychological Science* 18, no. 11 (2007): 965–70; M. Bonenberger et al., "Polymorphism in the μ-Opioid Receptor Gene (OPRM1) Modulates Neural Processing of Physical Pain, Social Rejection, and Error Processing," *Experimental Brain Research* (2015), doi:10.1007/s00221–015–4322–9. The fact that the A118G polymorphism makes those most vulnerable to social isolation or rejection most susceptible to addiction has led to the social connection theory of addiction: that the cure for addiction is an enriched environment. Mice raised in enriched environments who had access to morphine chose not to take it; it wasn't until they were deprived of social contact that they became addicts.

9 Hymel et al., "Social Status Among Peers"; Kelly, McCarty, and Iannone, "Interaction in Small Groups"; Davey et al., "Being Liked Activates Primary Reward and Midline Self-Related Brain Regions"; Julie Wargo Aikins and Scott D. Litwack, "Prosocial Skills, Social Competence, and Popularity," in *Popularity in the Peer System,* ed. Antonius H. N. Cillessen, David Schwartz, and Lara Mayeux (New York: Guilford Press, 2011), 151–52; Ville-Juhani Ilmarinen et al., "Why Are Extraverts More Popular? Oral Fluency Mediates the Effect of Extraversion on Popularity in Middle Childhood," *European Journal of Personality* 29, no. 2 (2015): 138–51.

10 Robert E. Kleck and Angelo Strenta, "Perceptions of the Impact of Negatively Valued Physical Characteristics on Social Interaction," *Journal of Personality and Social Psychology* 39, no. 5 (1980): 861–73.

11 Author interview, Aug. 7, 2015.

12 Carrie A. Bredow, Rodney M. Cate, and Ted L. Huston, "Have We Met Before? A Conceptual Model of First Romantic Encounters," in Sprecher, Wenzel, and Harvey, *Handbook of Relationship Initiation,* 3–28; Geraldine Downey et al., "The Self-Fulfilling Prophecy in Close Relationships: Rejection Sensitivity and Rejection by Romantic Partners," *Journal of Personality and Social Psychology* 75, no. 2 (1998): 545–60.

13 Author interview with Eastman, July 15, 2013.

14 Fiske, "Interpersonal Stratification," 946.

15 Carolyn C. Morf and Frederick Rhodewalt, "Unraveling the Paradoxes of Narcissism: A Dynamic Self-Regulatory Processing Model," *Psychological Inquiry* 12, no. 4 (2001): 177–96; W. Keith Campbell and Joshua D. Miller, eds., *The Handbook of Narcissism and Narcissistic Personality Disorder: Theoretical Approaches, Empirical Findings, and Treatments* (Hoboken, NJ: John Wiley & Sons, 2011); Ashton C. Southard, Amy Noser, and Virgil Zeigler-Hill, "Do Narcissists Really Love Themselves as Much as It Seems? The Psychodynamic Mask Model of Narcissistic Self-Worth," in *Handbook of the Psychology of Narcissism: Diverse Perspectives,* ed. Avi Besser (New York: Nova Science, 2014), 3–22; Anna Z. Czarna et al., "Do Narcissism and Emotional Intelligence Win Us Friends? Modeling Dynamics of Peer Popularity Using Inferential Network Analysis," *Personality and Social Psychology Bulletin* 42, no. 11 (2016): 1,588–99.

16 Danu Anthony Stinson, Jessica J. Cameron, and Kelley J. Robinson, "The Good, the Bad, and the Risky: Self-Esteem, Rewards and Costs, and Interpersonal Risk Regulation during Relationship Initiation," *Journal of Social and Personal Relationships* 32, no. 8 (2015): 1,109–36; Mark R. Leary, "Affiliation, Acceptance, and Belonging: The Pursuit of Interpersonal Connection," in Fiske, Gilbert, and Lindzey, *Handbook of Social Psychology,* 864–97; Eli J. Finkel and Roy F. Baumeister, "Attraction and Rejection," in *Advanced Social Psychology: The State of the Science,* ed. Roy F. Baumeister and Eli J. Finkel (New York: Oxford University Press, 2010), 419–59.

17 Michael Kosfeld et al., "Oxytocin Increases Trust in Humans," *Nature* 435 (2005): 673–76; René Hurlemann and Dirk Scheele, "Dissecting the Role of Oxytocin in the Formation and Loss of Social Relationships," *Biological Psychiatry* 79, no. 3 (2016): 185–93; Radhika Vaidyanathan and Elizabeth A. D. Hammock, "Oxytocin Receptor Dynamics in the Brain across Development and Species," *Developmental Neurobiology* 77, no. 2 (2017): 143–57; Michaela Pfundmair et al., "Oxytocin Promotes Attention to Social Cues Regardless of Group Membership," *Hormones and Behavior* 90 (2017): 136–40; Gül Dölen, "Autism: Oxytocin, Serotonin, and Social Reward," *Social Neuroscience* 10, no. 5 (2015): 450–65; Gül Dölen et al., "Correction of Fragile X Syndrome in Mice," *Neuron* 56, no. 6 (2007): 955–62; Simone G. Shamay-Tsoory et al., "Intranasal Administration of Oxytocin Increases Envy and Schadenfreude (Gloating)," *Biological Psychiatry* 66, no. 9 (2009): 864–70; Simone G. Shamay-Tsoory and Ahmad Abu-Akel, "The Social Salience Hypothesis of Oxytocin," *Biological Psychiatry* 79, no. 3 (2016): 194–202.

18 Linda Tickle-Degnen, "Nonverbal Behavior and Its Functions in the Ecosystem of Rapport," in Manusov and Patterson, *Sage Handbook of Nonverbal Communication*, 381–99; Keating, "Why and How the Silent Self Speaks Volumes"; Keating, "Charismatic Faces"; I. Altman and D. Taylor, *Social Penetration: The Development of Interpersonal Relationships* (New York: Holt, Rinehart & Winston, 1973); Linda Tickle-Degnen and Robert Rosenthal, "The Nature of Rapport and Its Nonverbal Correlates," *Psychological Inquiry* 1, no. 4 (1990): 285–93; Maggie Shiffrar, Martha D. Kaiser, and Areti Chouchourelou, "Seeing Human Movement as Inherently Social," in Adams et al., *Science of Social Vision*; Brooks and Freeman, "Psychology and Neuroscience of Person Perception."

19 Konstantin O. Tskhay et al., "Charisma in Everyday Life: Conceptualization and Validation of the General Charisma Inventory," *Journal of Personality and Social Psychology* 114, no. 1 (2018): 131–52.

20 Danu A. Stinson et al., "Deconstructing the 'Reign of Error': Interpersonal Warmth Explains the Self-Fulfilling Prophecy of Anticipated Acceptance," *Personality and Social Psychology Bulletin* 35, no. 9 (2009): 1,165–78; Danu Anthony Stinson et al., "Rewriting the Self-Fulfilling Prophecy of Social Rejection: Self-Affirmation Improves Relational Security and Social Behavior up to 2 Months Later," *Psychological Science* 22, no. 9 (2011): 1,145–49; Danielle Gaucher et al., "Perceived Regard Explains Self-Esteem Differences in Expressivity," *Personality and Social Psychology Bulletin* 38, no. 9 (2012): 1,144–56; Miranda Giacomin and Christian H. Jordan, "How Implicit Self-Esteem Influences Perceptions of Self-Esteem at Zero and Nonzero Acquaintance," *Self and Identity* 16, no. 6 (2016): 1–23; Stinson, Cameron, and Robinson, "The Good, the Bad, and the Risky"; Leary, "Affiliation, Acceptance, and Belonging"; Finkel and Baumeister, "Attraction and Rejection."

21 Author interview, March 24, 2015.

22 Chia-Jung Tsay, "Sight over Sound in the Judgment of Music Performance," *Proceedings of the National Academy of Sciences* 110, no. 36 (2013): 14,580–85.

23 Katherine A. Burson, Richard P. Larrick, and Joshua Klayman, "Skilled or Unskilled, but Still Unaware of It: How Perceptions of Difficulty Drive Miscalibration in Relative Comparisons," *Journal of Personality and Social Psychology* 90, no. 1 (2006): 60–77; Richard E. Nisbett and Timothy D. Wilson, "Telling More than We Can Know: Verbal Reports on Mental Processes," *Psychological Review* 84, no. 3 (1977): 231–59.

24 Nalini Ambady and Robert Rosenthal, "Thin Slices of Expressive Behavior as Predictors of Interpersonal Consequences: A Meta-analysis," *Psychological Bulletin* 111, no. 2 (1992): 256–74; Nalini Ambady, Frank J. Bernieri, and Jennifer A. Richeson, "Toward a Histology of Social Behavior: Judgmental Accuracy from Thin Slices of the Behavioral Stream," in *Advances in Experimental Social Psychology*, ed. Mark P. Zanna (San Diego: Academic Press, 2000), 32: 201–71; Nalini Ambady et al., "Surgeons' Tone of Voice: A Clue to Malpractice History," *Surgery* 132, no. 1 (2002): 5–9; Nalini Ambady and Robert Rosenthal, "Half a Minute: Predicting Teacher

Evaluations from Thin Slices of Nonverbal Behavior and Physical Attractiveness," *Journal of Personality and Social Psychology* 64, no. 3 (1993): 431–41.

25 Author interview, Aug. 7, 2013; Gaucher et al., "Perceived Regard Explains Self-Esteem Differences in Expressivity"; Giacomin and Jordan, "How Implicit Self-Esteem Influences Perceptions of Self-Esteem at Zero and Non-zero Acquaintance."

26 Eric R. Kandel et al., eds., *Principles of Neural Science,* 5th ed. (New York: McGraw-Hill, 2013), 888; Sook-Lei Liew and Lisa Aziz-Zadeh, "The Human Mirror Neuron System and Social Cognition," in *From DNA to Social Cognition,* ed. Richard Ebstein, Simone Shamay-Tsoory, and Soo Hong Chew, 1st ed. (New York: Wiley-Blackwell, 2011), 63–80; Tskhay et al., "Charisma in Everyday Life"; Cécile Emery, "Uncovering the Role of Emotional Abilities in Leadership Emergence: A Longitudinal Analysis of Leadership Networks," *Social Networks* 34, no. 4 (2012): 429–37; Melissa S. Cardon, "Is Passion Contagious? The Transference of Entrepreneurial Passion to Employees," *Human Resource Management Review* 18, no. 2 (2008): 77–86; Thomas Sy, Stéphane Côte, and Richard Saavedra, "The Contagious Leader: Impact of the Leader's Mood on the Mood of Group Members, Group Affective Tone, and Group Processes," *Journal of Applied Psychology* 90, no. 2 (2005): 295–305; Thomas Sy, Jin Nam Choi, and Stefanie K. Johnson, "Reciprocal Interactions between Group Perceptions of Leader Charisma and Group Mood through Mood Contagion," *Leadership Quarterly* 24, no. 4 (2013): 463–76; Sigal G. Barsade, "The Ripple Effect: Emotional Contagion and Its Influence on Group Behavior," *Administrative Science Quarterly* 47, no. 4 (2002): 644–75; Joyce E. Bono and Remus Ilies, "Charisma, Positive Emotions, and Mood Contagion," *Leadership Quarterly* 17 (2006): 317–34; Kristi Lewis Tyran, "Tell Me a Story: Emotional Responses to Emotional Expression during Leader 'Storytelling,'" in *Group Dynamics and Emotional Expression,* ed. Ursula Hess and Pierre Philippot (Cambridge, U.K.: Cambridge University Press, 2007), 118–39; Gerben A. Van Kleef et al., "Emotion Is for Influence," *European Review of Social Psychology* 22, no. 1 (2011): 114–63; Ronald E. Riggio and Rebecca J. Reichard, "The Emotional and Social Intelligences of Effective Leadership: An Emotional and Social Skill Approach," *Journal of Managerial Psychology* 23, no. 2 (2008): 169–85; Stéphane Côté et al., "Emotional Intelligence and Leadership Emergence in Small Groups," *Leadership Quarterly* 21, no. 3 (2010): 496–508; Kyongsik Yun, Katsumi Watanabe, and Shinsuke Shimojo, "Interpersonal Body and Neural Synchronization as a Marker of Implicit Social Interaction," *Scientific Reports* 2, no. 959 (2012); Riitta Hari et al., "Synchrony of Brains and Bodies during Implicit Interpersonal Interaction," *Trends in Cognitive Sciences* 17, no. 3 (2013): 105–6; Lauri Nummenmaa et al., "Emotions Promote Social Interaction by Synchronizing Brain Activity across Individuals," *Proceedings of the National Academy of Sciences* 109, no. 24 (2012): 9,599–604.

27 Nummenmaa et al., "Emotions Promote Social Interaction by Synchronizing Brain Activity across Individuals"; Piotr Winkielman et al., "Embodiment of Cognition and Emotion," in *APA Handbook of Personality and Social Psychology,* vol. 1,

Attitudes and Social Cognition, ed. M. Mikulincer and P. R. Shaver (Washington, D.C.: American Psychological Association, 2015), 151–75.

28 Edward P. Lemay Jr. and Rachel B. Venaglia, "Relationship Expectations and Relationship Quality," *Review of General Psychology* 20, no. 1 (2016): 57–70.

29 Tomas Chamorro-Premuzic, *Personality and Individual Differences,* 2nd ed. (West Sussex, U.K.: John Wiley & Sons, 2011), 42–62; Richard A. Depue, "Interpersonal Behavior and the Structure of Personality: Neurobehavioral Foundation of Agentic Extraversion and Affiliation," in *Biology of Personality and Individual Differences,* ed. Turhan Canli (New York: Guilford Press, 2006), 60–92; Benjamin M. Wilkowski and Elizabeth Louise Ferguson, "Just Loving These People: Extraverts Implicitly Associate People with Reward," *Journal of Research in Personality* 53 (2014): 93–102; cf. Edward P. Lemay and Noah R. Wolf, "Projection of Romantic and Sexual Desire in Opposite-Sex Friendships: How Wishful Thinking Creates a Self-Fulfilling Prophecy," *Personality and Social Psychology Bulletin* 42, no. 7 (2016): 864–78; Stinson et al., "Rewriting the Self-Fulfilling Prophecy of Social Rejection"; Gaucher et al., "Perceived Regard Explains Self-Esteem Differences in Expressivity"; Giacomin and Jordan, "How Implicit Self-Esteem Influences Perceptions of Self-Esteem at Zero and Non-zero Acquaintance"; Stinson, Cameron, and Robinson, "The Good, the Bad, and the Risky"; Leary, "Affiliation, Acceptance, and Belonging."

30 Joseph P. Forgas, "Feeling and Speaking: Affective Influences on Communication Strategies and Language Use," in *Social Cognition and Communication,* ed. Joseph P. Forgas, Orsolya Vincze, and János László (New York: Psychology Press, 2014); J. Salmi et al., "The Brains of High Functioning Autistic Individuals Do Not Synchronize with Those of Others," *NeuroImage: Clinical* 3 (2013): 489–97; Ishabel M. Vicaria and Leah Dickens, "Meta-analyses of the Intra- and Interpersonal Outcomes of Interpersonal Coordination," *Journal of Nonverbal Behavior* 40, no. 4 (2016): 335–61; Wolfgang Tschacher, Georg M. Rees, and Fabian Ramseyer, "Nonverbal Synchrony and Affect in Dyadic Interactions," *Frontiers in Psychology* 5, no. 1,323 (2014), journal.frontiersin.org/article/10.3389/fpsyg.2014.01323/full; Koban and Pourtois, "Brain Systems Underlying the Affective and Social Monitoring of Actions"; Linda Rose-Krasnor, "The Nature of Social Competence: A Theoretical Review," *Social Development* 6, no. 1 (1997): 111–35; Valerie Manusov and Miles L. Patterson, "Nonverbal Skills and Abilities," in Manusov and Patterson, *Sage Handbook of Nonverbal Communication.*

31 Cameron Anderson and Jon Cowan, "Personality and Status Attainment: A Micropolitics Perspective," in Cheng, Tracy, and Anderson, *Psychology of Social Status,* 99–117; M. Brent Donnellan and Richard W. Robins, "Development of Personality across the Lifespan," in *The Cambridge Handbook of Personality Psychology,* ed. Philip J. Corr and Gerald Matthews (New York: Cambridge University Press, 2012), 191–204. Leaders are better self-monitors: Ronald E. Riggio, "Business Applications of Nonverbal Communication," in *Applications of Nonverbal Communication,* ed. Ronald E. Riggio and Robert S. Feldman (Mahwah, NJ: Lawrence Erlbaum, 2005), 125; Cheri Ostroff and Yujie Zhan, "Person-Environment Fit in the Selection Process," in *The Oxford*

Handbook of Personnel Assessment and Selection, ed. Neal Schmitt (New York: Oxford University Press, 2012), 267; Mark Snyder and Steve Gangestad, "On the Nature of Self-Monitoring: Matters of Assessment, Matters of Validity," *Journal of Personality and Social Psychology* 51, no. 1 (1986): 125–39; Steven W. Gangestad and Mark Snyder, "Self-Monitoring: Appraisal and Reappraisal," *Psychological Bulletin* 126, no. 4 (2000): 530–55; Mark Snyder, "Self-Monitoring of Expressive Behavior," *Journal of Personality and Social Psychology* 30, no. 4 (1974): 526–37; Ajay Mehra, Martin Kilduff, and Daniel J. Brass, "The Social Networks of High and Low Self-Monitors: Implications for Workplace Performance," *Administrative Science Quarterly* 46, no. 1 (2001): 121–46; Martin Kilduff and David V. Day, "Do Chameleons Get Ahead? The Effects of Self-Monitoring on Managerial Careers," *Academy of Management Journal* 37, no. 4 (1994): 1,047–60; Hongseok Oh and Martin Kilduff, "The Ripple Effect of Personality on Social Structure: Self-Monitoring Origins of Network Brokerage," *Journal of Applied Psychology* 93, no. 5 (2008): 1,155–64; Ruolian Fang et al., "Integrating Personality and Social Networks: A Meta-analysis of Personality, Network Position, and Work Outcomes in Organizations," *Organization Science* 26, no. 4 (2015): 1,243–60; Davide Ponzi et al., "Social Network Centrality and Hormones: The Interaction of Testosterone and Cortisol," *Psychoneuroendocrinology* 68 (2016): 6–13; Taylor S. Bolt et al., "Integrating Personality/Character Neuroscience with Network Analysis," in Absher and Cloutier, *Neuroimaging Personality, Social Cognition, and Character,* 51–69.

32 Forgas, "Feeling and Speaking"; Salmi, "Brains of High Functioning Autistic Individuals Do Not Synchronize with Those of Others"; Vicaria and Dickens, "Meta-Analyses of the Intra- and Interpersonal Outcomes of Interpersonal Coordination"; Tschacher, Rees, and Ramseyer, "Nonverbal Synchrony and Affect in Dyadic Interactions"; Koban and Pourtois, "Brain Systems Underlying the Affective and Social Monitoring of Actions"; Rose-Krasnor, "Nature of Social Competence"; Manusov and Patterson, "Nonverbal Skills and Abilities."

33 R. Matthew Montoya and Robert S. Horton, "A Two-Dimensional Model for the Study of Interpersonal Attraction," *Personality and Social Psychology Review* 18, no. 1 (2014): 59–86; Kenneth H. Rubin, William M. Bukowski, and Jeffrey G. Parker, "Peer Interactions, Relationships, and Groups," in *Handbook of Child Psychology, vol. 3, Social, Emotional, and Personality Development,* ed. N. Eisenberg (Hoboken, NJ: John Wiley & Sons, 2006), 609.

34 Carl Richards, "Stop and Acknowledge How Much Luck Has to Do with Your Success," *New York Times,* Jan. 9, 2017, www.nytimes.com/2017/01/09/your-money/stop-and-acknowledge-how-much-luck-has-to-do-with-your-success.html.

35 Albert Bandura, "The Psychology of Chance Encounters and Life Paths," *American Psychologist* 37, no. 7 (1982): 747–55; Gifford-Smith and Brownell, "Childhood Peer Relationships."

36 Author interview, Aug. 18, 2009.

37 Cameron Anderson, Dacher Keltner, and Oliver P. John, "Emotional Convergence between People over Time," *Journal of Personality and Social Psychology* 84, no. 5 (2003): 1,054–68; Miller McPherson, Lynn Smith-Lovin, and James M. Cook,

"Birds of a Feather: Homophily in Social Networks," *Annual Review of Sociology* 27 (2001): 415–44; David Cwir et al., "Your Heart Makes My Heart Move: Cues of Social Connectedness Cause Shared Emotions and Physiological States among Strangers," *Journal of Experimental Social Psychology* 47, no. 3 (2011): 661–64; Rowland S. Miller, "Social Anxiousness, Shyness, and Embarrassability," in *Handbook of Individual Differences in Social Behavior,* ed. Mark R. Leary and Rick H. Hoyle (New York: Guilford Press, 2009), 176–91; cf. Leary, "Affiliation, Acceptance, and Belonging"; Owen Hargie, "Effects of Self-Disclosure Role on Liking, Closeness, and Other Impressions in Get-Acquainted Interactions," *Skilled Interpersonal Communication: Research, Theory, and Practice,* 5th ed. (New York: Routledge, 2010); Jean-Philippe Laurenceau et al., "Intimacy as an Interpersonal Process: Current Status and Future Directions," in *Handbook of Closeness and Intimacy,* ed. Debra J. Mashek and Arthur Aron (Mahwah, NJ: Lawrence Erlbaum, 2004), 61–78; Constantine Sedikides et al., "The Relationship Closeness Induction Task," *Representative Research in Social Psychology* 23 (1999): 1–4; Susan Sprecher et al., "Taking Turns: Reciprocal Self-Disclosure Promotes Liking in Initial Interactions," *Journal of Experimental Social Psychology* 49, no. 5 (2013): 860–66.

38 Joanne V. Wood and Amanda L. Forest, "Seeking Pleasure and Avoiding Pain in Interpersonal Relationships," in *Handbook of Self-Enhancement and Self-Protection,* ed. Mark D. Alicke and Constantine Sedikides (New York: Guilford Press, 2011), 258–78. Quotation on p. 269.

39 Anderson, Keltner, and John, "Emotional Convergence Between People over Time"; McPherson, Smith-Lovin, and Cook, "Birds of a Feather"; Cwir et al., "Your Heart Makes My Heart Move"; Miller, "Social Anxiousness, Shyness, and Embarrassability"; Leary, "Affiliation, Acceptance, and Belonging"; Hargie, "Effects of Self-Disclosure Role on Liking, Closeness, and Other Impressions in Get-Acquainted Interactions"; Laurenceau et al., "Intimacy as an Interpersonal Process"; Sedikides et al., "Relationship Closeness Induction Task"; Sprecher et al., "Taking Turns."

40 R. Matthew Montoya, Robert S. Horton, and Jeffrey Kirchner, "Is Actual Similarity Necessary for Attraction? A Meta-analysis of Actual and Perceived Similarity," *Journal of Social and Personal Relationships* 25, no. 6 (2008): 889–922; R. Matthew Montoya and Robert S. Horton, "A Meta-analytic Investigation of the Processes Underlying the Similarity-Attraction Effect," *Journal of Social and Personal Relationships* 30, no. 1 (2012): 64–94; Bhatia, "Associations and the Accumulation of Preference"; Tina Strombach, "Social Discounting Involves Modulation of Neural Value Signals by Temporoparietal Junction," *Proceedings of the National Academy of Sciences* 112, no. 5 (2015): 1,619–24; D. Mobbs et al., "A Key Role for Similarity in Vicarious Reward," *Science* 324, no. 5929 (2009): 900. Perceived similarity fosters coordination: Tim Cole and J. C. Bruno Teboul, "Non-zero-sum Collaboration, Reciprocity, and the Preference for Similarity: Developing an Adaptive Model of Close Relational Functioning," *Personal Relationships* 11, no. 2 (2004): 135–60.

41 Katherine Giuffre, "Sandpiles of Opportunity: Success in the Art World," *Social Forces* 77, no. 3 (1999): 815–32.

42 Chamorro-Premuzic, *Personality and Individual Differences,* 42–62; Depue, "Interpersonal Behavior and the Structure of Personality"; Wilkowski and Ferguson, "Just Loving These People"; cf. Lemay and Wolf, "Projection of Romantic and Sexual Desire in Opposite-Sex Friendships"; Stinson et al., "Rewriting the Self-Fulfilling Prophecy of Social Rejection"; Gaucher et al., "Perceived Regard Explains Self-Esteem Differences in Expressivity"; Giacomin and Jordan, "How Implicit Self-Esteem Influences Perceptions of Self-Esteem at Zero and Non-zero Acquaintance"; Stinson, Cameron, and Robinson, "The Good, The Bad, and The Risky"; Leary, "Affiliation, Acceptance, and Belonging."

43 Katherine Giuffre, "Mental Maps: Social Networks and the Language of Critical Reviews," *Sociological Inquiry* 71, no. 3 (2001): 381–93; Richard Swedberg, "Economic Sociology," in *Encyclopedia of Sociology,* ed. Edgar F. Borgatta and Rhonda J. V. Montgomery, 2nd ed. (New York: Macmillan, 2000), 737; Yuval Kalish, "Bridging in Social Networks: Who Are the People in Structural Holes and Why Are They There?," *Asian Journal of Social Psychology* 11, no. 1 (2008): 53–66; Matthew S. Bothner, Edward Bishop Smith, and Harrison C. White, "A Model of Robust Positions in Social Networks," *American Journal of Sociology* 116, no. 3 (2010): 943–92; Ronald S. Burt, "The Network Structure of Social Capital," *Research in Organizational Behaviour* 22 (2000): 345–423; Zhen Zhang et al., "The Genetic Basis of Entrepreneurship: Effects of Gender and Personality," *Organizational Behavior and Human Decision Processes* 110, no. 2 (2009): 93–107.

44 Michael Woolcock, "The Place of Social Capital in Understanding Social and Economic Outcomes," *Canadian Journal of Policy Research* 2, no. 1 (2001): 11–17.

45 Mark S. Granovetter, "The Strength of Weak Ties," *American Journal of Sociology* 78, no. 6 (1973): 1,360–80; Ronald S. Burt, "Bridge Decay," *Social Networks* 24, no. 4 (2002): 333–63; J. L. Martin and K. Yeung, "Persistence of Close Personal Ties over a 12-Year Period," *Social Networks* 28, no. 4 (2006): 331–62; A. Zaheer and G. Soda, "Network Evolution: The Origins of Structural Holes," *Administrative Science Quarterly* 54, no. 1 (2009): 1–31; Z. Sasovova et al., "Network Churn: The Effects of Self-Monitoring Personality on Brokerage Dynamics," *Administrative Science Quarterly* 55, no. 4 (2010): 639–70; E. Quintane et al., "How Do Brokers Broker: An Investigation of the Temporality of Structural Holes," *Academy of Management Proceedings* (Jan. 2012).

46 Andrew Abbott, *Time Matters: On Theory and Method* (Chicago: University of Chicago Press, 2001), 247. Also quoted in Bothner, Smith, and White, "Model of Robust Positions in Social Networks."

47 Matthew A. Andersson, "Dispositional Optimism and the Emergence of Social Network Diversity," *Sociological Quarterly* 53, no. 1 (2012): 92–115; Gillian M. Sandstrom and Elizabeth W. Dunn, "Social Interactions and Well-Being: The Surprising Power of Weak Ties," *Personality and Social Psychology Bulletin* 40, no. 7 (2014): 910–22; Ian Brissette, Michael F. Scheier, and Charles S. Carver, "The Role of Optimism in Social Network Development, Coping, and Psychological Adjustment during a Life Transition," *Journal of Personality and Social Psychology* 82, no. 1 (2002): 102–11.

48 Susan M. Bögels and Warren Mansell, "Attention Processes in the Maintenance and Treatment of Social Phobia: Hypervigilance, Avoidance, and Self-Focused Attention," *Clinical Psychology Review* 24, no. 7 (2004): 827–56; David M. Clark and Adrian Wells, "A Cognitive Model of Social Phobia," in *Social Phobia: Diagnosis, Assessment, and Treatment,* ed. Richard G. Heimberg et al. (New York: Guilford Press, 1995), 69–93; Colette R. Hirsch and David M. Clark, "Information-Processing Bias in Social Phobia," *Clinical Psychology Review* 24, no. 7 (2004): 799–825; Stefan G. Hofmann, "Cognitive Factors That Maintain Social Anxiety Disorder: A Comprehensive Model and Its Treatment Implications," *Cognitive Behaviour Therapy* 36, no. 4 (2007): 193–209; Todd B. Kashdan, "Social Anxiety Spectrum and Diminished Positive Experiences: Theoretical Synthesis and Meta-analysis," *Clinical Psychology Review* 27, no. 3 (2007): 348–65; Bethany A. Teachman and Joseph P. Allen, "Development of Social Anxiety: Social Interaction Predictors of Implicit and Explicit Fear of Negative Evaluation," *Journal of Abnormal Child Psychology* 35, no. 1 (2007): 63–78; Luke T. Schultz and Richard G. Heimberg, "Attentional Focus in Social Anxiety Disorder: Potential for Interactive Processes," *Clinical Psychology Review* 28, no. 7 (2008): 1,206–21; Brandon L. Pearson, D. Caroline Blanchard, and Robert J. Blanchard, "Social Stress Effects on Defensive Behavior and Anxiety," in *The Handbook of Stress: Neuropsychological Effects on the Brain,* ed. Cheryl D. Conrad, 1st ed. (West Sussex, U.K.: Blackwell, 2011), 369–87; Alexandre Heeren et al., "Biased Cognitions and Social Anxiety: Building a Global Framework for Integrating Cognitive, Behavioral, and Neural Processes," *Frontiers in Human Neuroscience* 8, no. 538 (2014); Stephanie Cacioppo, Stephen Balogh, and John T. Cacioppo, "Implicit Attention to Negative Social, in Contrast to Nonsocial, Words in the Stroop Task Differs between Individuals High and Low in Loneliness: Evidence from Event-Related Brain Microstates," *Cortex* 70 (2015): 213–33; Hussain Y. Khdour et al., "Generalized Anxiety Disorder and Social Anxiety Disorder, but Not Panic Anxiety Disorder, Are Associated with Higher Sensitivity to Learning from Negative Feedback: Behavioral and Computational Investigation," *Frontiers in Integrative Neuroscience* 10, no. 20 (2016); Marcel Badra et al., "The Association between Ruminative Thinking and Negative Interpretation Bias in Social Anxiety," *Cognition and Emotion*, 31, no. 6 (2016): 1–9.

49 David A. Moscovitch, Thomas L. Rodebaugh, and Benjamin D. Hesch, "How Awkward! Social Anxiety and the Perceived Consequences of Social Blunders," *Behaviour Research and Therapy* 50, no. 2 (2012): 142–9.

50 Nummenmaa et al., "Emotions Promote Social Interaction by Synchronizing Brain Activity across Individuals"; Winkielman et al., "Embodiment of Cognition and Emotion."

51 Author interview, Aug. 18, 2009.

52 R. Matthew Montoya and Robert S. Horton, "A Two-Dimensional Model for the Study of Interpersonal Attraction," *Personality and Social Psychology Review* 18, no. 1 (2014): 59–86.

CHAPTER 9: MY FUTURE'S BRIGHT, I GOTTA WEAR SHADES

1 On O'Donnell, see "This Is Going to Be Big," Charlie O'Donnell (blog), www .thisisgoingtobebig.com/blog/2014/5/12/the-economics-of-a-small-vc-fund.html, accessed June 6, 2014.

2 Not his real name.

3 Anderson, Hildreth, and Howland, "Is the Desire for Status a Fundamental Human Motive?"; Waclaw Bak, "Self-Standards and Self-Discrepancies: A Structural Model of Self-Knowledge," *Current Psychology* 33, no. 2 (2014): 155–73; E. Tory Higgins, "Self-Discrepancy: A Theory Relating Self and Affect," *Psychological Review* 94, no. 3 (1987): 319–40; Edward L. Deci and Richard M. Ryan, "A Motivational Approach to Self: Integration in Personality," in *Nebraska Symposium on Motivation: Perspectives on Motivation* (Lincoln: University of Nebraska Press, 1991), 237–88; Allan Wigfield and Jacquelynne S. Eccles, "Expectancy-Value Theory of Achievement Motivation," *Contemporary Educational Psychology* 25, no. 1 (2000): 68–81; Robert J. Vallerand, "Toward a Hierarchical Model of Intrinsic and Extrinsic Motivation," *Advances in Experimental Social Psychology* 29 (1997): 271–360; Ellen J. Langer, "The Illusion of Control," *Journal of Personality and Social Psychology* 32, no. 2 (1975): 311–28.

4 See www.youtube.com/watch?v=9gtIHcWa6HU.

5 Noreen Y. R. Geenen et al., "BIS and BAS: Biobehaviorally Rooted Drivers of Entrepreneurial Intent," *Personality and Individual Differences* 95 (2016): 204–13; Shelley E. Taylor et al., "Neural Bases of Moderation of Cortisol Stress Responses by Psychosocial Resources," *Journal of Personality and Social Psychology* 95, no. 1 (2008): 197–211; Zhou Jiang, "Core Self-Evaluation and Career Decision Self-Efficacy: A Mediation Model of Value Orientations," *Personality and Individual Differences* 86 (2015): 450–54; Keith M. Hmieleski and Robert A. Baron, "Entrepreneurs' Optimism and New Venture Performance: A Social Cognitive Perspective," *Academy of Management Journal* 52, no. 3 (2009): 473–88; Timothy A. Judge, Amir Erez, and Joyce E. Bono, "The Power of Being Positive: The Relation between Positive Self-Concept and Job Performance," *Human Performance* 11, no. 2–3 (1998): 167–87; Brissette, Scheier, and Carver, "Role of Optimism in Social Network Development, Coping, and Psychological Adjustment during a Life Transition"; Shelley E. Taylor and Annette L. Stanton, "Coping Resources, Coping Processes, and Mental Health," *Annual Review of Clinical Psychology* 3 (2007): 377–401; Emma Mosley and Sylvain Laborde, "Performing under Pressure: Influence of Personality-Trait-Like Individual Differences," in Raab et al., *Performance Psychology,* 291–308.

6 Anderson and Cowan, "Personality and Status Attainment"; Carlos J. Torelli et al., "Cultural Determinants of Status: Implications for Workplace Evaluations and Behaviors," *Organizational Behavior and Human Decision Processes* 123, no. 1 (2014): 34–48; David Melamed, "Do Magnitudes of Difference on Status Characteristics Matter for Small Group Inequalities?," *Social Science Research* 42, no. 1 (2013): 217–29; Cecilia L.

Ridgeway and Joseph Berger, "Expectations, Legitimation, and Dominance Behavior in Task Groups," *American Sociological Review* 51, no. 5 (1986): 603–17.

7 Biernat and Kobrynowicz, "Gender- and Race-Based Standards of Competence"; Crandall and Eshleman, "Justification-Suppression Model of the Expression and Experience of Prejudice"; Uhlmann and Cohen, "Constructed Criteria"; Castilla, "Gender, Race, and Meritocracy in Organizational Careers"; Biernat, *Standards and Expectancies*; C. Neil Macrae and Galen V. Bodenhausen, "Social Cognition: Thinking Categorically about Others," *Annual Review of Psychology* 51 (2000): 93–120; Foy et al., "Emotions and Affect as Source, Outcome, and Resistance to Inequality"; Biernat, "Stereotypes and Shifting Standards"; Walton and Cohen, "Question of Belonging"; Magee and Galinsky, "Social Hierarchy"; Kimberly A. Quinn and Harriet E. S. Rosenthal, "Categorizing Others and the Self: How Social Memory Structures Guide Social Perception and Behavior," *Learning and Motivation* 43, no. 4 (2012): 247–58; Pager, Western, and Bonikowski, "Discrimination in a Low-Wage Labor Market"; Foschi, "Double Standards for Competence"; Biernat and Fuegen, "Shifting Standards and the Evaluation of Competence"; Castilla and Benard, "Paradox of Meritocracy in Organizations."

8 Jessica M. Nolan et al., "Normative Social Influence Is Underdetected," *Personality and Social Psychology Bulletin* 34, no. 7 (2008): 913–23; P. Wesley Schultz, Jennifer J. Tabanico, and Tania Rendón, "Normative Beliefs as Agents of Influence: Basic Processes and Real-World Applications," in *Attitudes and Attitude Change,* ed. William D. Crano and Radmila Prislin (New York: Psychology Press, 2008), 385–410.

9 Alex Mesoudi, Andrew Whiten, and Robin Dunbar, "A Bias for Social Information in Human Cultural Transmission," *British Journal of Psychology* 97, no. 3 (2006): 405–23; Stefan Voigt and Daniel Kiwit, "The Role and Evolution of Beliefs, Habits, Moral Norms, and Institutions," in *Merits and Limits of Markets,* ed. Herbert Giersch (Heidelberg: Springer, 1998), 83–106.

10 Author interview, May 13, 2015.

11 Treadway et al., "Dopaminergic Mechanisms of Individual Differences in Human Effort-Based Decision-Making"; Michael J. Frank, Lauren C. Seeberger, and Randall C. O'Reilly, "By Carrot or by Stick: Cognitive Reinforcement Learning in Parkinsonism," *Science* 306, no. 5703 (2004): 1,940–43; Bradley B. Doll and Michael J. Frank, "The Basal Ganglia in Reward and Decision Making: Computational Models and Empirical Studies," in Dreher and Tremblay, *Handbook of Reward and Decision-Making,* 399–425; Jan Wacker et al., "Dopamine-D2-Receptor Blockade Reverses the Association between Trait Approach Motivation and Frontal Asymmetry in an Approach-Motivation Context," *Psychological Science* 24, no. 4 (2013): 489–97; Cox et al., "Striatal D1 and D2 Signaling Differentially Predict Learning from Positive and Negative Outcomes"; David M. Hughes et al., "Asymmetric Frontal Cortical Activity Predicts Effort Expenditure for Reward," *Social Cognitive and Affective Neuroscience* 10, no. 7 (2015): 1,015–19.

12 Richard Contrada and Andrew Baum, ed., *The Handbook of Stress Science: Biology, Psychology, and Health* (New York: Springer, 2011); Barry S. Oken, Irina Chamine,

and Wayne Wakeland, "A Systems Approach to Stress, Stressors, and Resilience in Humans," *Behavioural Brain Research* 282 (2015): 144–54; McEwen, "Brain on Stress"; Juster, McEwen, and Lupien, "Allostatic Load Biomarkers of Chronic Stress and Impact on Health and Cognition"; Thomas Frodl and Veronica O'Keane, "How Does the Brain Deal with Cumulative Stress? A Review with Focus on Developmental Stress, HPA Axis Function, and Hippocampal Structure in Humans," *Neurobiology of Disease* 52 (2013): 24–37; Christiaan H. Vinkers et al., "Stress Exposure across the Life Span Cumulatively Increases Depression Risk and Is Moderated by Neuroticism," *Depression and Anxiety* 31, no. 9 (2014): 737–45.

13 Michael Sheard, *Mental Toughness: The Mindset Behind Sporting Achievement* (New York: Routledge, 2012); Thomas W. Britt et al., "How Much Do We Really Know about Employee Resilience?," *Industrial and Organizational Psychology: Perspectives on Science and Practice* 9, no. 2 (2016): 378–404; Elizabeth L. Shoenfelt, "How Much Do We Really Know about Employee Resilience? More, If We Include the Sport Psychology Resilience Research," *Industrial and Organizational Psychology* 9, no. 2 (2016): 442–46; Andrew E. Skodol, "The Resilient Personality," in *Handbook of Adult Resilience,* ed. John W. Reich, Alex J. Zautra, and John Stuart Hall (New York: Guilford Press, 2010), 112–25; Lee Crust and Peter J. Clough, "Developing Mental Toughness: From Research to Practice," *Journal of Sport Psychology in Action* 2, no. 1 (2011): 21–32; Sarah P. McGeown, Helen St. Clair-Thompson, and Peter Clough, "The Study of Non-cognitive Attributes in Education: Proposing the Mental Toughness Framework," *Educational Review* 68, no. 1 (2016): 96–113; B. P. F. Rutten et al., "Resilience in Mental Health: Linking Psychological and Neurobiological Perspectives," *Acta Psychiatrica Scandinavica* 128, no. 1 (2013): 3–20.

14 Alison Wood Brooks et al., "Don't Stop Believing: Rituals Improve Performance by Decreasing Anxiety," *Organizational Behavior and Human Decision Processes* 137 (2016): 71–85; Malte Friese and Michaela Wänke, "Personal Prayer Buffers Self-Control Depletion," *Journal of Experimental Social Psychology* 51 (2014): 56–59; Michael E. McCullough and Brian L. B. Willoughby, "Religion, Self-Regulation, and Self-Control: Associations, Explanations, and Implications," *Psychological Bulletin* 135, no. 1 (2009): 69–93; Kevin Rounding et al., "Religion Replenishes Self-Control," *Psychological Science* 23, no. 6 (2012): 635–42.

15 Charity Anderson et al., "On the Meaning of Grit . . . and Hope . . . and Fate Control . . . and Alienation . . . and Locus of Control . . . and . . . Self-Efficacy . . . and . . . Effort Optimism . . . and . . . ," *Urban Review* 48, no. 2 (2016): 198–219; Peter R. Darke and Jonathan L. Freedman, "The Belief in Good Luck Scale," *Journal of Research in Personality* 31, no. 4 (1997): 486–511; Liza Day and John Maltby, "Belief in Good Luck and Psychological Well-Being: The Mediating Role of Optimism and Irrational Beliefs," *Journal of Psychology* 137, no. 1 (2003): 99–110; Liza Day and John Maltby, "'With Good Luck': Belief in Good Luck and Cognitive Planning," *Personality and Individual Differences* 39, no. 7 (2005): 1,217–26; Briony D. Pulford, "Is Luck on My Side? Optimism, Pessimism, and Ambiguity Aversion," *Quarterly Journal of Experimental Psychology* 62, no. 6 (2009): 1,079–87; Lysann

Damisch, Barbara Stoberock, and Thomas Mussweiler, "Keep Your Fingers Crossed! How Superstition Improves Performance," *Psychological Science* 21, no. 7 (2010): 1,014–20; Carol K. Sigelman, "Age Differences in Perceptions of Rich and Poor People: Is It Skill or Luck?," *Social Development* 22, no. 1 (2013): 1–18; Peter R. Darke and Jonathan L. Freedman, "Lucky Events and Beliefs in Luck: Paradoxical Effects on Confidence and Risk-Taking," *Personality and Social Psychology Bulletin* 23, no. 4 (1997): 378–88.

16 Russell E. Johnson, Christopher C. Rosen, and Szu-Han Joanna Lin, "Assessing the Status of Locus of Control as an Indicator of Core Self-Evaluations," *Personality and Individual Differences* 90 (2016): 155–62; Carolyn H. Declerck, Christophe Boone, and Bert De Brabander, "On Feeling in Control: A Biological Theory for Individual Differences in Control Perception," *Brain and Cognition* 62, no. 2 (2006): 143–76; Anderson et al., "Status-Enhancement Account of Overconfidence"; Diemo Urbig and Erik Monsen, "The Structure of Optimism: 'Controllability Affects the Extent to Which Efficacy Beliefs Shape Outcome Expectancies,'" *Journal of Economic Psychology* 33, no. 4 (2012): 854–67; Zhou Jiang et al., "Core Self-Evaluation: Linking Career Social Support to Life Satisfaction," *Personality and Individual Differences* 112 (2017): 128–35; Kennon M. Sheldon, "Becoming Oneself: The Central Role of Self-Concordant Goal Selection," *Personality and Social Psychology Review* 18, no. 4 (2014): 349–65.

17 Tweet: twitter.com/jack/status/295280990836891648. Alexis C. Madrigal, "And Now Let Us Praise, and Consider the Absurd Luck of, Famous Men: A Lesson about the Success of Great Men from Intel Co-founder Bob Noyce's Life Story," *Atlantic,* Feb. 6, 2013, www.theatlantic.com/technology/archive/2013/02/and-now-let-us-praise-and-consider-the-absurd-luck-of-famous-men/272917/.

18 Jacob B. Hirsh and Sonia K. Kang, "Mechanisms of Identity Conflict: Uncertainty, Anxiety, and the Behavioral Inhibition System," *Personality and Social Psychology Review* 20, no. 3 (2015): 1–22.

19 Francesca Gino, Caroline Ashley Wilmuth, and Alison Wood Brooks, "Compared to Men, Women View Professional Advancement as Equally Attainable, but Less Desirable," *Proceedings of the National Academy of Sciences* 112, no. 40 (2015): 12,354–59; Kaitlyn M. Werner et al., "Some Goals Just Feel Easier: Self-Concordance Leads to Goal Progress through Subjective Ease, Not Effort," *Personality and Individual Differences* 96 (2016): 237–42.

20 John Maltby et al., "Beliefs in Being Unlucky and Deficits in Executive Functioning," *Consciousness and Cognition* 22, no. 1 (2013): 137–47.

21 Marco Caliendo, Frank Fossen, and Alexander S. Kritikos, "Personality Characteristics and the Decisions to Become and Stay Self-Employed," *Small Business Economics* 42, no. 4 (2014): 787–814; Alexander S. Browman, Mesmin Destin, and Daniel C. Molden, "Identity-Specific Motivation: How Distinct Identities Direct Self-Regulation across Distinct Situations," *Journal of Personality and Social Psychology* 113, no. 6 (2017): 835–57.

22 Andrew P. Hill and Thomas Curran, "Multidimensional Perfectionism and Burn-out: A Meta-analysis," *Personality and Social Psychology Review* 20, no. 3 (2016): 269–88; Suh, Gnilka, and Rice, "Perfectionism and Well-Being."

23 Joyce Ehrlinger and David Dunning, "How Chronic Self-Views Influence (and Potentially Mislead) Estimates of Performance," *Journal of Personality and Social Psychology* 84, no. 1 (2003): 5–17; Shelley J. Correll, "Gender and the Career Choice Process: The Role of Biased Self-Assessments," *American Journal of Sociology* 106, no. 6 (2001): 1,691–730; Guimond et al., "Social Comparison, Self-Stereotyping, and Gender Differences in Self-Construals"; J. E. O. Blakemore, "Children's Beliefs about Violating Gender Norms: Boys Shouldn't Look Like Girls, and Girls Shouldn't Act Like Boys," *Sex Roles* 48, no. 9–10 (2003): 411–19; Justin V. Cavallo and Gráinne M. Fitzsimons, "Goal Competition, Conflict, Coordination, and Completion: How Intergoal Dynamics Affect Self-Regulation," in Aarts and Elliot, *Goal-Directed Behavior,* 267–99; Shane W. Bench et al., "Gender Gaps in Overestimation of Math Performance," *Sex Roles* 72, no. 11–12 (2015): 536–46; Ernesto Reuben, Paola Sapienza, and Luigi Zingales, "How Stereotypes Impair Women's Careers in Science," *Proceedings of the National Academy of Sciences* 111, no. 12 (2014): 4,403–8; Koban and Pourtois, "Brain Systems Underlying the Affective and Social Monitoring of Actions"; M. Hausmann, "Arts versus Science: Academic Background Implicitly Activates Gender Stereotypes on Cognitive Abilities with Threat Raising Men's (but Lowering Women's) Performance," *Intelligence* 46 (2014): 235–45; Gert Jan Hofstede et al., "Gender Differences: The Role of Nature, Nurture, Social Identity, and Self-Organization," in *International Workshop on Multi-agent Systems and Agent-Based Simulation* (Berlin: Springer, 2014), 72–87.

24 Cimpian and Salomon, "Inherence Heuristic." Easier for us to think of white men as leaders and start-up founders: Michael A. Hogg, "Influence and Leadership," in Fiske, Gilbert, and Lindzey, *Handbook of Social Psychology,* 1,195; Aimee Groth, "Entrepreneurs Don't Have a Special Gene for Risk—They Come from Families with Money," *Quartz,* July 17, 2015, https://qz.com/455109/entrepreneurs-dont-have-a-special-gene-for-risk-they-come-from-families-with-money/; Jordan Weissmann, "Entrepreneurship: The Ultimate White Privilege?," *Atlantic,* Aug. 16, 2013, www.theatlantic.com/business/archive/2013/08/entrepreneurship-the-ultimate-white-privilege/278727/.

25 Correll, "Gender and the Career Choice Process."

26 Ana Guinote, Megan Brown, and Susan T. Fiske, "Minority Status Decreases Sense of Control and Increases Interpretive Processing," *Social Cognition* 24, no. 2 (2006): 169–86; Jacqueline M. Chen and David L. Hamilton, "Understanding Diversity: The Importance of Social Acceptance," *Personality and Social Psychology Bulletin* 41, no. 4 (2015): 586–98.

27 Walton and Cohen, "Question of Belonging"; Biernat, "Stereotypes and Shifting Standards."

28 Biernat and Kobrynowicz, "Gender- and Race-Based Standards of Competence"; Crandall and Eshleman, "Justification-Suppression Model of the Expression and Experience of Prejudice"; Uhlmann and Cohen, "Constructed Criteria"; Castilla, "Gender, Race, and Meritocracy in Organizational Careers"; Biernat, *Standards and Expectancies*; Macrae and Bodenhausen, "Social Cognition"; Ridgeway and Nakagawa, "Status"; Foy et al., "Emotions and Affect as Source, Outcome, and Resistance to Inequality"; Magee and Galinsky, "Social Hierarchy"; Pager, Western, and Bonikowski, "Discrimination in a Low-Wage Labor Market"; Foschi, "Double Standards for Competence"; Biernat and Fuegen, "Shifting Standards and the Evaluation of Competence"; Castilla and Benard, "Paradox of Meritocracy in Organizations."

29 Zakary L. Tormala, Jayson S. Jia, and Michael I. Norton, "The Preference for Potential," *Journal of Personality and Social Psychology* 103, no. 4 (2012): 567–83.

30 Chia-Jung Tsay and Mahzarin R. Banaji, "Naturals and Strivers: Preferences and Beliefs about Sources of Achievement," *Journal of Experimental Social Psychology* 47, no. 2 (2011): 460–65.

31 Author interview, March 24, 2015.

32 Nathan C. Pettit et al., "Rising Stars and Sinking Ships: Consequences of Status Momentum," *Psychological Science* 24, no. 8 (2013): 1,579–84.

33 Groth, "Entrepreneurs Don't Have a Special Gene for Risk."

34 Davidai and Gilovich, "Headwinds/Tailwinds Asymmetry"; Sendhil Mullainathan, "To Help Tackle Inequality, Remember the Advantages You've Had," *New York Times,* April 28, 2017, www.nytimes.com/2017/04/28/upshot/income-equality -isnt-just-about-headwinds-tailwinds-count-too.html; Ridgeway, "Social Construction of Status Value"; Fiske, "Interpersonal Stratification"; Laurie A. Rudman et al., "Reactions to Vanguards: Advances in Backlash Theory," in *Advances in Experimental Social Psychology* (San Diego: Elsevier, 2012), 45: 167–227; Daniel Sullivan et al., "Competitive Victimhood as a Response to Accusations of Ingroup Harm Doing," *Journal of Personality and Social Psychology* 102, no. 4 (2012): 778–95.

35 Robert A. Baron and Gideon D. Markman, "Beyond Social Capital: How Social Skills Can Enhance Entrepreneurs' Success," *Academy of Management Executive* 14, no. 1 (2000): 106–16; Robert A. Baron and Gideon D. Markman, "Beyond Social Capital: The Role of Entrepreneurs' Social Competence in Their Financial Success," *Journal of Business Venturing* 18, no. 1 (2003): 41–60; Peter Witt, "Entrepreneurs' Networks and the Success of Start-Ups," *Entrepreneurship and Regional Development* 16, no. 5 (2004): 391–412; Robert A. Baron, "Psychological Perspectives on Entrepreneurship: Cognitive and Social Factors in Entrepreneurs' Success," *Current Directions in Psychological Science* 9, no. 1 (2000): 15–18.

36 (This is a cheesy turn of phrase adapted from the actual psychological theory known as the broaden-and-build theory of positive emotions.) Barbara L. Fredrickson, "What Good Are Positive Emotions?," *Review of General Psychology* 2, no. 3 (1998): 300–319; Barbara L. Fredrickson, "Cultivating Positive Emotions to Optimize Health and Well-Being," *Prevention and Treatment* 3, no. 1 (2000): 1a;

Barbara L. Fredrickson, "The Role of Positive Emotions in Positive Psychology: The Broaden-and-Build Theory of Positive Emotions," *American Psychologist* 56, no. 3 (2001): 218–26; Barbara L. Fredrickson and T. Joiner, "Positive Emotions Trigger Upward Spirals Toward Emotional Well-Being," *Psychological Science* 13, no. 2 (2002): 172–75; Shelley E. Taylor and Joelle I. Broffman, "Psychosocial Resources: Functions, Origins, and Links to Mental and Physical Health," *Advances in Experimental Social Psychology* 44 (2011): 1–57; Michael A. Cohn et al., "Happiness Unpacked: Positive Emotions Increase Life Satisfaction by Building Resilience," *Emotion* 9, no. 3 (2009): 361–68.

37 Rotter, "Generalized Expectancies for Internal versus External Control of Reinforcement"; Robert Merton, *Mass Persuasion* (New York: Harpers, 1946).

38 Xiao-Ping Chen, Xin Yao, and Suresh Kotha, "Entrepreneur Passion and Preparedness in Business Plan Presentations: A Persuasion Analysis of Venture Capitalists' Funding Decisions," *Academy of Management Journal* 52, no. 1 (2009): 199–214; Melissa S. Cardon et al., "The Nature and Experience of Entrepreneurial Passion," *Academy of Management Review* 34, no. 3 (2009): 511–32.

39 Author interview, Nov. 10, 2015.

40 Monica Soliman and Roger Buehler, "Why Improvement Can Trump Consistent Strong Performance: The Role of Effort Perceptions." *Journal of Behavioral Decision Making* 31, no. 1 (2018): 52–64.

41 John M. Malouff and Nicola S. Schutte, "Can Psychological Interventions Increase Optimism? A Meta-analysis," *Journal of Positive Psychology* 12, no. 6 (2016): 1–11; Kennon M. Sheldon and Sonja Lyubomirsky, "How to Increase and Sustain Positive Emotion: The Effects of Expressing Gratitude and Visualizing Best Possible Selves," *Journal of Positive Psychology* 1, no. 2 (2006): 73–82; Joachim T. Geaney, Michael T. Treadway, and Luke D. Smillie, "Trait Anticipatory Pleasure Predicts Effort Expenditure for Reward," *PLoS ONE* 10, no. 6 (2015): e0131357, doi:10.1371/journal.pone.0131357.

42 Juan-Carlos Ayala and Guadalupe Manzano, "The Resilience of the Entrepreneur: Influence on the Success of the Business: A Longitudinal Analysis," *Journal of Economic Psychology* 42 (2014): 126–35.

43 Author interview, July 31, 2009.

44 Moto Shimizu, Yu Niiya, and Eri Shigemasu, "Achievement Goals and Improvement Following Failure: Moderating Roles of Self-Compassion and Contingency of Self-Worth," *Self and Identity* 15, no. 1 (2016): 107–15; Kelley J. Robinson et al., "Resisting Self-Compassion: Why Are Some People Opposed to Being Kind to Themselves?," *Self and Identity* 15, no. 5 (2016): 505–24; Lisa E. Kim et al., "Evidence for Three Factors of Perfectionism: Perfectionistic Strivings, Order, and Perfectionistic Concerns," *Personality and Individual Differences* 84 (2015): 16–22.

CHAPTER 10: YES, AND

1 The idea of "surface area of luck" is credited to Jason Roberts: www.codusoperandi .com/posts/increasing-your-luck-surface-area.

2 Tony Hsieh, *Delivering Happiness* (New York: Grand Central Publishing, 2013), loc. 147–49, Kindle.

3 Ibid., loc. 305–6.

4 Adam Lashinsky, "Why Amazon Tolerates Zappos' Extreme Management Experiment," *Fortune*, March 4, 2016. Available at http://fortune.com/2016/03/04/amazon -zappos-holacracy/

5 Ibid., loc. 181–83, 335–36.

6 Austin, *Chase, Chance, and Creativity*, 75–76.

7 Donald O. Hebb, *The Organization of Behavior* (New York: Wiley, 1949); Joe Z. Tsien, "Learning and Memory," in Brady et al., *Basic Neurochemistry*, 956–65; Donald O. Hebb, "The Effects of Early Experience on Problem Solving at Maturity," *American Psychologist* 2 (1947): 306–7.

8 Mark R. Rosenzweig, "Historical Perspective," in *Neurobiology of Learning and Memory*, ed. Joe L. Martinez Jr. and Raymond P. Kesner, 2nd ed. (New York: Elsevier, 2007), 18–19; Hebb, *Organization of Behavior*, 298–99.

9 Email exchange with author, Jan. 3, 2017.

10 Colin G. DeYoung et al., "Openness to Experience, Intellect, and Cognitive Ability," *Journal of Personality Assessment* 96, no. 1 (2014): 46–52; Philip J. Corr, Colin G. DeYoung, and Neil McNaughton, "Motivation and Personality: A Neuropsychological Perspective," *Social and Personality Psychology Compass* 7, no. 3 (2013): 158–175; Colin G. DeYoung, "Openness/Intellect: A Dimension of Personality Reflecting Cognitive Exploration," in *APA Handbook of Personality and Social Psychology, vol. 3: Personality Processes and Individual Differences* 4 (2014): 369–99; Robert K. McCrae and Angelina R. Sutin, "Openness to Experience," in Leary and Hoyle, *Handbook of Individual Differences in Social Behavior*, 257–73; Benjamin D. Hill et al., "The Interaction of Ability and Motivation: Average Working Memory Is Required for Need for Cognition to Positively Benefit Intelligence and the Effect Increases with Ability," *Personality and Individual Differences* 98 (2016): 225–28; Colin G. DeYoung et al., "Intellect as Distinct from Openness: Differences Revealed by fMRI of Working Memory," *Journal of Personality and Social Psychology* 97, no. 5 (2009): 883–92; Adrian Furnham and Jeremy D. Thorne, "Need for Cognition: Its Dimensionality and Personality and Intelligence Correlates," *Journal of Individual Differences* 34 (2015): 230–40.

11 Elliot M. Tucker-Drob and K. Paige Harden, "Intellectual Interest Mediates Gene-by-Socioeconomic Status Interaction on Adolescent Academic Achievement," *Child Development* 83, no. 2 (2012): 743–57; Elliot M. Tucker-Drob and K. Paige Harden, "Learning Motivation Mediates Gene-by-Socioeconomic Status Interaction on Mathematics Achievement in Early Childhood," *Learning and Individual Differences* 22, no. 1 (2012): 37–45; Artur Pokropek, Francesca Borgonovi, and

Maciej Jakubowski, "Socio-economic Disparities in Academic Achievement: A Comparative Analysis of Mechanisms and Pathways," *Learning and Individual Differences* 42 (2015): 10–18.

12 Todd B. Kashdan and Paul J. Silvia, "Curiosity and Interest: The Benefits of Thriving on Novelty and Challenge," in Snyder and Lopez, *Oxford Handbook of Positive Psychology,* 368. For the sake of brevity, curiosity here encompasses other forms of "cognitive exploration," or ideas such as openness to experience and need for cognition. Sophie von Stumm and Philip L. Ackerman, "Investment and Intellect: A Review and Meta-analysis," *Psychological Bulletin* 139, no. 4 (2013): 841–69; Sophie von Stumm, "Investment Traits and Intelligence in Adulthood: Assessment and Associations," *Journal of Individual Differences* 34, no. 2 (2013): 82–89; Monika Fleischhauer et al., "Same or Different? Clarifying the Relationship of Need for Cognition to Personality and Intelligence," *Personality and Social Psychology Bulletin* 36, no. 1 (2010): 82–96.

13 Amitai Shenhav, Lisa Feldman Barrett, and Moshe Bar, "Affective Value and Associative Processing Share a Cortical Substrate," *Cognitive and Affective Behavioral Neuroscience* 13, no. 1 (2013): 46–59.

14 Brunyé et al., "Happiness by Association"; Trapp et al., "Human Preferences Are Biased Towards Associative Information"; Bar, "Cognitive Neuroscience Hypothesis of Mood and Depression"; John Kounios and Mark Beeman, "The Cognitive Neuroscience of Insight," *Annual Review of Psychology* 65 (2014): 71–93.

15 Email exchange with author, Aug. 1, 2014.

16 Kevin B. Meehan et al., "Rejection Sensitivity and Interpersonal Behavior in Daily Life," *Personality and Individual Differences* 126 (2018): 109–15.

17 R. Nicholas Carleton, "Fear of the Unknown: One Fear to Rule Them All?," *Journal of Anxiety Disorders* 41 (2016): 5–21; Hirsh, Mar, and Peterson, "Psychological Entropy"; Jonas et al., "Threat and Defense"; Tullett, Kay, and Inzlicht, "Randomness Increases Self-Reported Anxiety and Neurophysiological Correlates of Performance Monitoring."

18 Jos F. Brosschot, Bart Verkuil, and Julian F. Thayer, "The Default Response to Uncertainty and the Importance of Perceived Safety in Anxiety and Stress: An Evolution-Theoretical Perspective," *Journal of Anxiety Disorders* 41 (2016): 22–34.

19 Author interview, April 13, 2015.

20 Anna Rabinovich and Thomas A. Morton, "Coping with Identity Conflict: Perceptions of Self as Flexible versus Fixed Moderate the Effect of Identity Conflict on Well-Being," *Self and Identity* 15, no. 2 (2016): 224–44; Stephen Joseph and Kate Hefferon, "Post-traumatic Growth: Eudaimonic Happiness in the Aftermath of Adversity," in *The Oxford Handbook of Happiness,* ed. Susan A. David, Ilona Boniwell, and Amanda Conley Ayers (New York: Oxford University Press, 2013), 926–40.

21 Mark L. Savickas and Erik J. Porfeli, "Career Adapt-Abilities Scale: Construction, Reliability, and Measurement Equivalence across 13 Countries," *Journal of Vocational Behavior* 80, no. 3 (2012): 661–73; Yuhui Li et al., "Big-Five Personality and

BIS/BAS Traits as Predictors of Career Exploration: The Mediation Role of Career Adaptability," *Journal of Vocational Behavior* 89 (2015): 39–45; Hannes Zacher, "Career Adaptability Predicts Subjective Career Success above and beyond Personality Traits and Core Self-Evaluations," *Journal of Vocational Behavior* 84, no. 1 (2014): 21–30.

22 Bandura, "Psychology of Chance Encounters and Life Paths."

23 Andreas Hirschi, "The Role of Chance Events in the School-to-Work Transition: The Influence of Demographic, Personality, and Career Development Variables," *Journal of Vocational Behavior* 77, no. 1 (2010): 39–49; Robert G. L. Pryor and Jim E. H. Bright, "The Chaos Theory of Careers (CTC): Ten Years on and Only Just Begun," *Australian Journal of Career Development* 23, no. 1 (2014): 4–12; Jerome G. Manis and Bernard N. Meltzer, "Chance in Human Affairs," *Sociological Theory* 12, no. 1 (1994): 45–56.

24 Author interview, Sept. 15, 2016.

25 Frank E. Walter, Stefano Battiston, and Frank Schweitzer, "Coping with Information Overload through Trust-Based Networks," in *Managing Complexity: Insights, Concepts, Applications,* ed. D. Helbing (Berlin: Springer, 2008), 273–300; Frédéric C. Godart and Ashley Mears, "How Do Cultural Producers Make Creative Decisions? Lessons from the Catwalk," *Social Forces* 88, no. 2 (2009): 671–92.

26 Ada Ferrer-i-Carbonell, "Income and Well-Being: An Empirical Analysis of the Comparison Income Effect," *Journal of Public Economics* 89, no. 5 (2005): 997–1,019; Anderson et al., "Local-Ladder Effect"; Hedonic treadmill: cf. Ian McGregor and Brian R. Little, "Personal Projects, Happiness, and Meaning: On Doing Well and Being Yourself," *Journal of Personality and Social Psychology* 74, no. 2 (1998): 494–512; P. Brickman and D. T. Campbell, "Hedonic Relativism and Planning the Good Society," in *Adaptation Level Theory: A Symposium,* ed. M. H. Appley (London: Academic Press, 1971), 287–302; P. Brickman, D. Coates, and R. Janoff-Bulman, "Lottery Winners and Accident Victims: Is Happiness Relative?," *Journal of Personality and Social Psychology* 36, no. 8 (1978): 917–27.

27 Halttunen, *Confidence Men and Painted Women,* 2.

28 Author interview, June 24, 2014.

29 Author interview, May 28, 2015.

30 Bandura, "Psychology of Chance Encounters and Life Paths"; Gifford-Smith and Brownell, "Childhood Peer Relationships."

31 David Scott Yeager et al., "The Far-Reaching Effects of Believing People Can Change: Implicit Theories of Personality Shape Stress, Health, and Achievement during Adolescence," *Journal of Personality and Social Psychology* 106, no. 6 (2014): 867–84; Todd B. Kashdan and Jonathan Rottenberg, "Psychological Flexibility as a Fundamental Aspect of Health," *Clinical Psychology Review* 30, no. 7 (2010): 865–78; Patricia W. Linville, "Self-Complexity as a Cognitive Buffer against Stress-Related Illness and Depression," *Journal of Personality and Social Psychology* 52, no. 4 (1987): 663–76; Sonia Roccas and Marilynn B. Brewer, "Social Identity Complexity," *Personality and Social Psychology Review* 6, no. 2 (2002): 88–106.

32 William Hart et al., "Feeling Validated versus Being Correct: A Meta-analysis of Selective Exposure to Information," *Psychological Bulletin* 135, no. 4 (2009): 555–88; Kashdan and Rottenberg, "Psychological Flexibility as a Fundamental Aspect of Health."

33 Gloria Steinem, *Revolution from Within: A Book of Self-Esteem* (Boston: Little, Brown, 1992), 38.

34 Avshalom Caspi, Daryl J. Bem, and Glen H. Elder, "Continuities and Consequences of Interactional Styles across the Life Course," *Journal of Personality* 57, no. 2 (1989): 375–406; Jens B. Asendorpf and Susanne Wilpers, "Personality Effects on Social Relationships," *Journal of Personality and Social Psychology* 74, no. 6 (1998): 1,531–44; Avshalom Caspi, "The Child Is Father of the Man: Personality Continuities from Childhood to Adulthood," *Journal of Personality and Social Psychology* 78, no. 1 (2000): 158–72; Avshalom Caspi and Brent W. Roberts, "Personality Development across the Life Course: The Argument for Change and Continuity," *Psychological Inquiry* 12, no. 2 (2001): 49–66; Donnellan and Robins, "Development of Personality across the Lifespan"; Sandra Scarr and Kathleen McCartney, "How People Make Their Own Environments: A Theory of Genotype → Environment Effects," *Child Development* 54, no. 2 (1983): 424–35; Avshalom Caspi, Brent W. Roberts, and Rebecca L. Shiner, "Personality Development: Stability and Change," *Annual Review of Psychology* 56 (2005): 453–84.

35 Email exchange with author, July 17, 2015.

36 Peter Bossaerts and Carsten Murawski, "Decision Neuroscience: Why We Become More Cautious with Age," *Current Biology* 26, no. 12 (2016): R495–R497; Robb B. Rutledge et al., "Risk Taking for Potential Reward Decreases across the Lifespan," *Current Biology* 26, no. 12 (2016): 1,634–39.

37 Laura L. Carstensen, Derek M. Isaacowitz, and Susan T. Charles, "Taking Time Seriously: A Theory of Socioemotional Selectivity," *American Psychologist* 54, no. 3 (1999): 165–81; Ezekiel J. Emanuel, "Why I Hope to Die at 75," *Atlantic,* Oct. 2014, www.theatlantic.com/magazine/archive/2014/10/why-i-hope-to-die-at-75/379329/.

38 Amitai Shenhav et al., "Anterior Cingulate Engagement in a Foraging Context Reflects Choice Difficulty, Not Foraging Value," *Nature Neuroscience* 17, no. 9 (2014): 1,249–54; Joshua W. Brown, "Models of Anterior Cingulate Cortex Function in Cognitive Control," in *The Wiley Handbook of Cognitive Control,* ed. Tobias Egner, 1st ed. (Malden, MA: John Wiley & Sons, 2017), 259–73; Nils Kolling et al., "Neural Mechanisms of Foraging," *Science* 336, no. 6077 (2012): 95–98.

39 June Price Tangney, "Humility," in Snyder and Lopez, *Oxford Handbook of Positive Psychology,* 411–19; Christopher Peterson and Martin E. P. Seligman, "Humility and Modesty," in *Character Strengths and Virtues: A Handbook and Classification* (New York: Oxford University Press, 2004), 1: 461–75.

40 Hsieh, *Delivering Happiness,* loc. 305–6.

41 Kashdan and Rottenberg, "Psychological Flexibility as a Fundamental Aspect of Health."

42 McKay and Dennett, "Evolution of Misbelief"; Martie G. Haselton, Daniel Nettle, and Damian R. Murray, "The Evolution of Cognitive Bias," in *The Handbook of Evolutionary Psychology vol. 2, Integrations*, ed. D.M. Buss, 2nd ed. (Hoboken, NJ: John Wiley & Sons, 2016), 968–87.

43 Stellar et al., "Self-Transcendent Emotions and Their Social Functions"; Pargament and Mahoney, "Spirituality: Discovering and Conserving the Sacred," 646–59.

44 McKay and Dennett, "Evolution of Misbelief"; Elliott Kruse et al., "An Upward Spiral between Gratitude and Humility," *Social Psychological and Personality Science* 5, no. 7 (2014): 805–14; Cohn et al., "Happiness Unpacked"; Barbara L. Fredrickson et al., "Open Hearts Build Lives: Positive Emotions, Induced through Loving-Kindness Meditation, Build Consequential Personal Resources," *Journal of Personality and Social Psychology* 95, no. 5 (2008): 1,045–62; Skodol, "Resilient Personality"; Mark R. Leary et al., "Cognitive and Interpersonal Features of Intellectual Humility," *Personality and Social Psychology Bulletin* 43, no. 6 (2017): 793–813.

INDEX